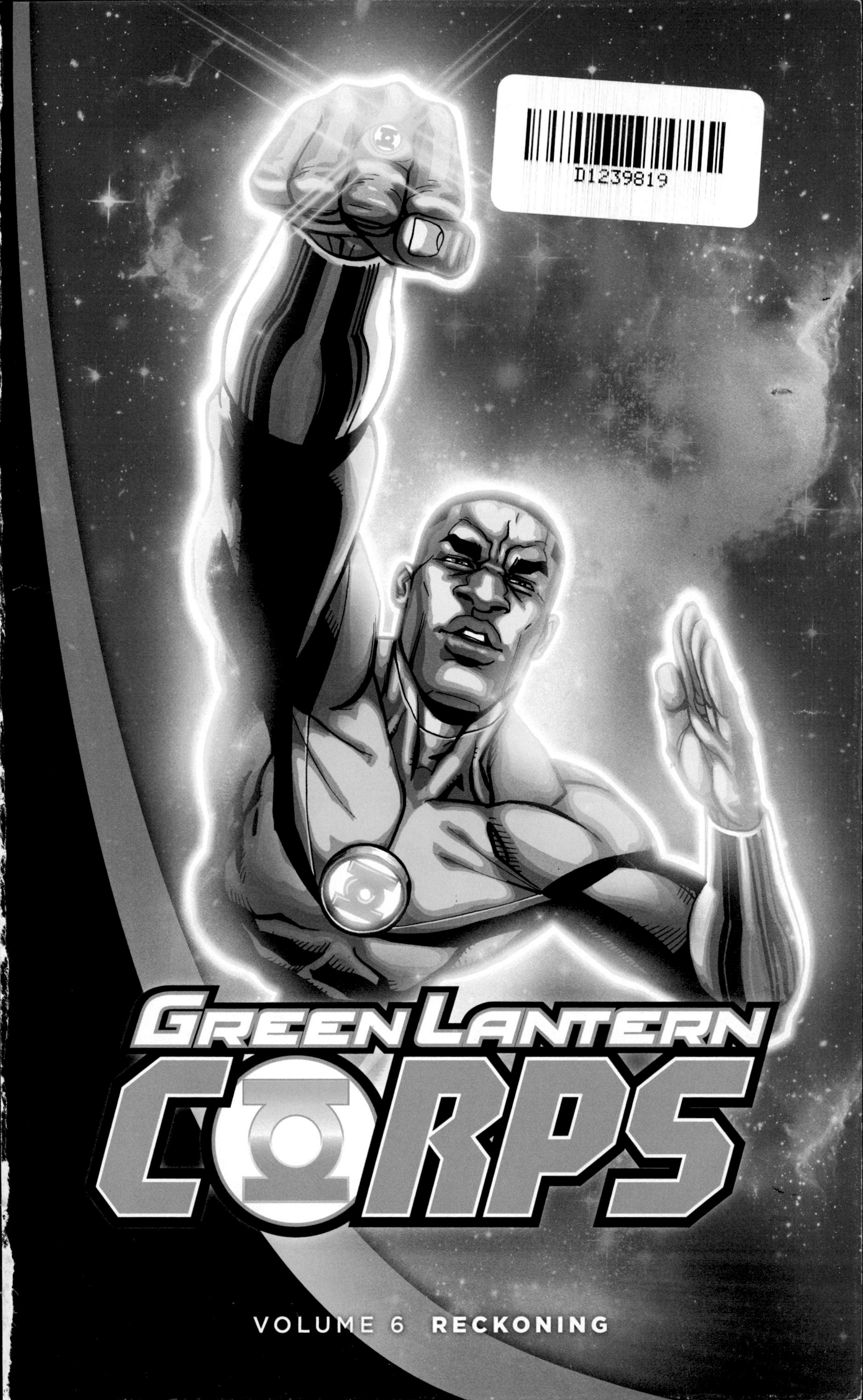
GREEN LANTERN
CORPS
VOLUME 6 RECKONING

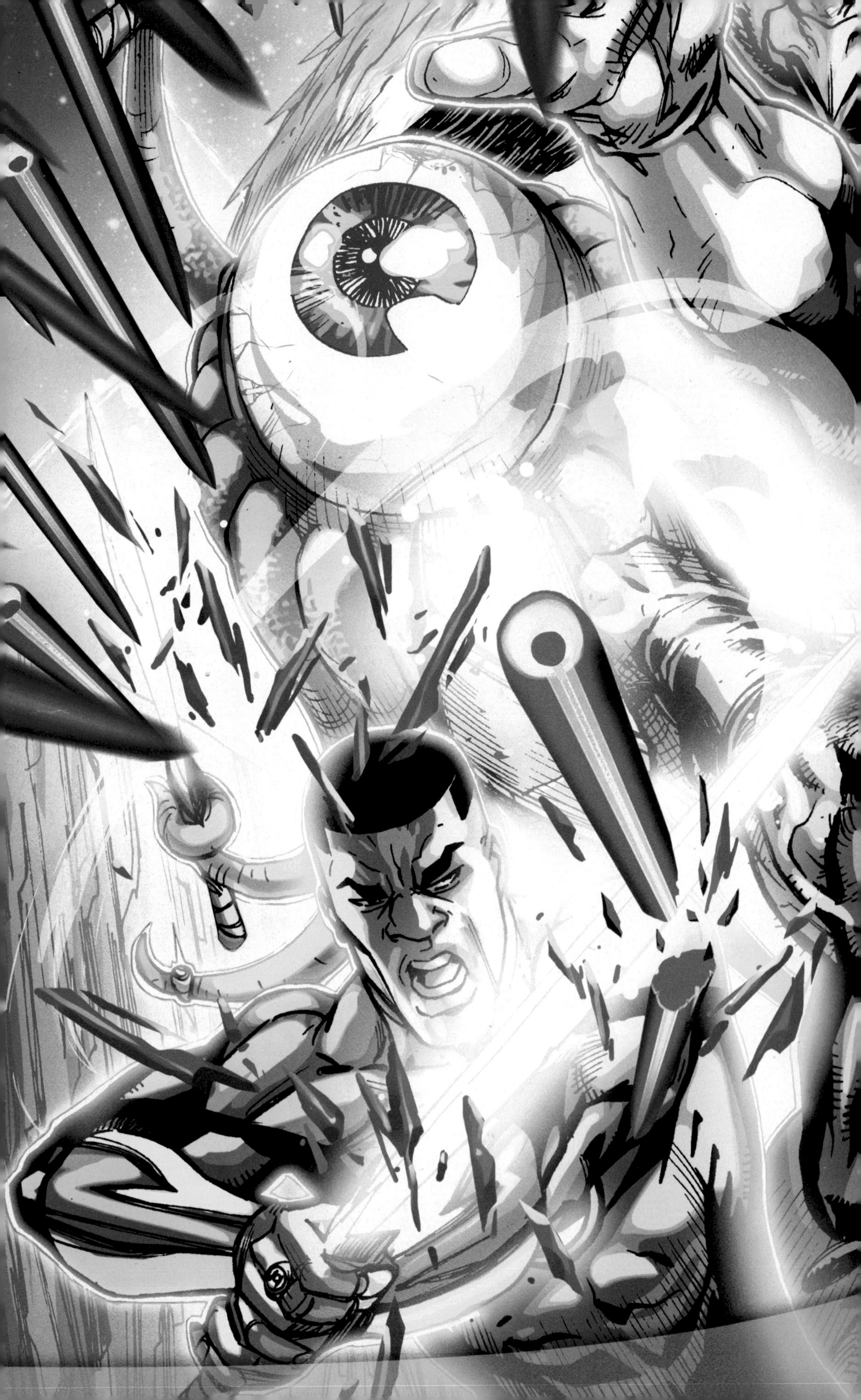

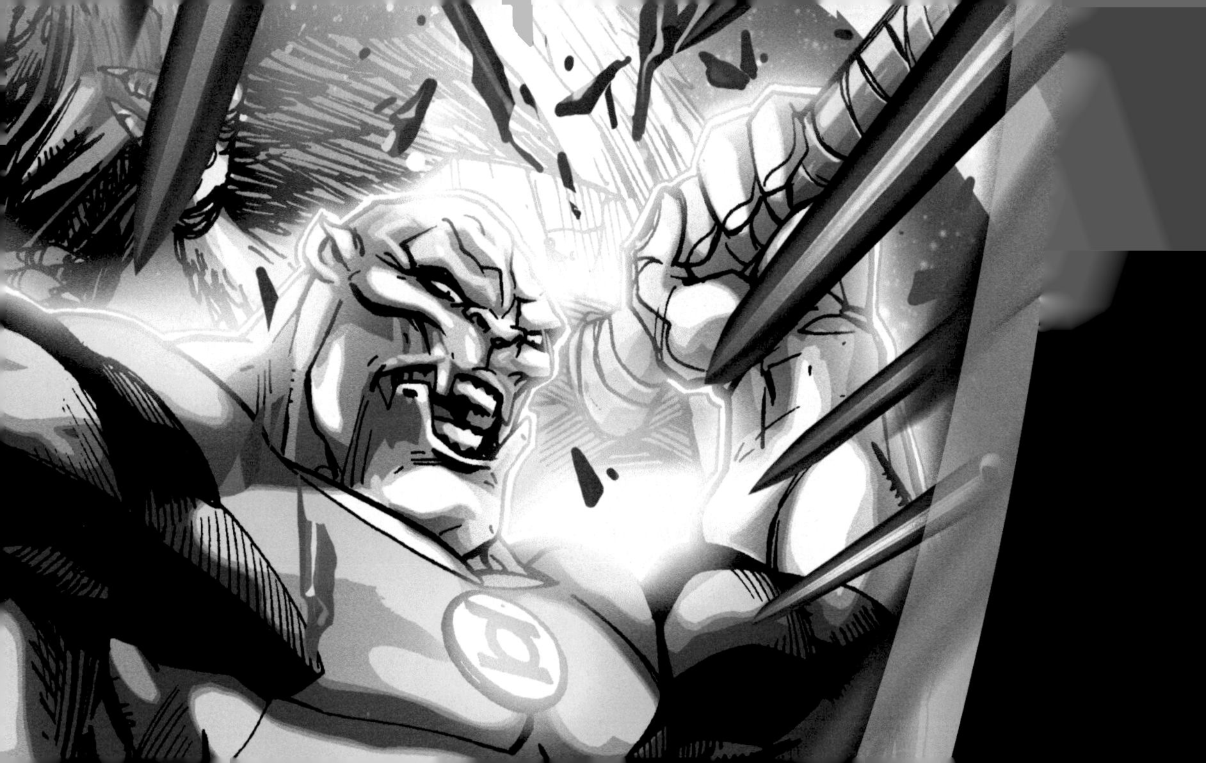

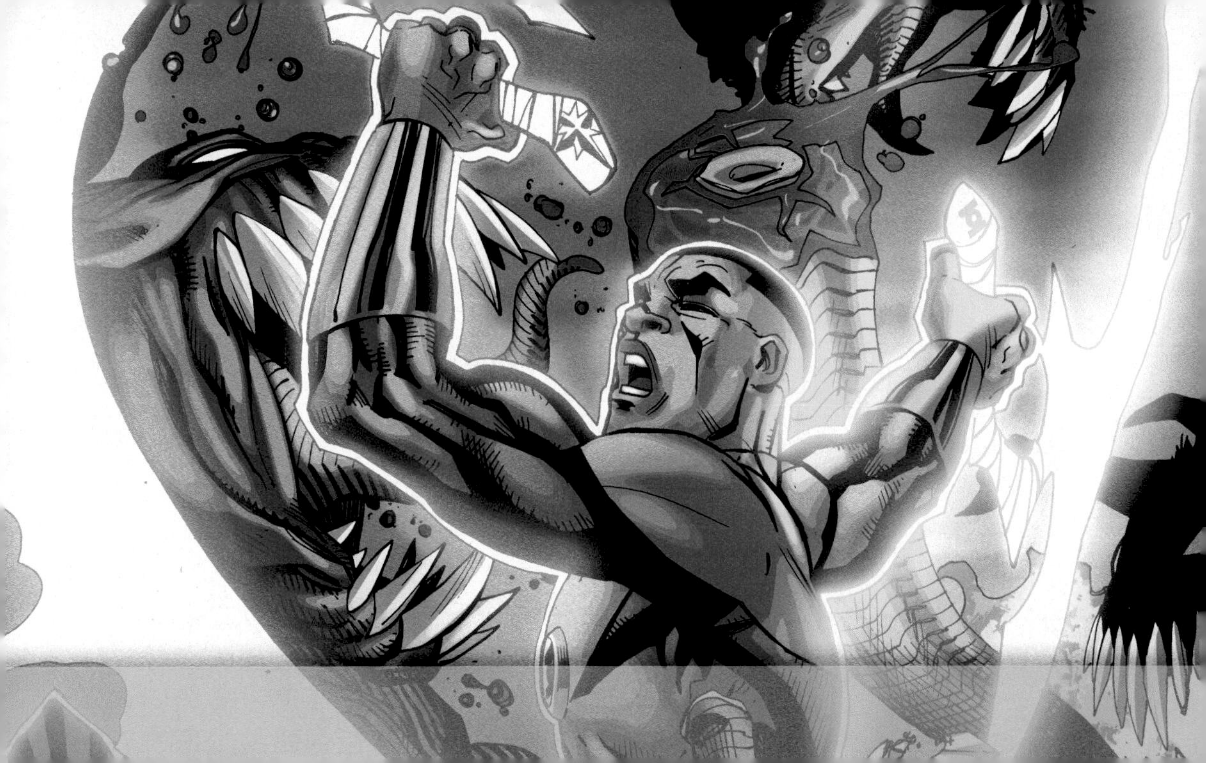

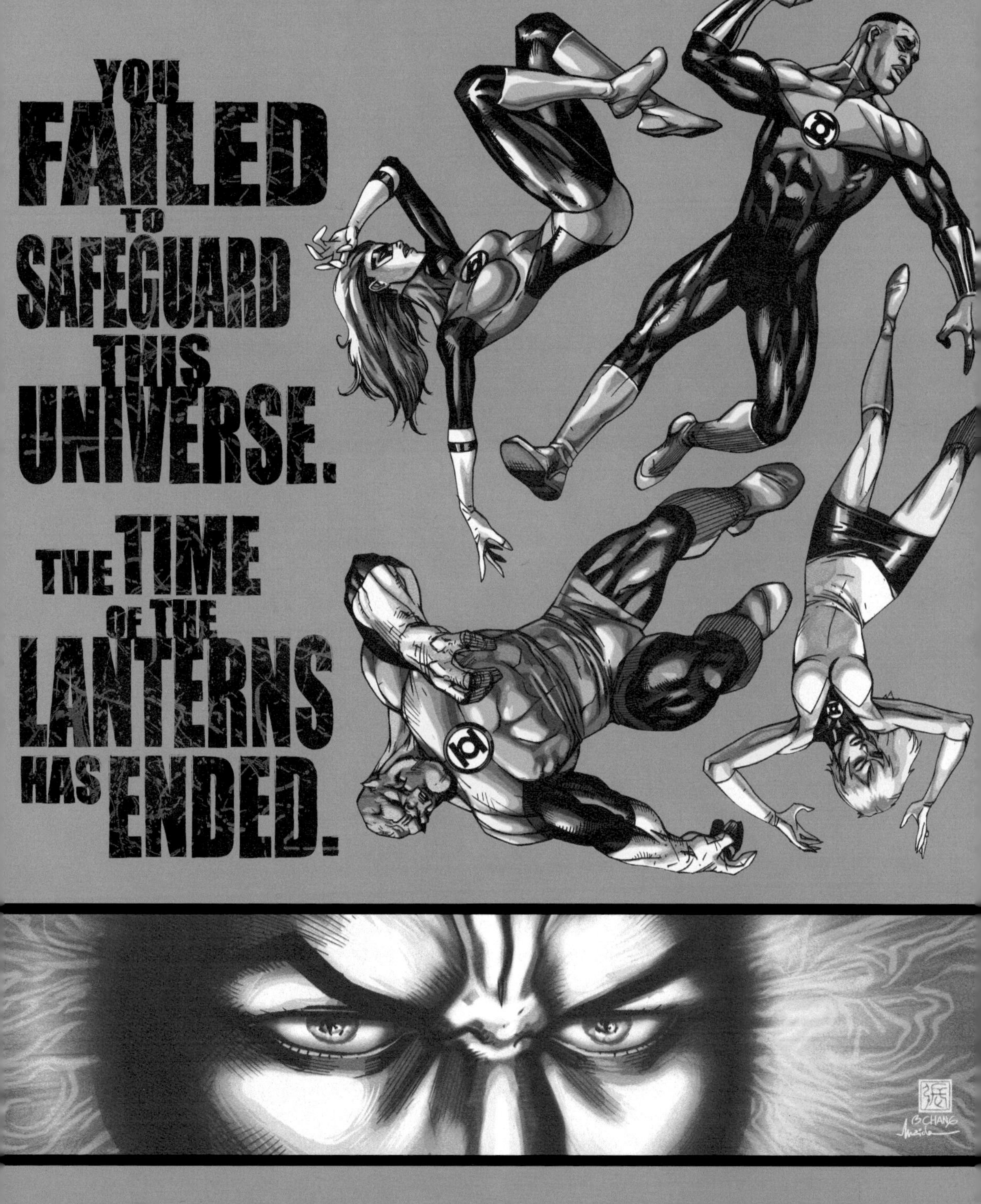
YOU FAILED TO SAFEGUARD THIS UNIVERSE.
THE TIME OF THE LANTERNS HAS ENDED.

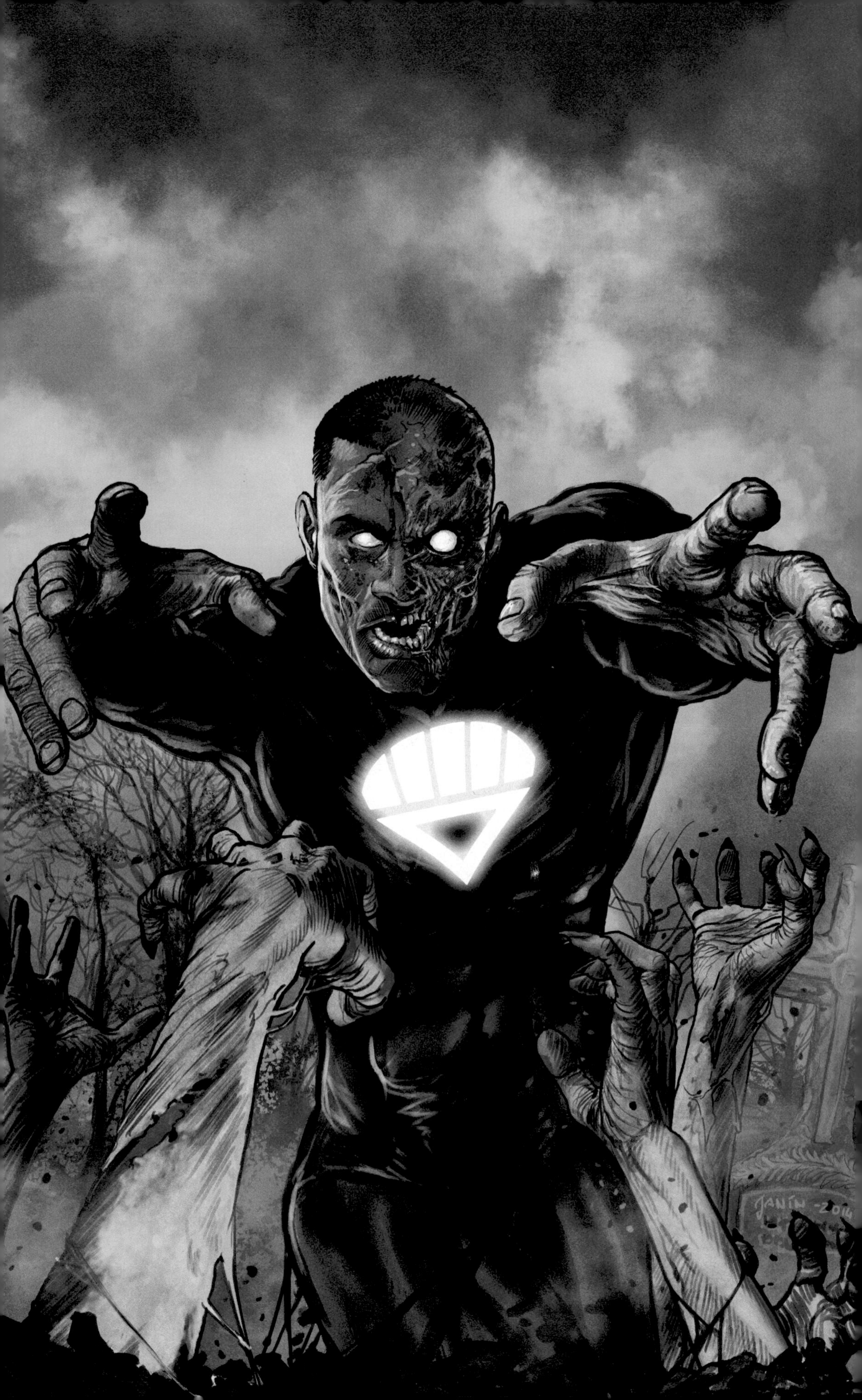

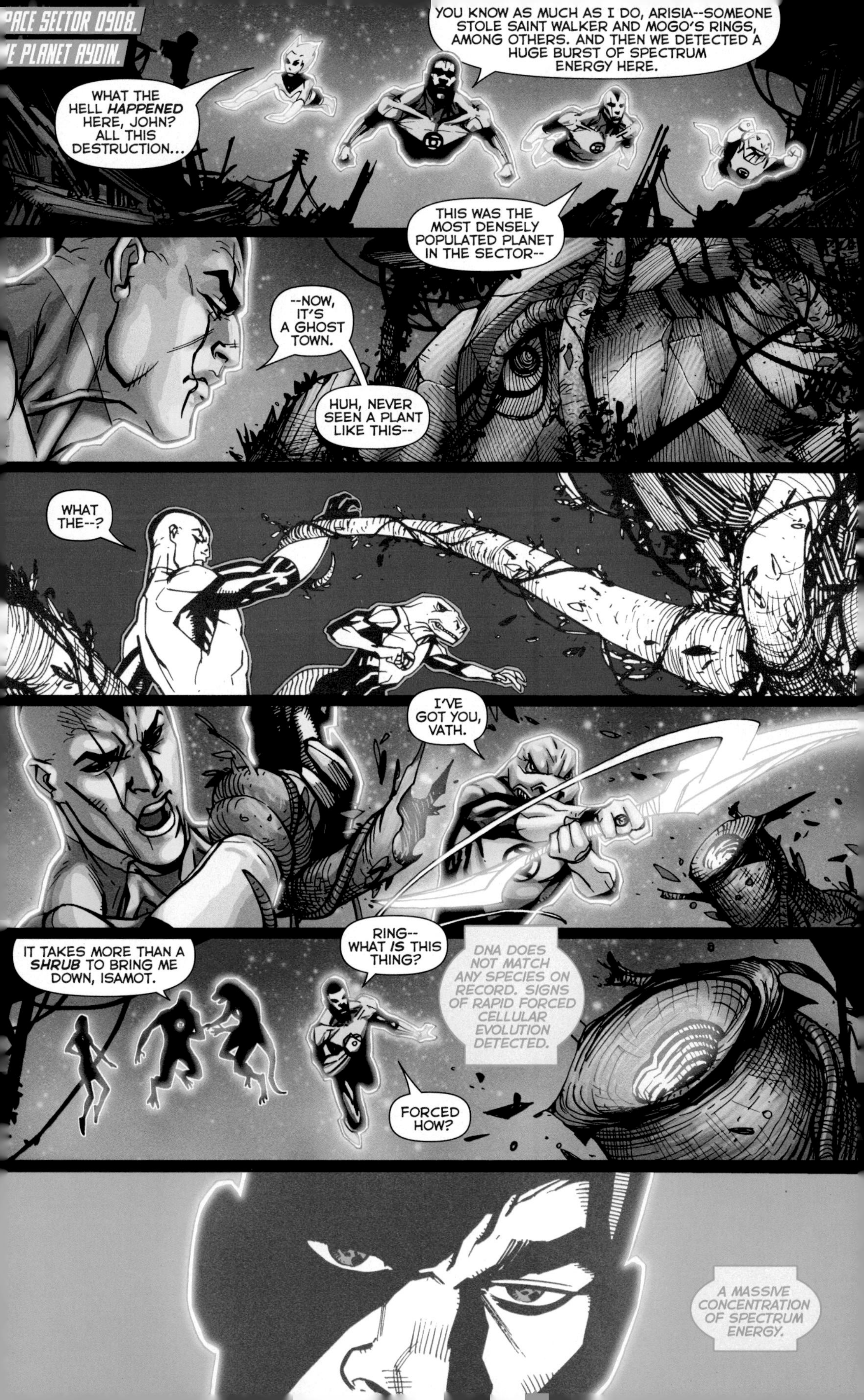

PACE SECTOR 0908.
E PLANET AYDIN.
WHAT THE HELL *HAPPENED* HERE, JOHN? ALL THIS DESTRUCTION...
YOU KNOW AS MUCH AS I DO, ARISIA--SOMEONE STOLE SAINT WALKER AND MOGO'S RINGS, AMONG OTHERS. AND THEN WE DETECTED A HUGE BURST OF SPECTRUM ENERGY HERE.
THIS WAS THE MOST DENSELY POPULATED PLANET IN THE SECTOR--
--NOW, IT'S A GHOST TOWN.
HUH, NEVER SEEN A PLANT LIKE THIS--
WHAT THE--?
I'VE GOT YOU, VATH.
IT TAKES MORE THAN A *SHRUB* TO BRING ME DOWN, ISAMOT.
RING--WHAT *IS* THIS THING?
DNA DOES NOT MATCH ANY SPECIES ON RECORD. SIGNS OF RAPID FORCED CELLULAR EVOLUTION DETECTED.
FORCED HOW?
A MASSIVE CONCENTRATION OF SPECTRUM ENERGY.

RINGS DID THIS?

MAYBE THE ONES THAT WERE STOLEN.

RING-- WHAT *KIND* OF SPECTRUM ENERGY?

ALL SPECTRUM ENERGY DETECTED-- RED, ORANGE, YELLOW, GREEN--

I GET IT.

WHOEVER DID THIS HAS A RING FROM EACH OF THE SEVEN COLORS OF THE SPECTRUM...

THAT STILL DOESN'T EXPLAIN WHAT HAPPENED TO THE PEOPLE. WHERE DID EVERYONE GO?

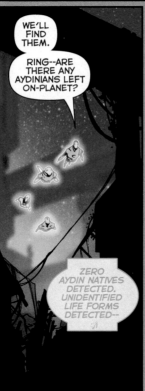

WE'LL FIND THEM.

RING--ARE THERE ANY AYDINIANS LEFT ON-PLANET?

ZERO AYDIN NATIVES DETECTED. UNIDENTIFIED LIFE FORMS DETECTED--

HUH. THE RING SAYS THERE ARE SOME INSIDE HERE, BUT I DON'T SEE--

--WITH DNA THAT IS A *98.9%* MATCH FOR AYDINIAN.

--ANYONE.

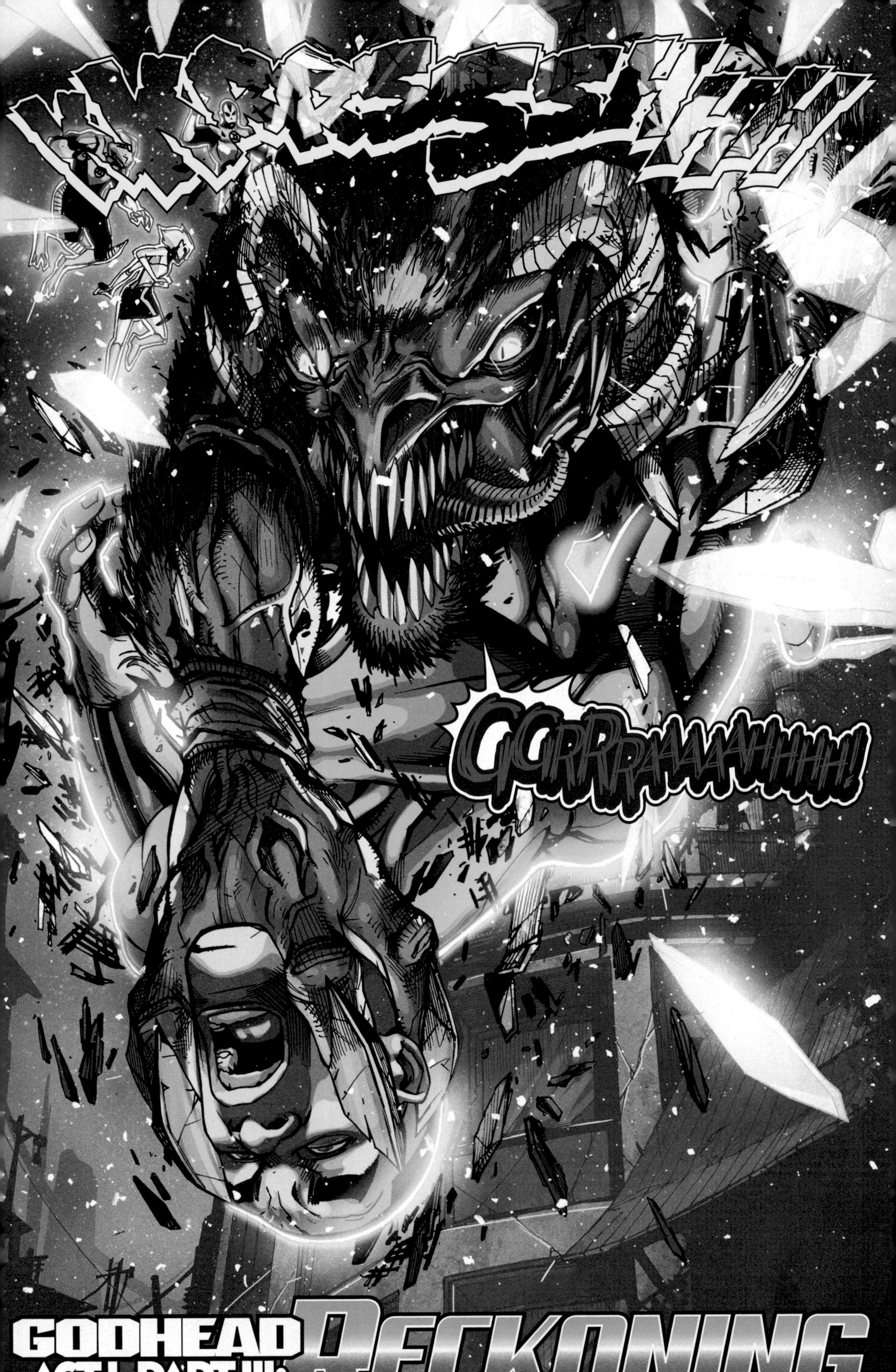
GGRRRAAAAHHHH!

GODHEAD ACT I, PART III: RECKONING

WRITER: VAN JENSEN ARTIST BERNARD CHANG COLORIST: MARCELO MAIOLO LETTERER: DAVE SHARPE
COVER: CHANG & MAIOLO MONSTERS VARIANT COVER: MIKEL JANIN

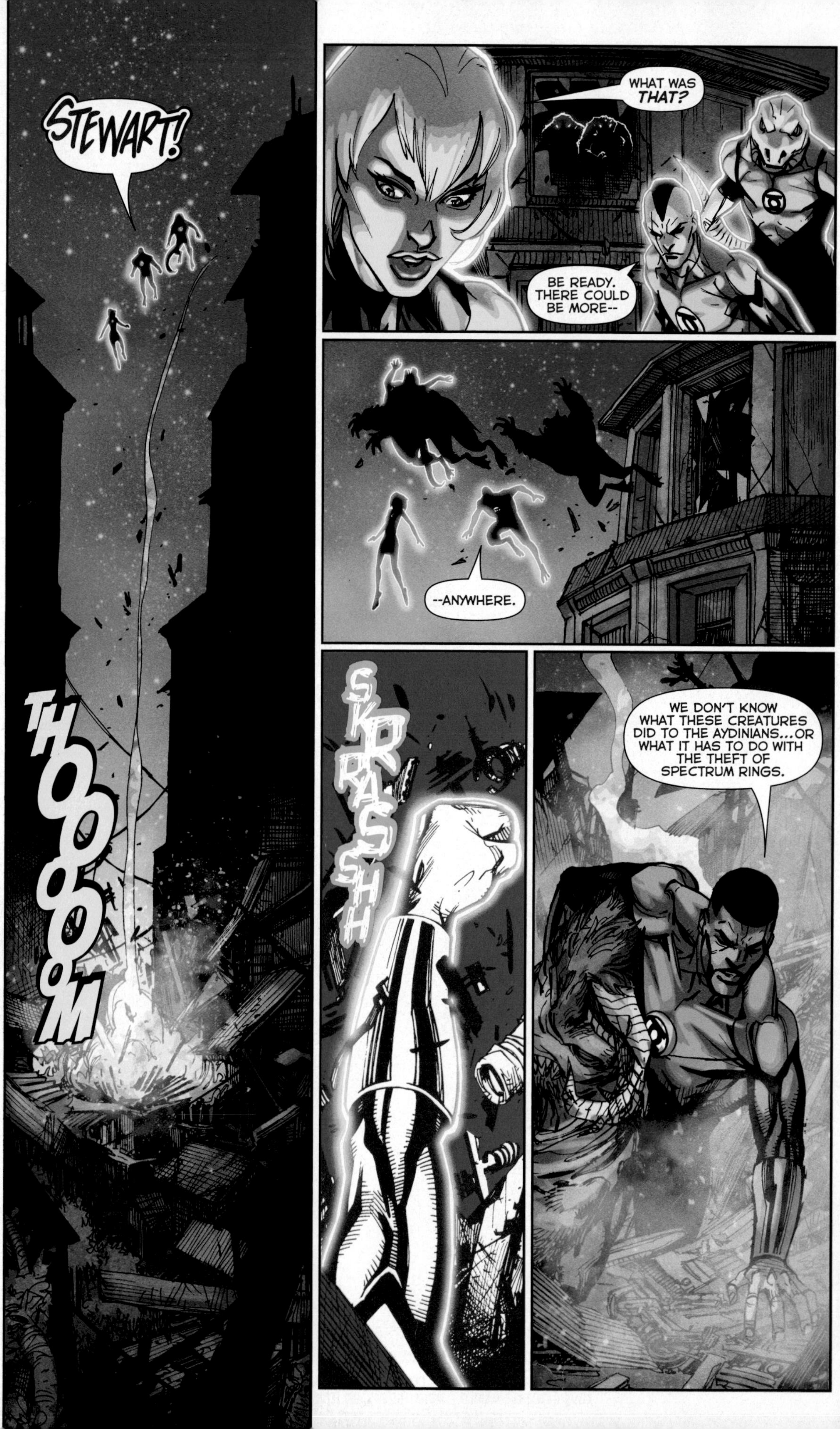
STEWART!
THOOOOOM
WHAT WAS THAT?
BE READY. THERE COULD BE MORE--
--ANYWHERE.
SKRASHH
WE DON'T KNOW WHAT THESE CREATURES DID TO THE AYDINIANS...OR WHAT IT HAS TO DO WITH THE THEFT OF SPECTRUM RINGS.

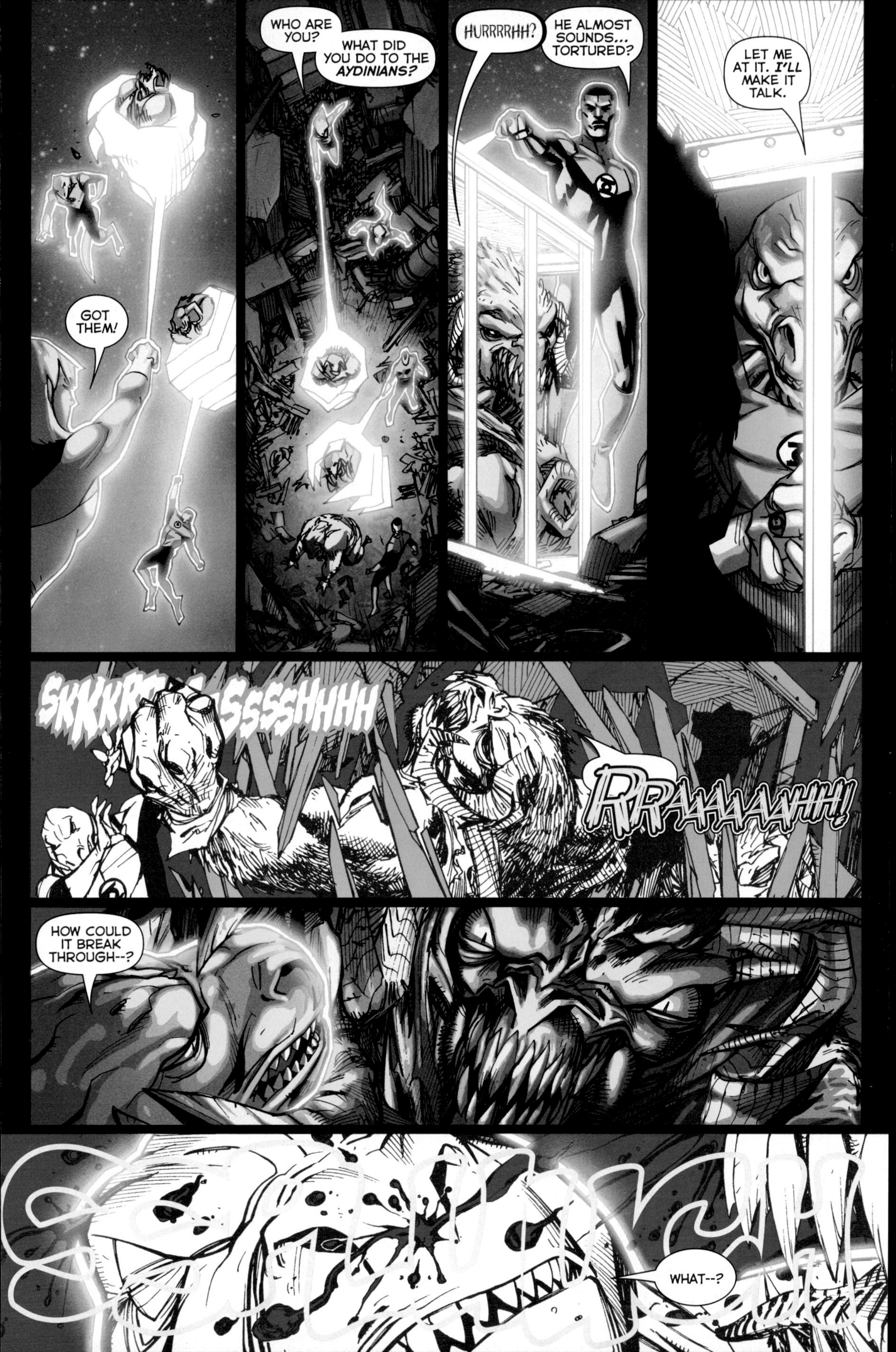
GOT THEM!
WHO ARE YOU?
WHAT DID YOU DO TO THE *AYDINIANS?*
HURRRRHH?
HE ALMOST SOUNDS... TORTURED?
LET ME AT IT. *I'LL* MAKE IT TALK.
SKKRR
SSSSHHHH
RRAAAAAAHH!
HOW COULD IT BREAK THROUGH--?
WHAT--?

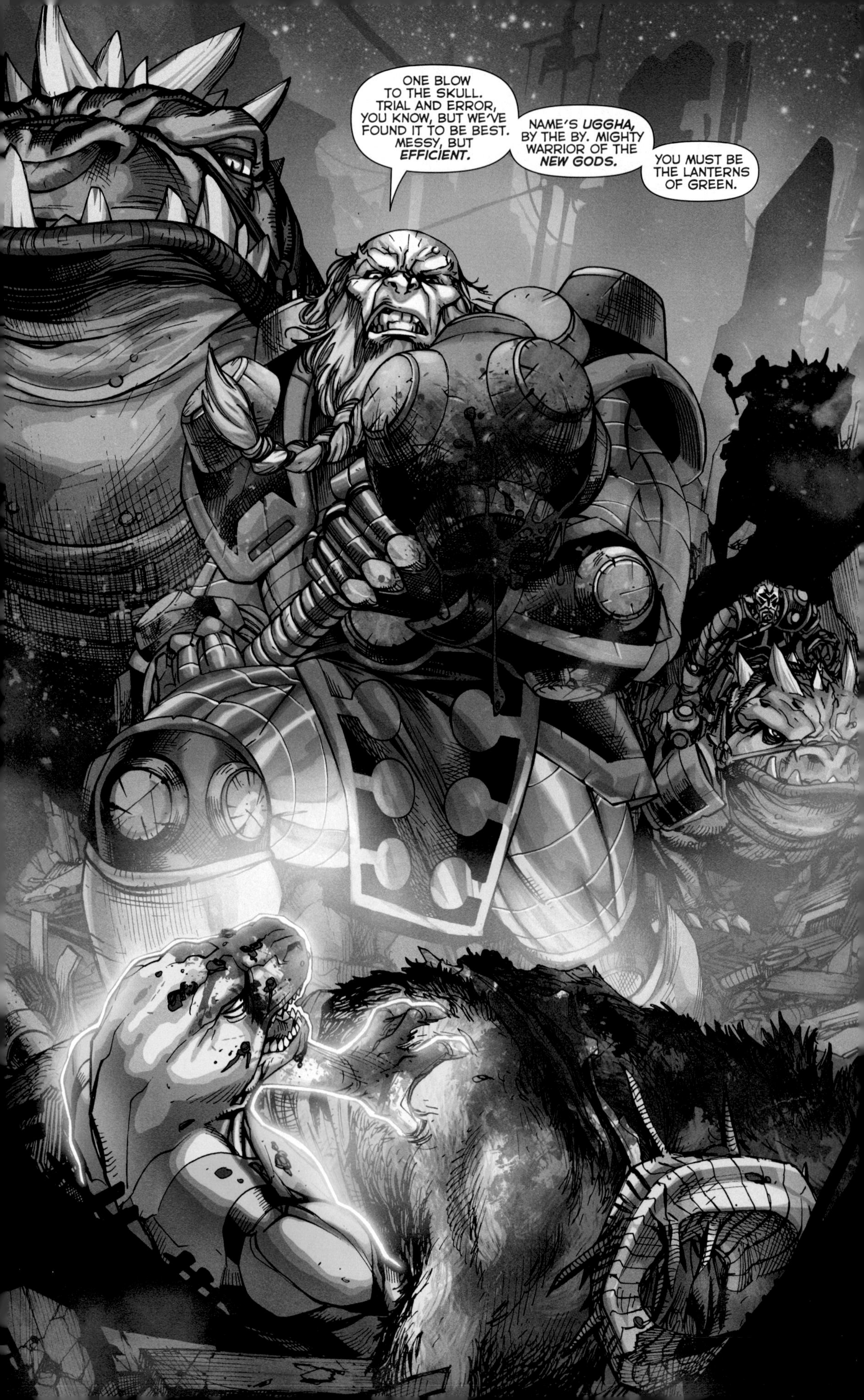
ONE BLOW TO THE SKULL. TRIAL AND ERROR, YOU KNOW, BUT WE'VE FOUND IT TO BE BEST. MESSY, BUT *EFFICIENT.*
NAME'S *UGGHA,* BY THE BY. MIGHTY WARRIOR OF THE *NEW GODS.*
YOU MUST BE THE LANTERNS OF GREEN.

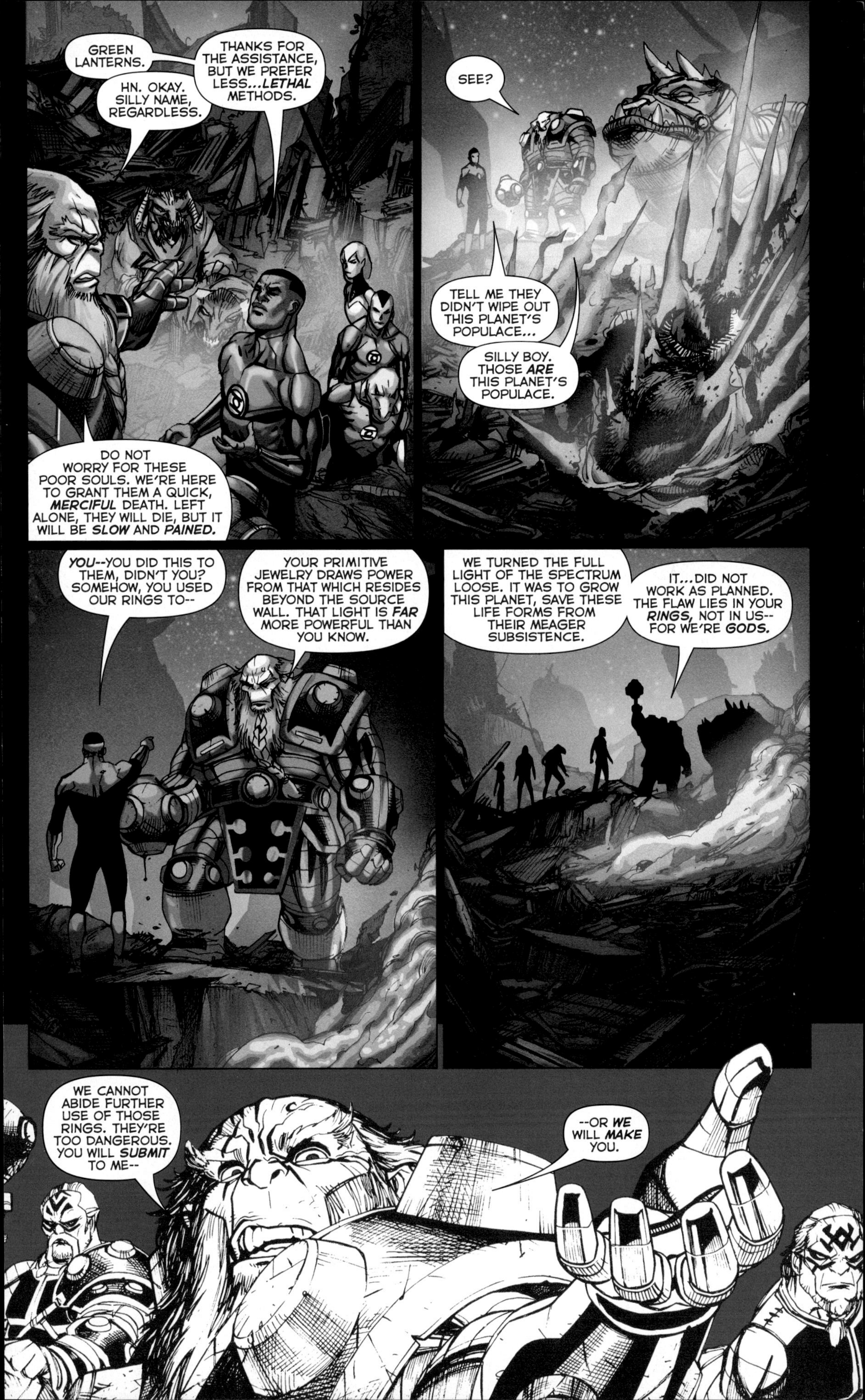

GREEN LANTERNS.
HN. OKAY. SILLY NAME, REGARDLESS.
THANKS FOR THE ASSISTANCE, BUT WE PREFER LESS...LETHAL METHODS.
DO NOT WORRY FOR THESE POOR SOULS. WE'RE HERE TO GRANT THEM A QUICK, MERCIFUL DEATH. LEFT ALONE, THEY WILL DIE, BUT IT WILL BE SLOW AND PAINED.
SEE?
TELL ME THEY DIDN'T WIPE OUT THIS PLANET'S POPULACE...
SILLY BOY. THOSE ARE THIS PLANET'S POPULACE.
YOU--YOU DID THIS TO THEM, DIDN'T YOU? SOMEHOW, YOU USED OUR RINGS TO--
YOUR PRIMITIVE JEWELRY DRAWS POWER FROM THAT WHICH RESIDES BEYOND THE SOURCE WALL. THAT LIGHT IS FAR MORE POWERFUL THAN YOU KNOW.
WE TURNED THE FULL LIGHT OF THE SPECTRUM LOOSE. IT WAS TO GROW THIS PLANET, SAVE THESE LIFE FORMS FROM THEIR MEAGER SUBSISTENCE.
IT...DID NOT WORK AS PLANNED. THE FLAW LIES IN YOUR RINGS, NOT IN US--FOR WE'RE GODS.
WE CANNOT ABIDE FURTHER USE OF THOSE RINGS. THEY'RE TOO DANGEROUS. YOU WILL SUBMIT TO ME--
--OR WE WILL MAKE YOU.

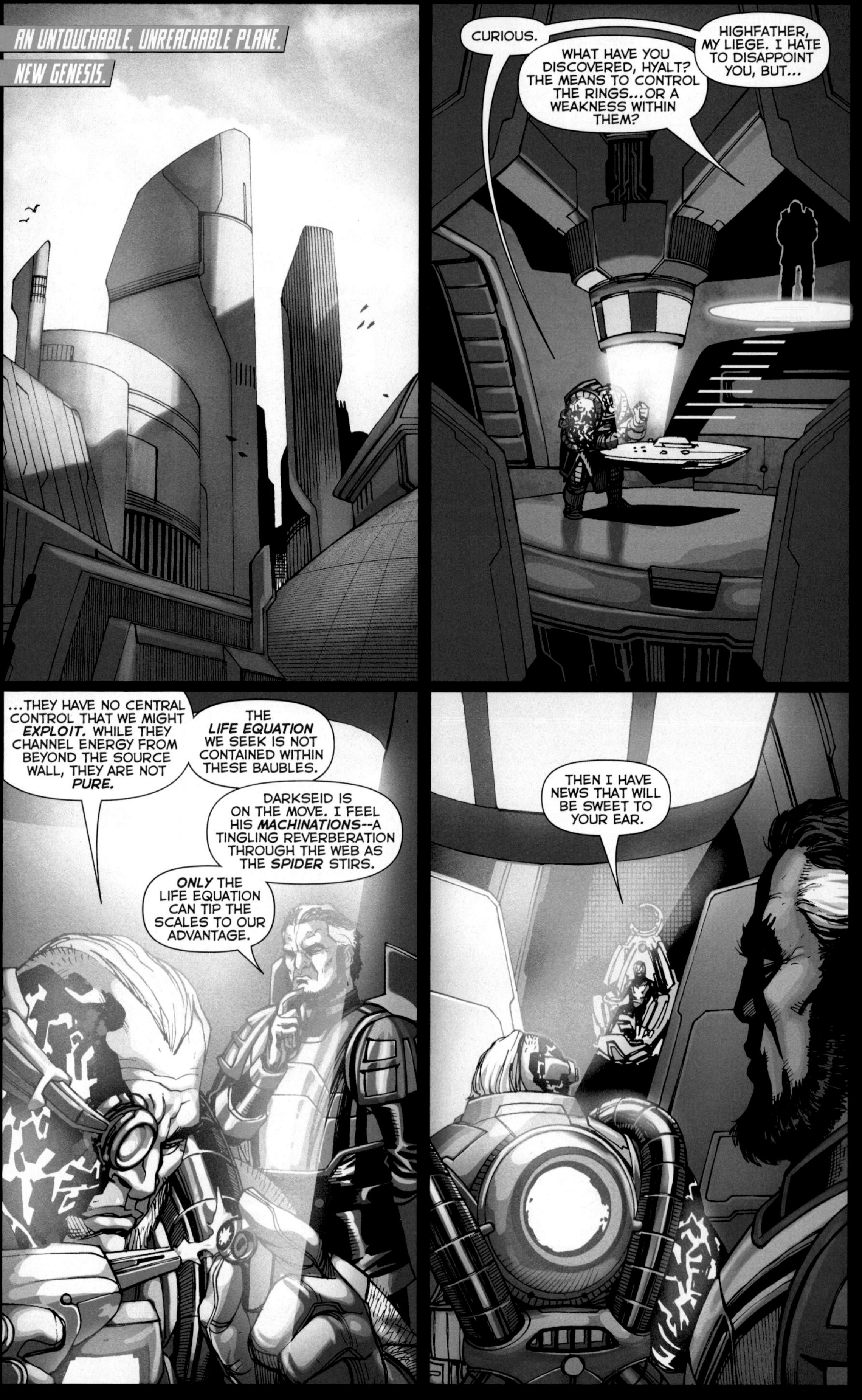

AN UNTOUCHABLE, UNREACHABLE PLANE.
NEW GENESIS.
CURIOUS.
WHAT HAVE YOU DISCOVERED, HYALT? THE MEANS TO CONTROL THE RINGS...OR A WEAKNESS WITHIN THEM?
HIGHFATHER, MY LIEGE. I HATE TO DISAPPOINT YOU, BUT...
...THEY HAVE NO CENTRAL CONTROL THAT WE MIGHT EXPLOIT. WHILE THEY CHANNEL ENERGY FROM BEYOND THE SOURCE WALL, THEY ARE NOT PURE.
THE LIFE EQUATION WE SEEK IS NOT CONTAINED WITHIN THESE BAUBLES.
DARKSEID IS ON THE MOVE. I FEEL HIS MACHINATIONS--A TINGLING REVERBERATION THROUGH THE WEB AS THE SPIDER STIRS.
ONLY THE LIFE EQUATION CAN TIP THE SCALES TO OUR ADVANTAGE.
THEN I HAVE NEWS THAT WILL BE SWEET TO YOUR EAR.

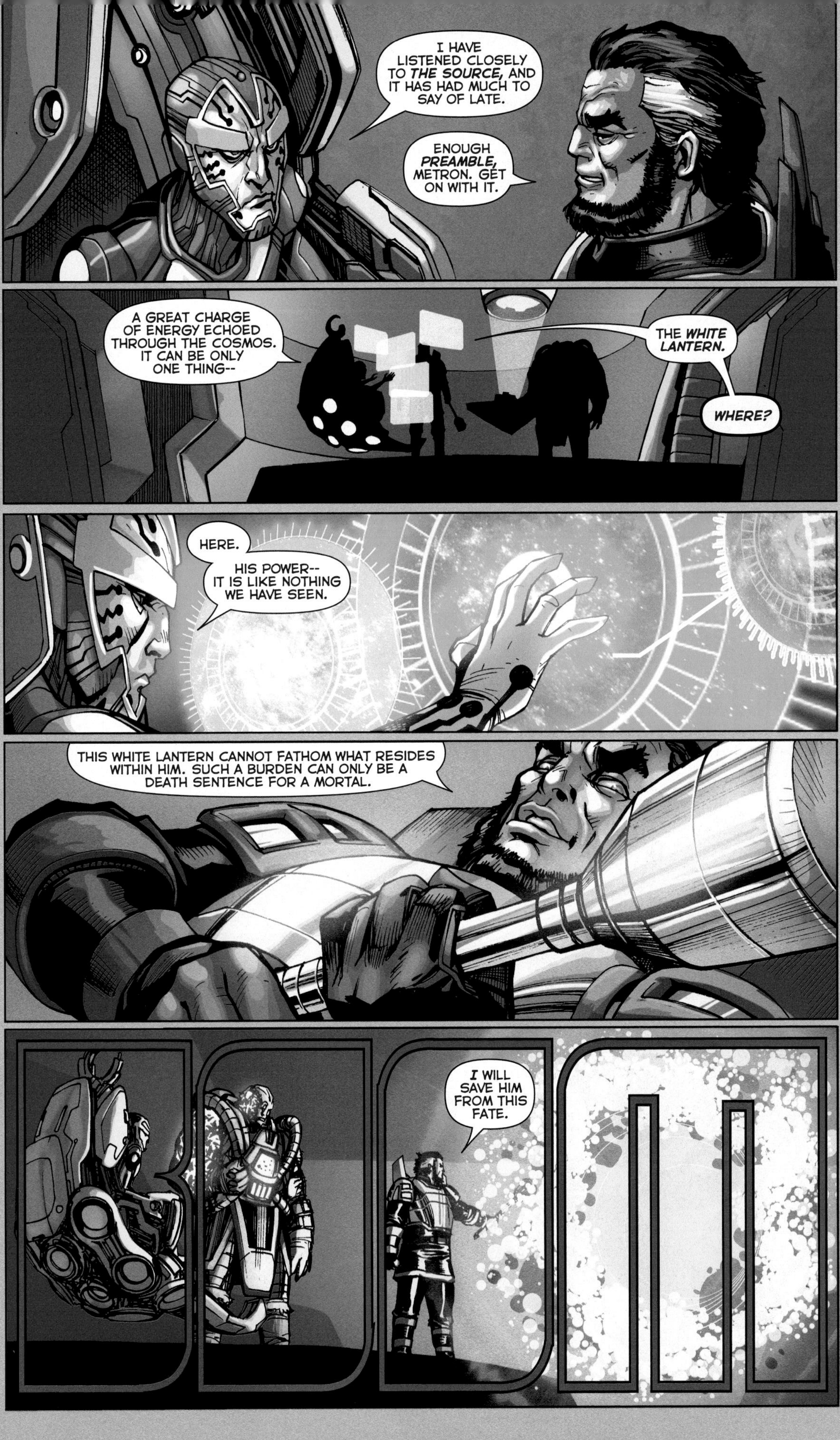
I HAVE LISTENED CLOSELY TO *THE SOURCE,* AND IT HAS HAD MUCH TO SAY OF LATE.
ENOUGH *PREAMBLE,* METRON. GET ON WITH IT.
A GREAT CHARGE OF ENERGY ECHOED THROUGH THE COSMOS. IT CAN BE ONLY ONE THING--
THE *WHITE LANTERN.*
WHERE?
HERE.
HIS POWER-- IT IS LIKE NOTHING WE HAVE SEEN.
THIS WHITE LANTERN CANNOT FATHOM WHAT RESIDES WITHIN HIM. SUCH A BURDEN CAN ONLY BE A DEATH SENTENCE FOR A MORTAL.
I WILL SAVE HIM FROM THIS FATE.

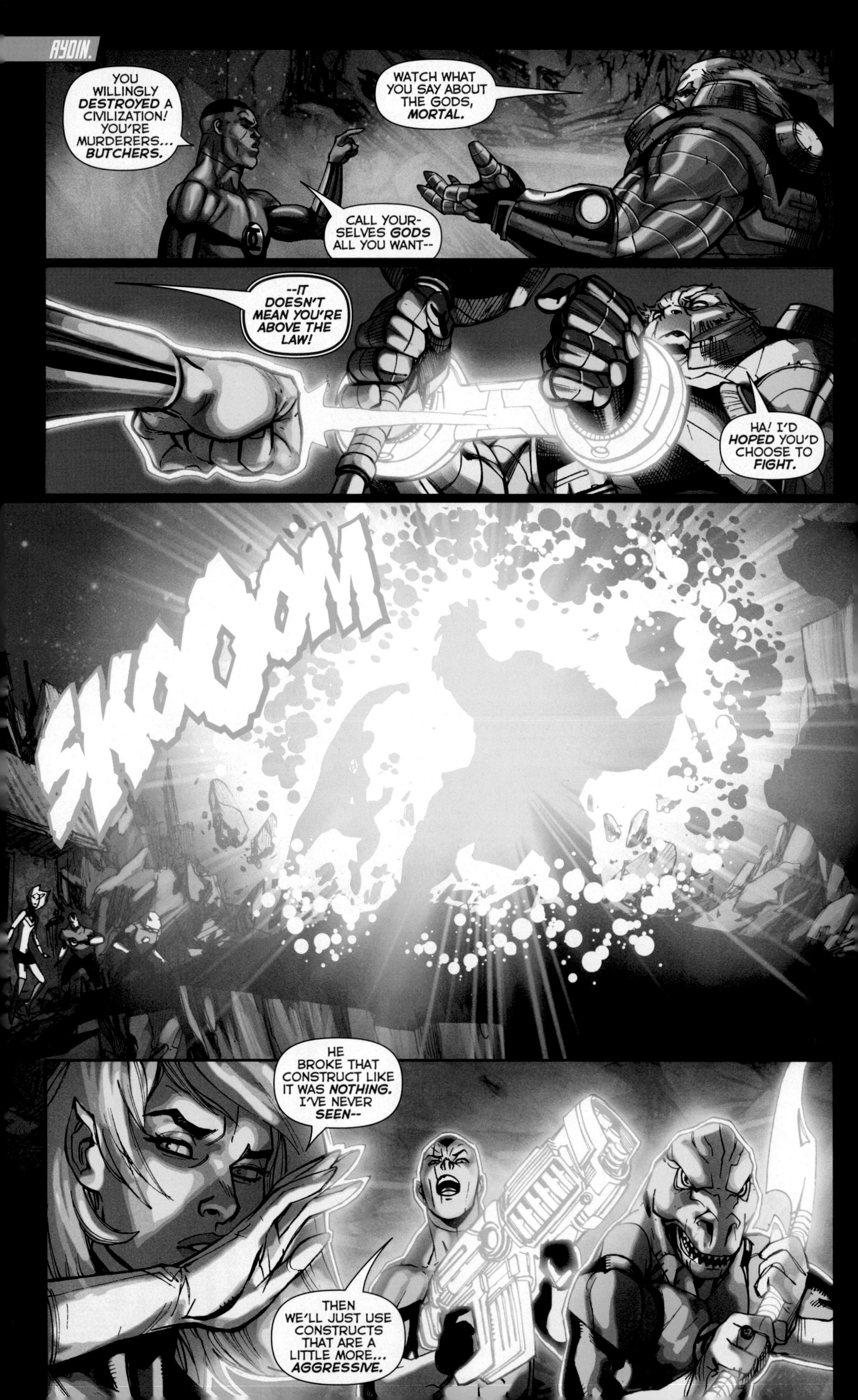
AYDIN.
YOU WILLINGLY DESTROYED A CIVILIZATION! YOU'RE MURDERERS... BUTCHERS.
WATCH WHAT YOU SAY ABOUT THE GODS, MORTAL.
CALL YOURSELVES GODS ALL YOU WANT--
--IT DOESN'T MEAN YOU'RE ABOVE THE LAW!
HA! I'D HOPED YOU'D CHOOSE TO FIGHT.
SKOOOM
HE BROKE THAT CONSTRUCT LIKE IT WAS NOTHING. I'VE NEVER SEEN--
THEN WE'LL JUST USE CONSTRUCTS THAT ARE A LITTLE MORE... AGGRESSIVE.

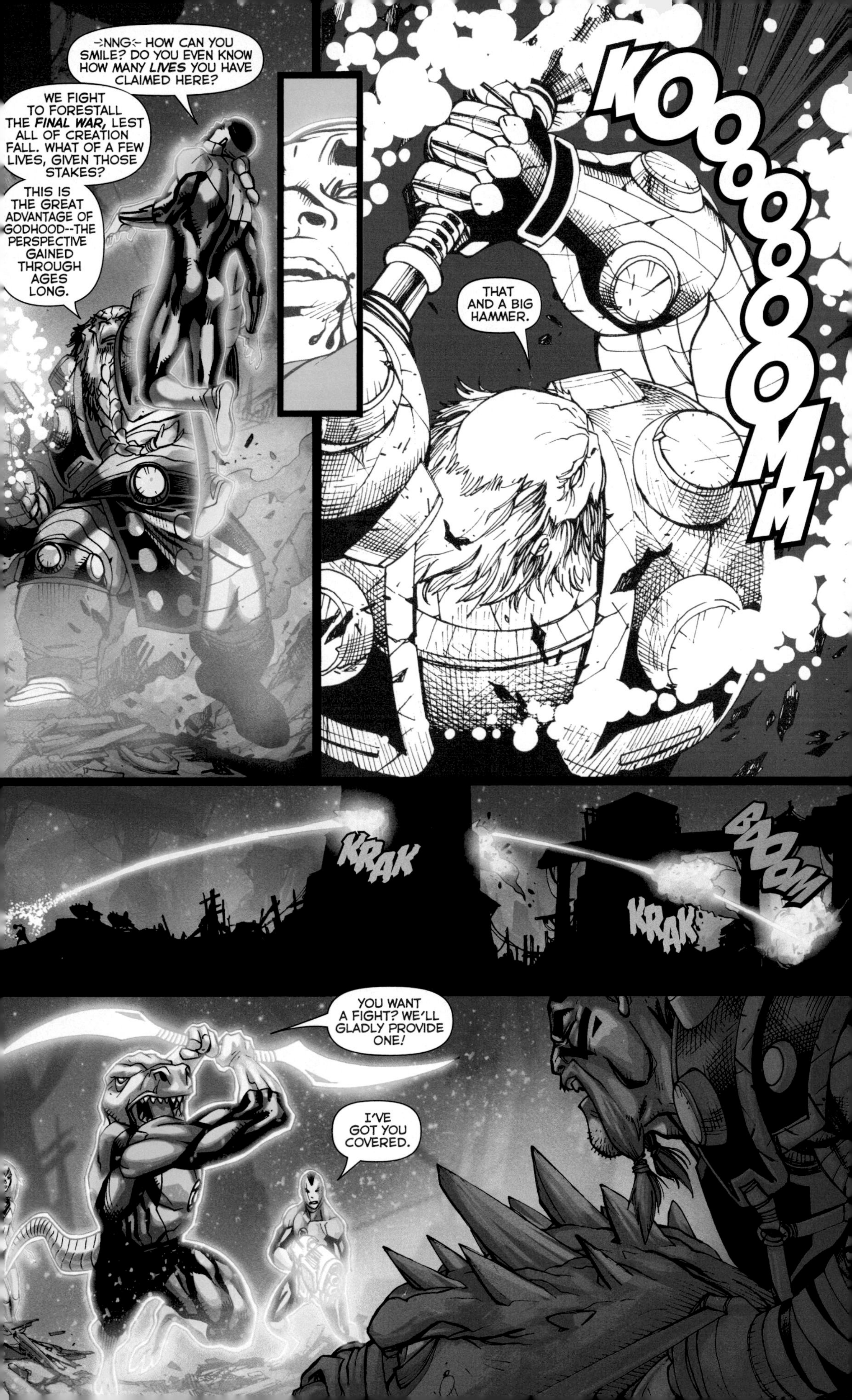

–NNG– HOW CAN YOU SMILE? DO YOU EVEN KNOW HOW MANY LIVES YOU HAVE CLAIMED HERE?
WE FIGHT TO FORESTALL THE FINAL WAR, LEST ALL OF CREATION FALL. WHAT OF A FEW LIVES, GIVEN THOSE STAKES?
THIS IS THE GREAT ADVANTAGE OF GODHOOD--THE PERSPECTIVE GAINED THROUGH AGES LONG.
KOOOOOOOOMM
THAT AND A BIG HAMMER.
KRAK
BOOOM
KRAK
YOU WANT A FIGHT? WE'LL GLADLY PROVIDE ONE!
I'VE GOT YOU COVERED.

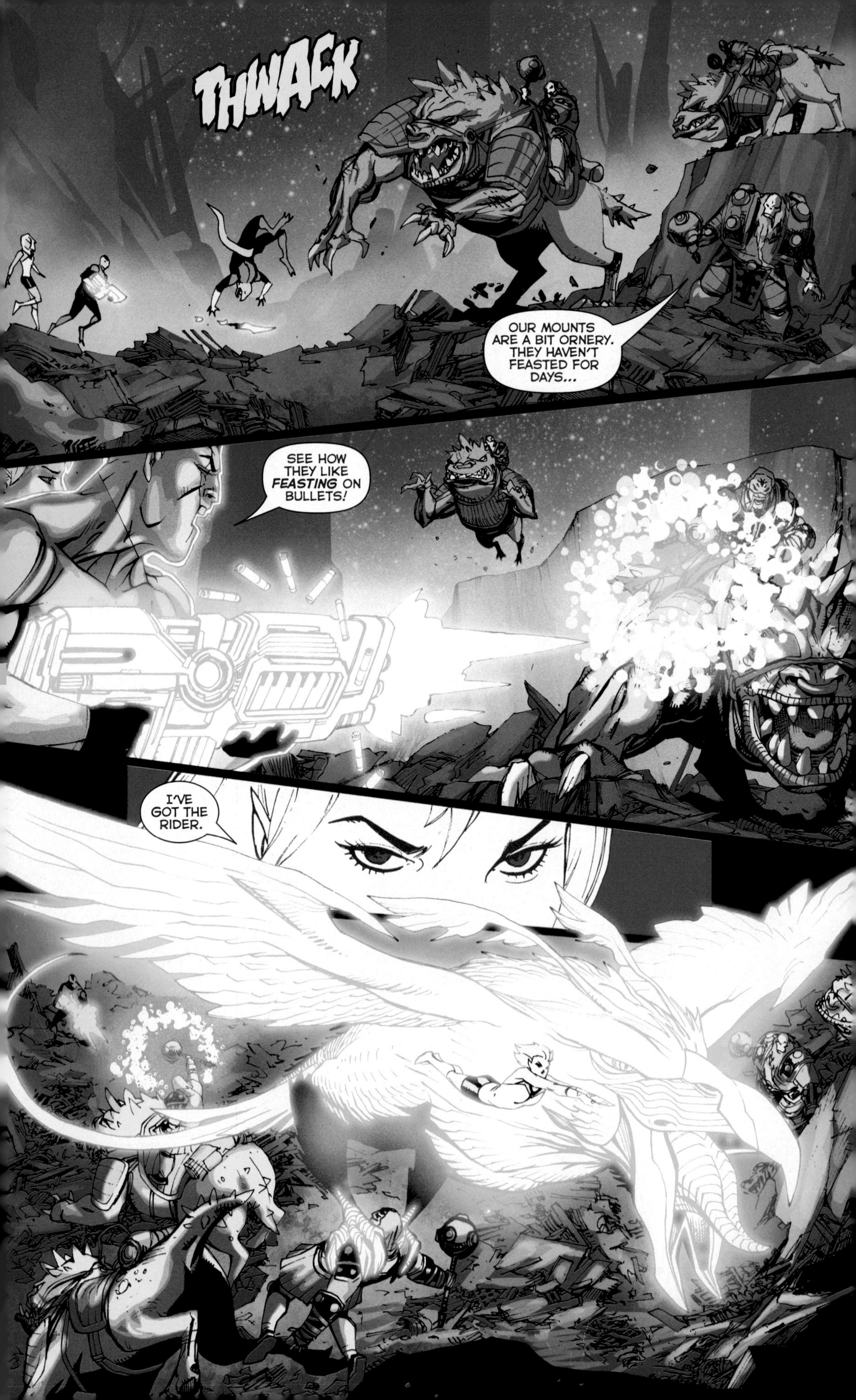
THWACK
OUR MOUNTS ARE A BIT ORNERY. THEY HAVEN'T FEASTED FOR DAYS...
SEE HOW THEY LIKE *FEASTING* ON BULLETS!
I'VE GOT THE RIDER.

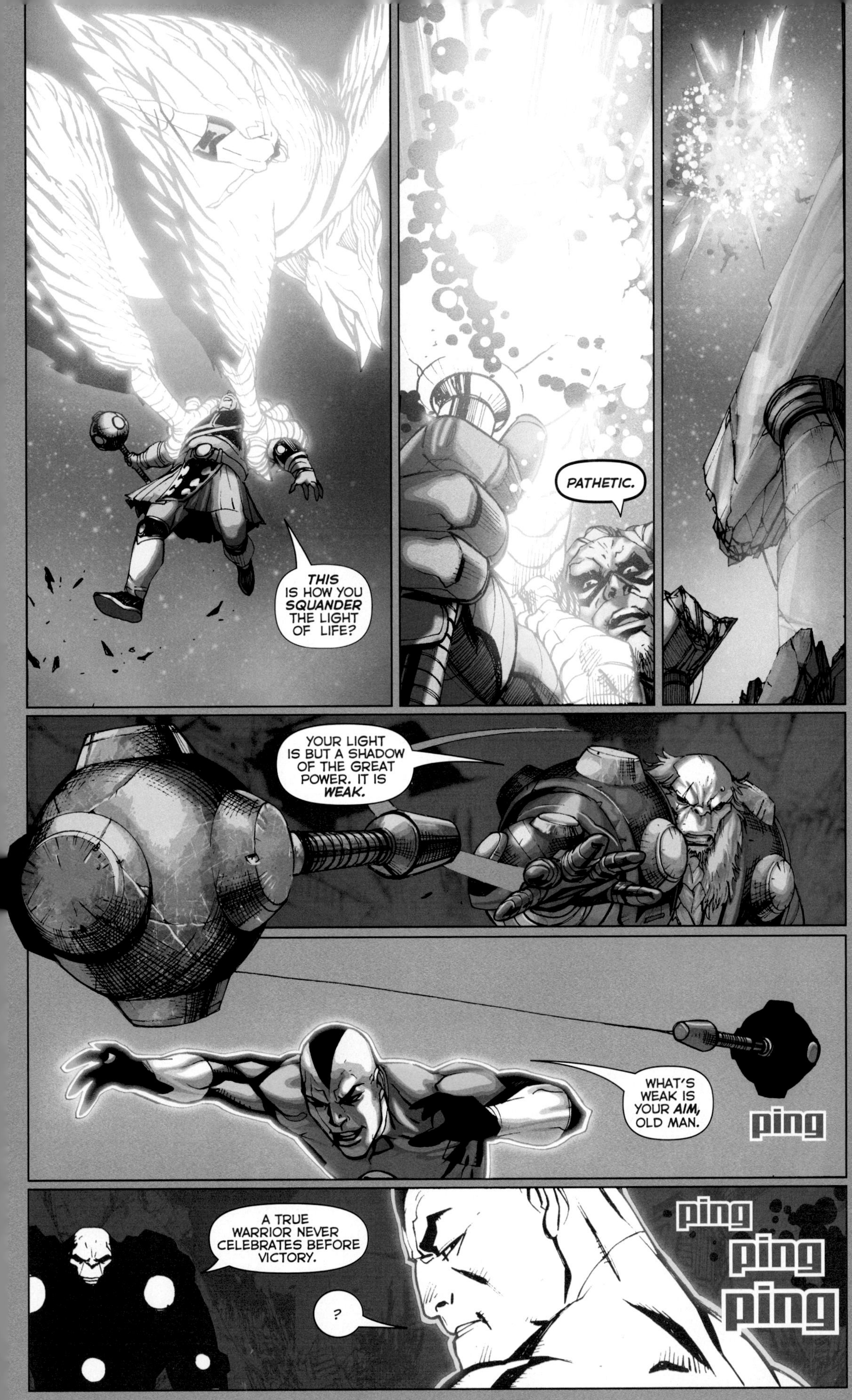
THIS IS HOW YOU SQUANDER THE LIGHT OF LIFE?
PATHETIC.
YOUR LIGHT IS BUT A SHADOW OF THE GREAT POWER. IT IS WEAK.
WHAT'S WEAK IS YOUR AIM, OLD MAN.
ping
A TRUE WARRIOR NEVER CELEBRATES BEFORE VICTORY.
?
ping
ping
ping

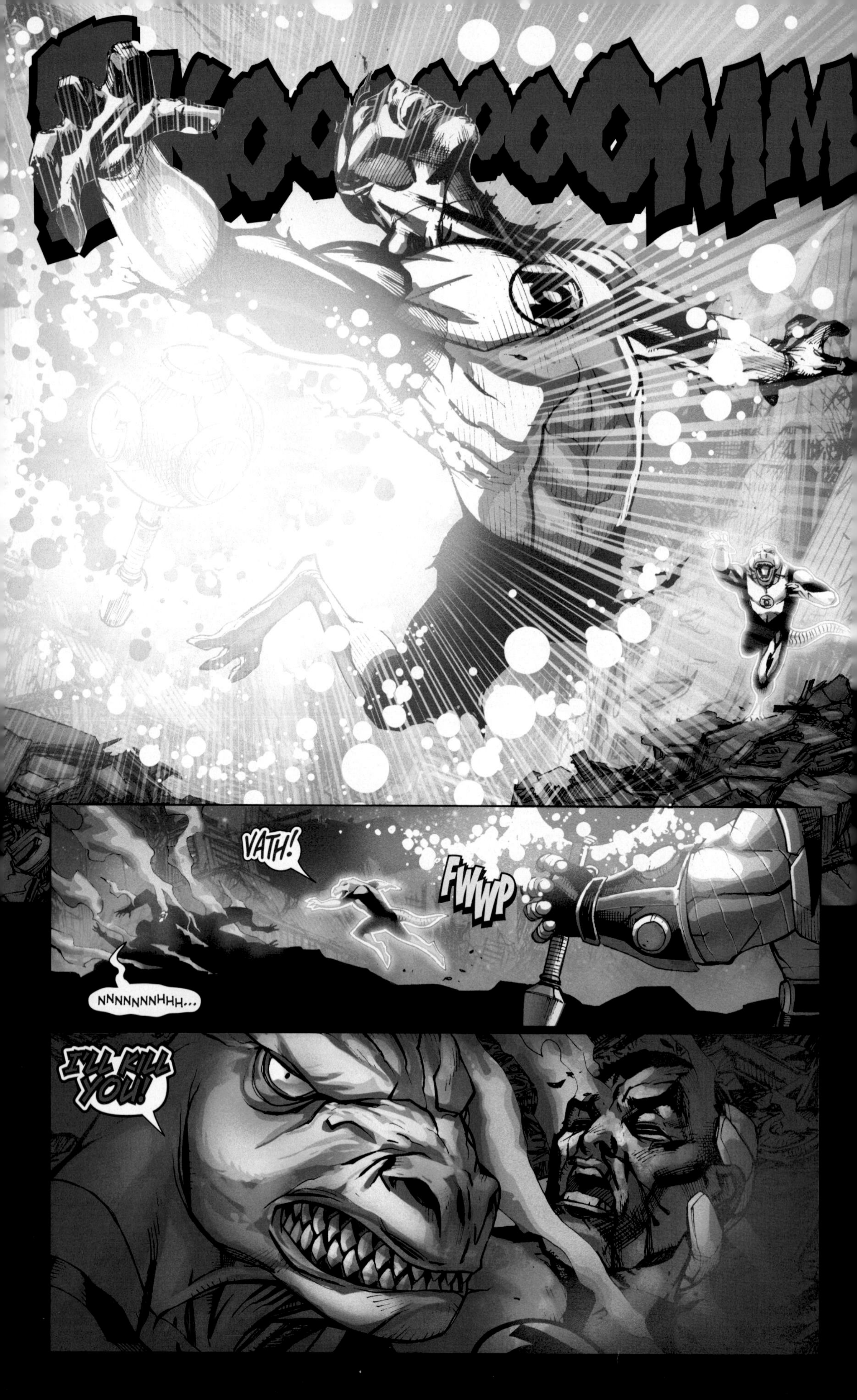

KROOOOOOOMM
VATH!
FWWP
NNNNNNNHHH...
I'LL KILL YOU!

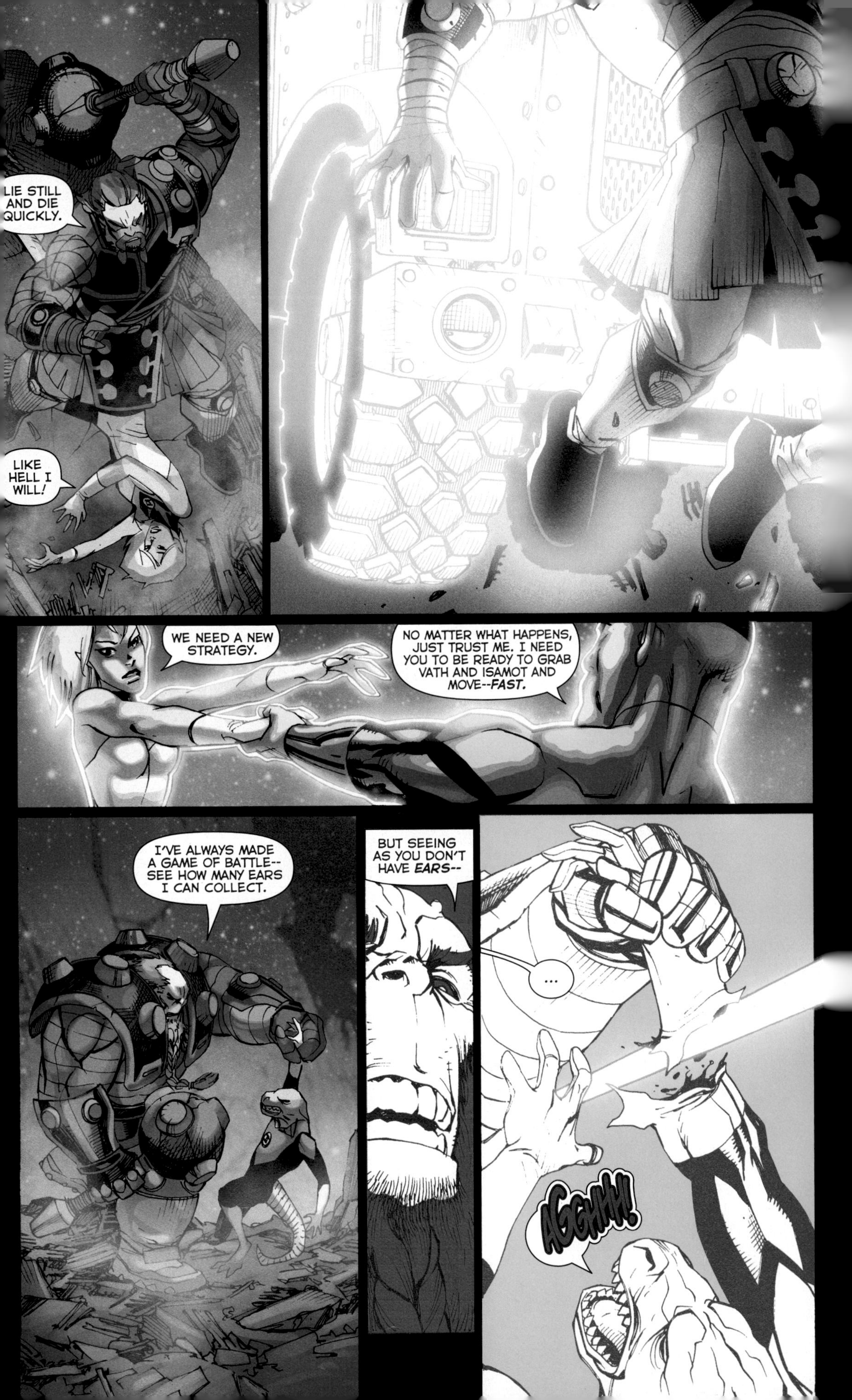

LIE STILL AND DIE QUICKLY.
LIKE HELL I WILL!
WE NEED A NEW STRATEGY.
NO MATTER WHAT HAPPENS, JUST TRUST ME. I NEED YOU TO BE READY TO GRAB VATH AND ISAMOT AND MOVE--*FAST.*
I'VE ALWAYS MADE A GAME OF BATTLE-- SEE HOW MANY EARS I CAN COLLECT.
BUT SEEING AS YOU DON'T HAVE *EARS*--
...
AGGHHH!

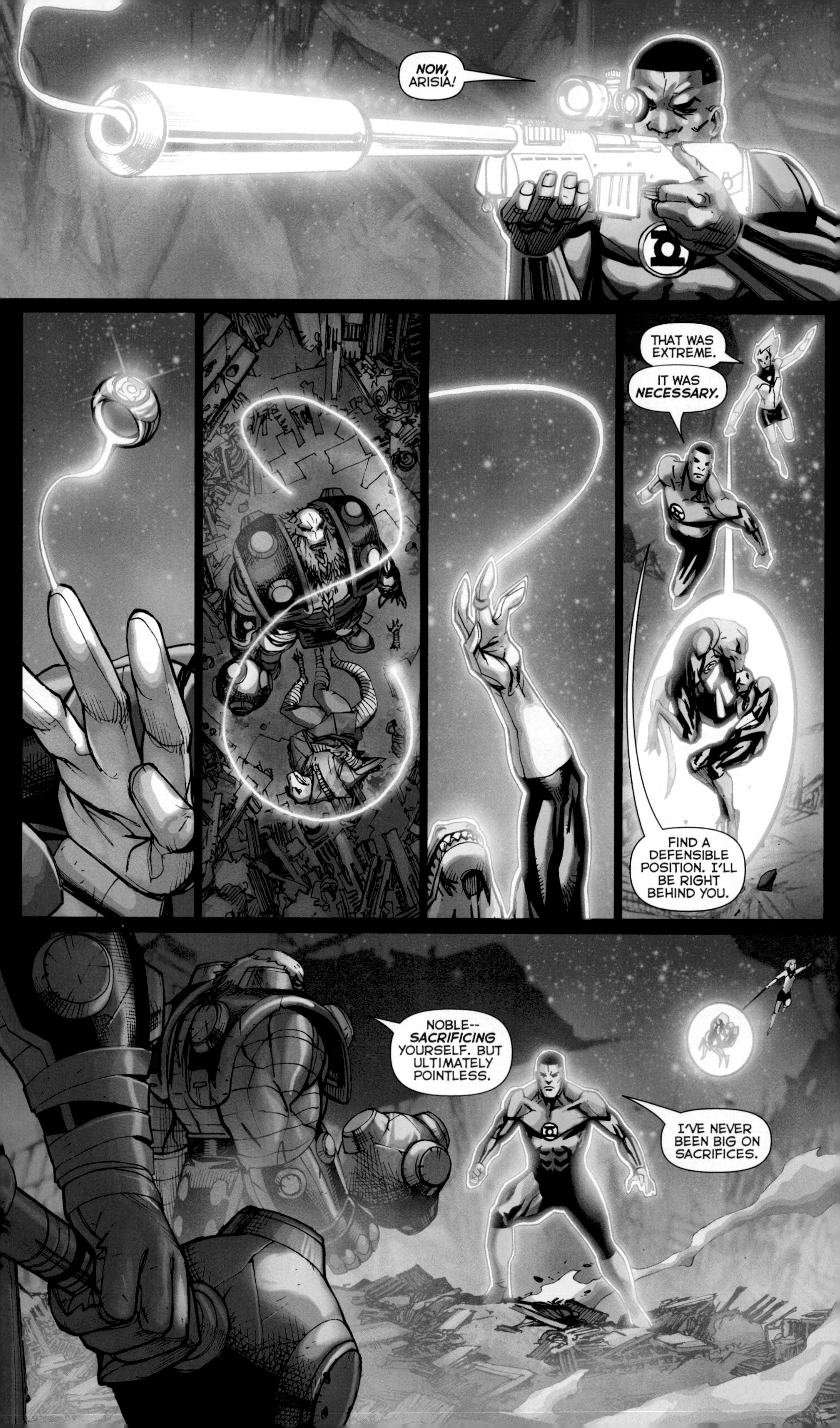
NOW, ARISIA!
THAT WAS EXTREME.
IT WAS NECESSARY.
FIND A DEFENSIBLE POSITION. I'LL BE RIGHT BEHIND YOU.
NOBLE-- SACRIFICING YOURSELF. BUT ULTIMATELY POINTLESS.
I'VE NEVER BEEN BIG ON SACRIFICES.

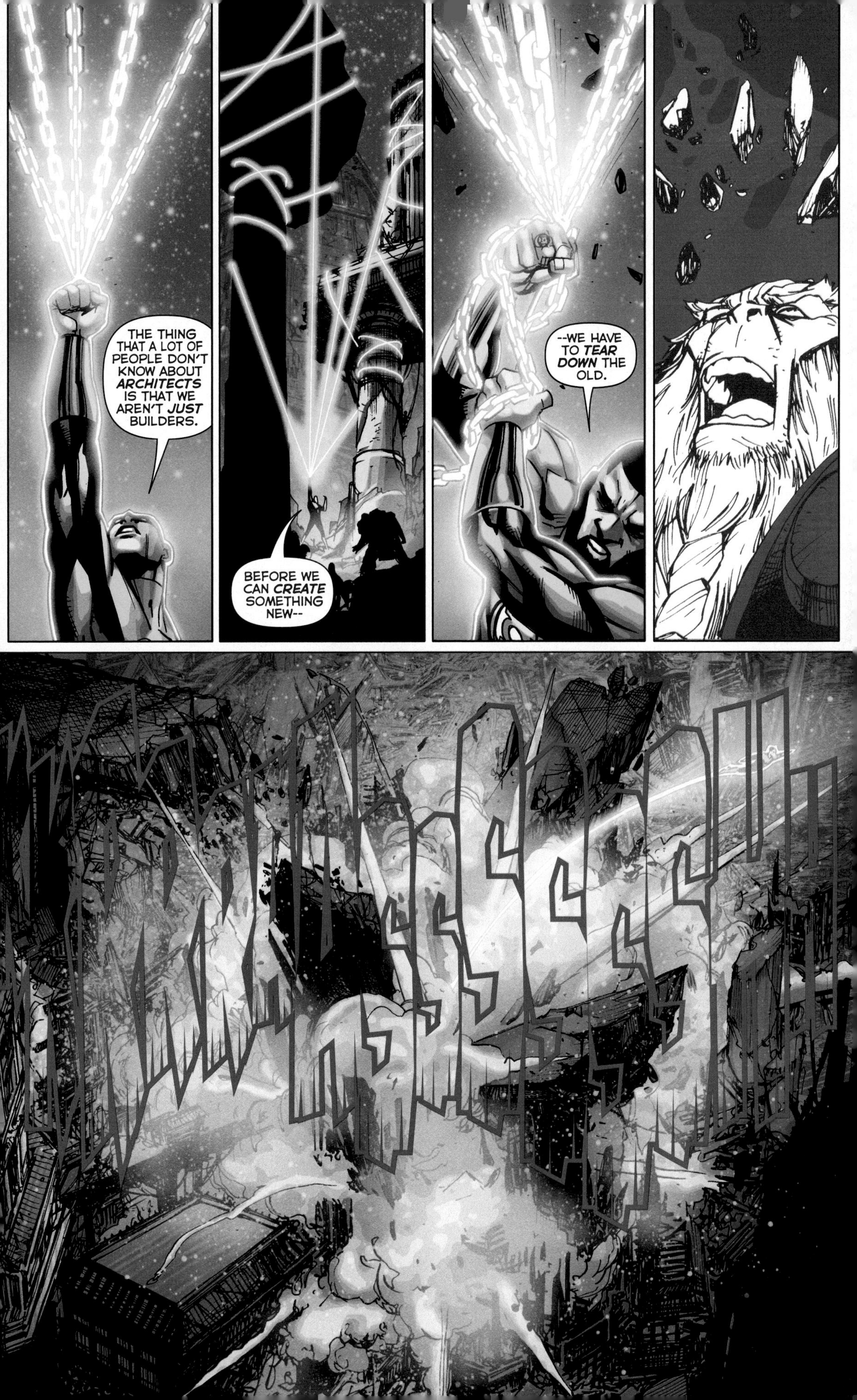
THE THING THAT A LOT OF PEOPLE DON'T KNOW ABOUT *ARCHITECTS* IS THAT WE AREN'T *JUST* BUILDERS.
BEFORE WE CAN *CREATE* SOMETHING NEW--
--WE HAVE TO *TEAR DOWN* THE OLD.

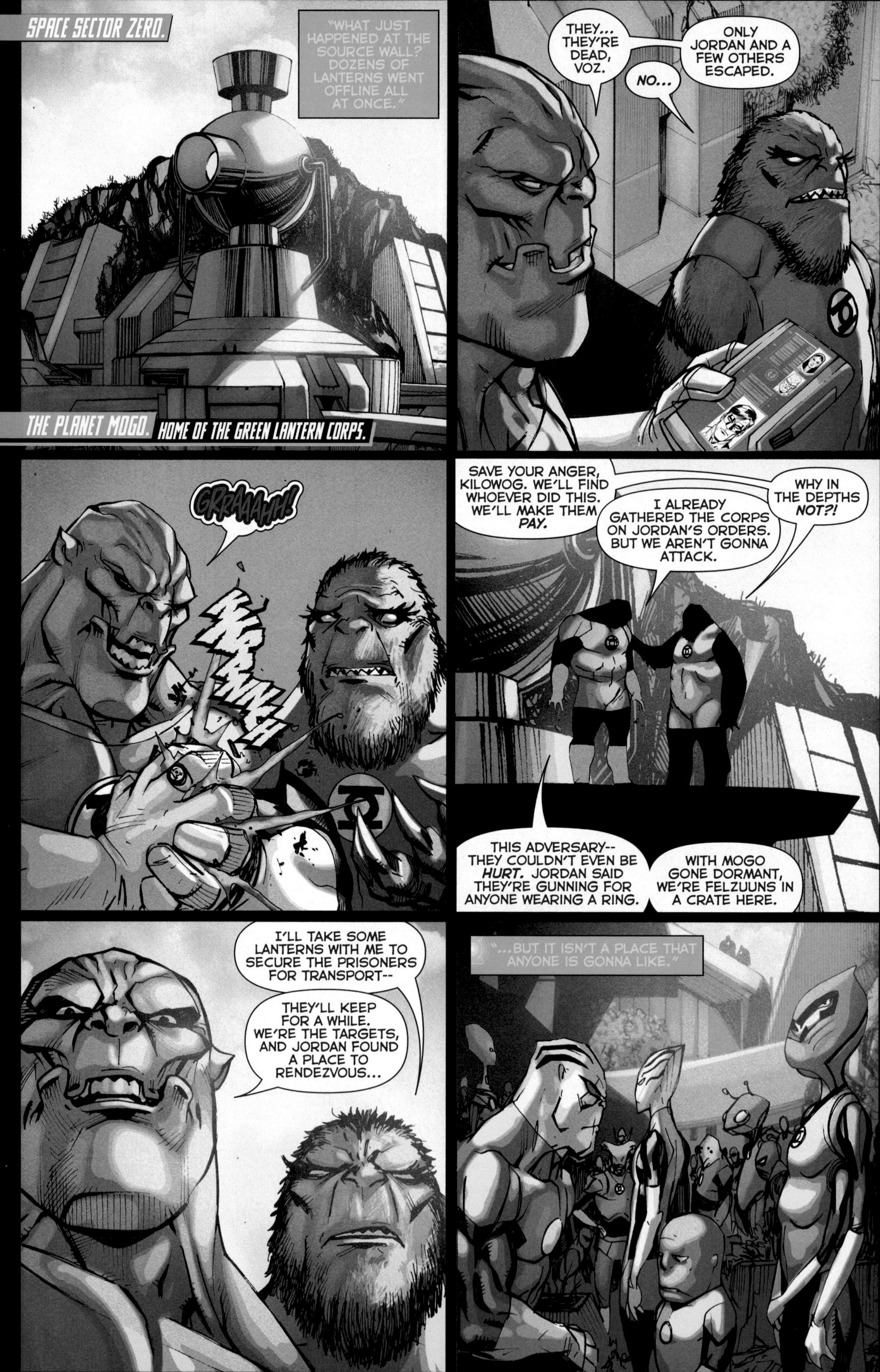
SPACE SECTOR ZERO.
"WHAT JUST HAPPENED AT THE SOURCE WALL? DOZENS OF LANTERNS WENT OFFLINE ALL AT ONCE."
THE PLANET MOGO.
HOME OF THE GREEN LANTERN CORPS.
THEY... THEY'RE DEAD, VOZ.
ONLY JORDAN AND A FEW OTHERS ESCAPED.
NO...
GRRAAAHH!
SAVE YOUR ANGER, KILOWOG. WE'LL FIND WHOEVER DID THIS. WE'LL MAKE THEM PAY.
I ALREADY GATHERED THE CORPS ON JORDAN'S ORDERS. BUT WE AREN'T GONNA ATTACK.
WHY IN THE DEPTHS NOT?!
THIS ADVERSARY-- THEY COULDN'T EVEN BE HURT. JORDAN SAID THEY'RE GUNNING FOR ANYONE WEARING A RING.
WITH MOGO GONE DORMANT, WE'RE FELZUUNS IN A CRATE HERE.
I'LL TAKE SOME LANTERNS WITH ME TO SECURE THE PRISONERS FOR TRANSPORT--
THEY'LL KEEP FOR A WHILE. WE'RE THE TARGETS, AND JORDAN FOUND A PLACE TO RENDEZVOUS...
"...BUT IT ISN'T A PLACE THAT ANYONE IS GONNA LIKE."

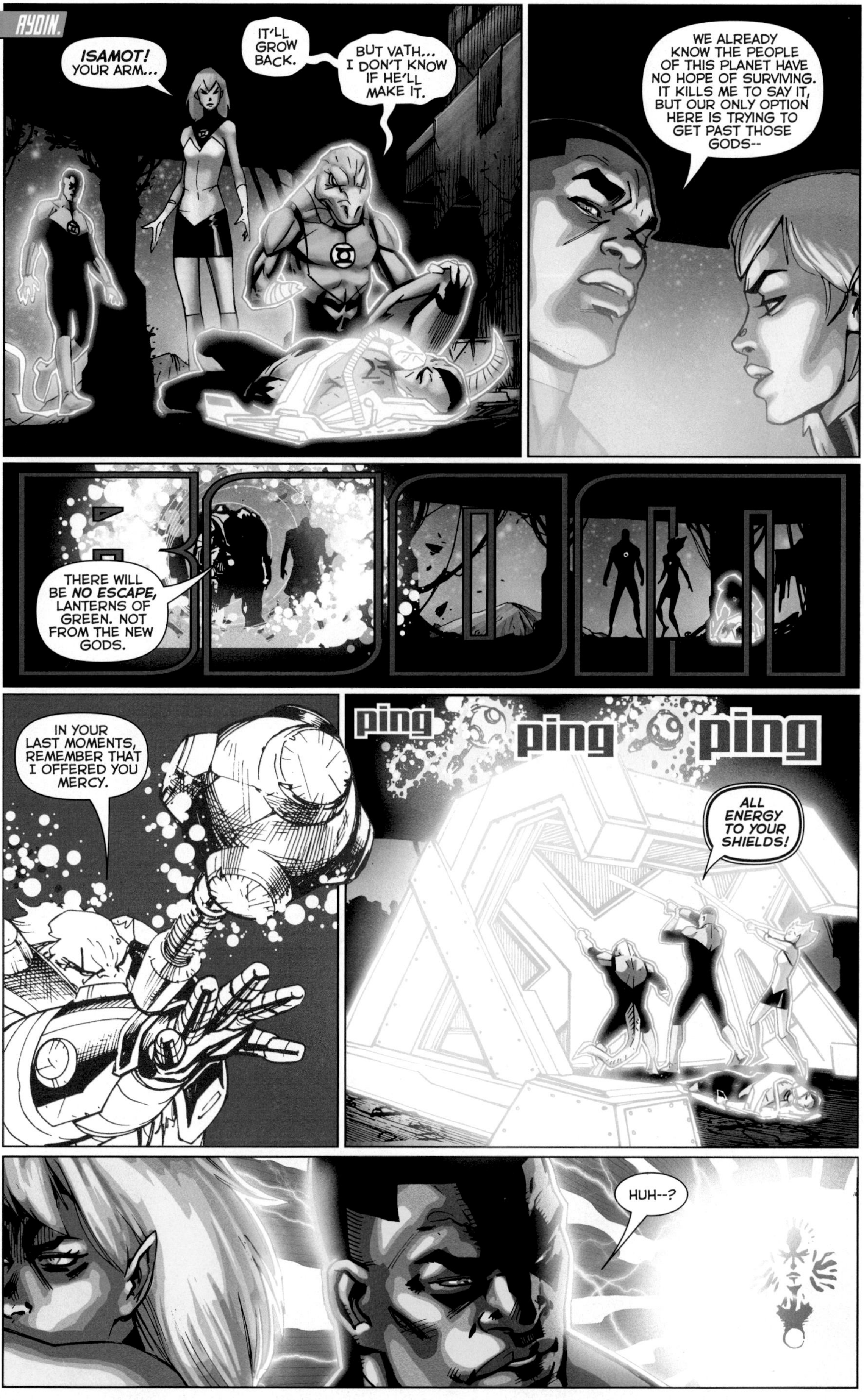
AYDIN.
ISAMOT! YOUR ARM...
IT'LL GROW BACK.
BUT VATH... I DON'T KNOW IF HE'LL MAKE IT.
WE ALREADY KNOW THE PEOPLE OF THIS PLANET HAVE NO HOPE OF SURVIVING. IT KILLS ME TO SAY IT, BUT OUR ONLY OPTION HERE IS TRYING TO GET PAST THOSE GODS--
THERE WILL BE NO ESCAPE, LANTERNS OF GREEN. NOT FROM THE NEW GODS.
IN YOUR LAST MOMENTS, REMEMBER THAT I OFFERED YOU MERCY.
ping
ping
ping
ALL ENERGY TO YOUR SHIELDS!
HUH--?

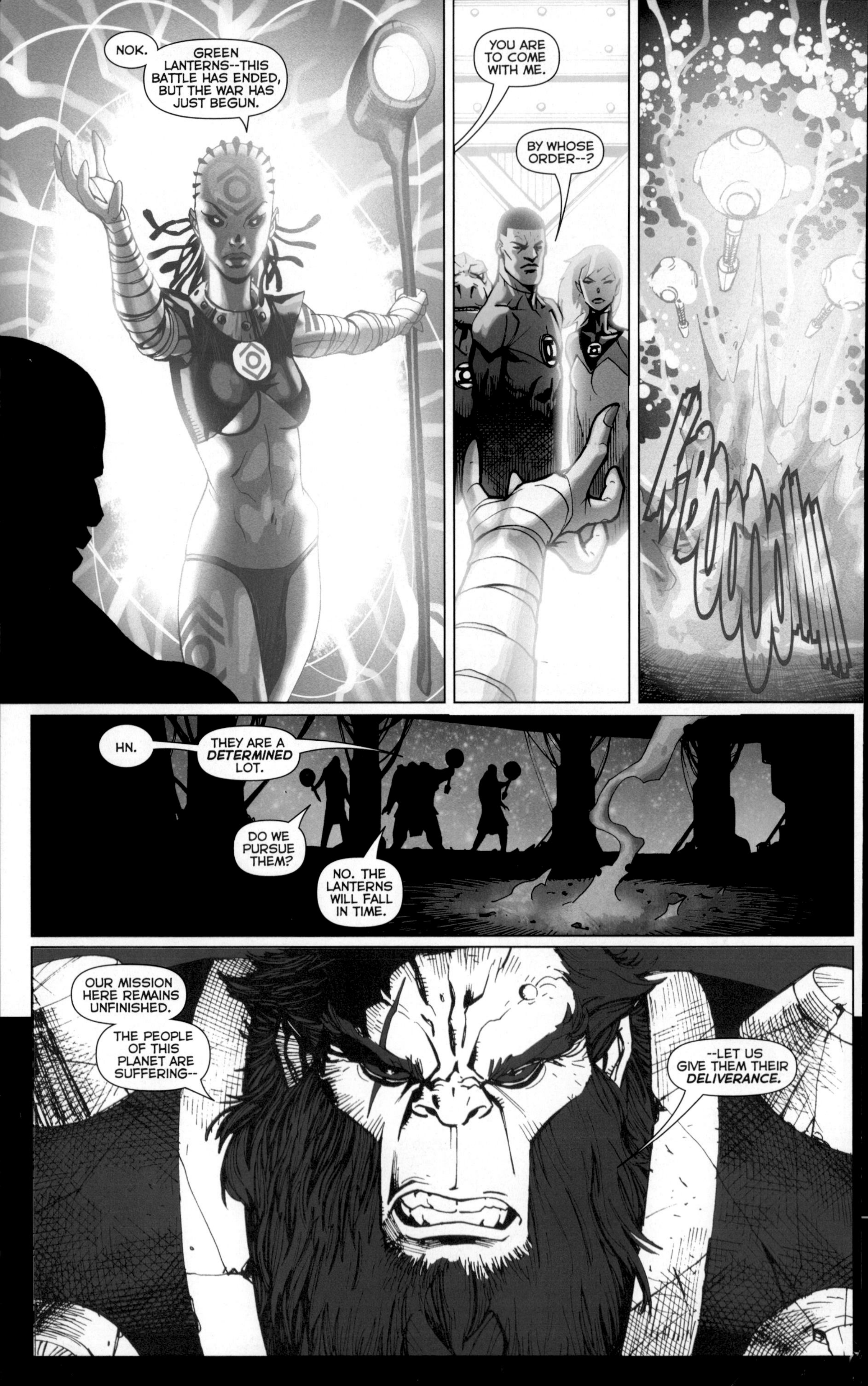
NOK.
GREEN LANTERNS--THIS BATTLE HAS ENDED, BUT THE WAR HAS JUST BEGUN.
YOU ARE TO COME WITH ME.
BY WHOSE ORDER--?
HN.
THEY ARE A *DETERMINED* LOT.
DO WE PURSUE THEM?
NO. THE LANTERNS WILL FALL IN TIME.
OUR MISSION HERE REMAINS UNFINISHED.
THE PEOPLE OF THIS PLANET ARE SUFFERING--
--LET US GIVE THEM THEIR *DELIVERANCE.*

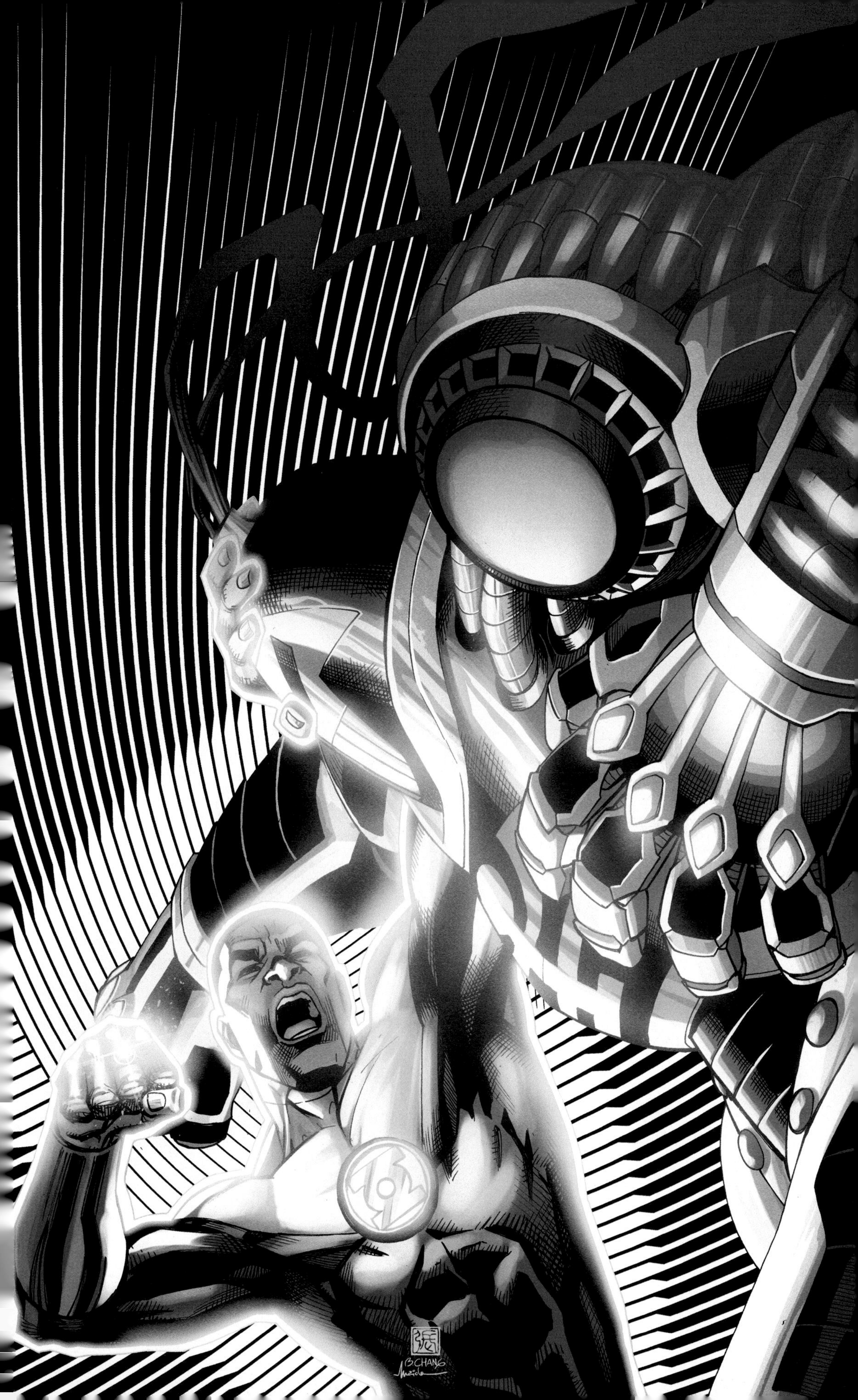
B CHANG

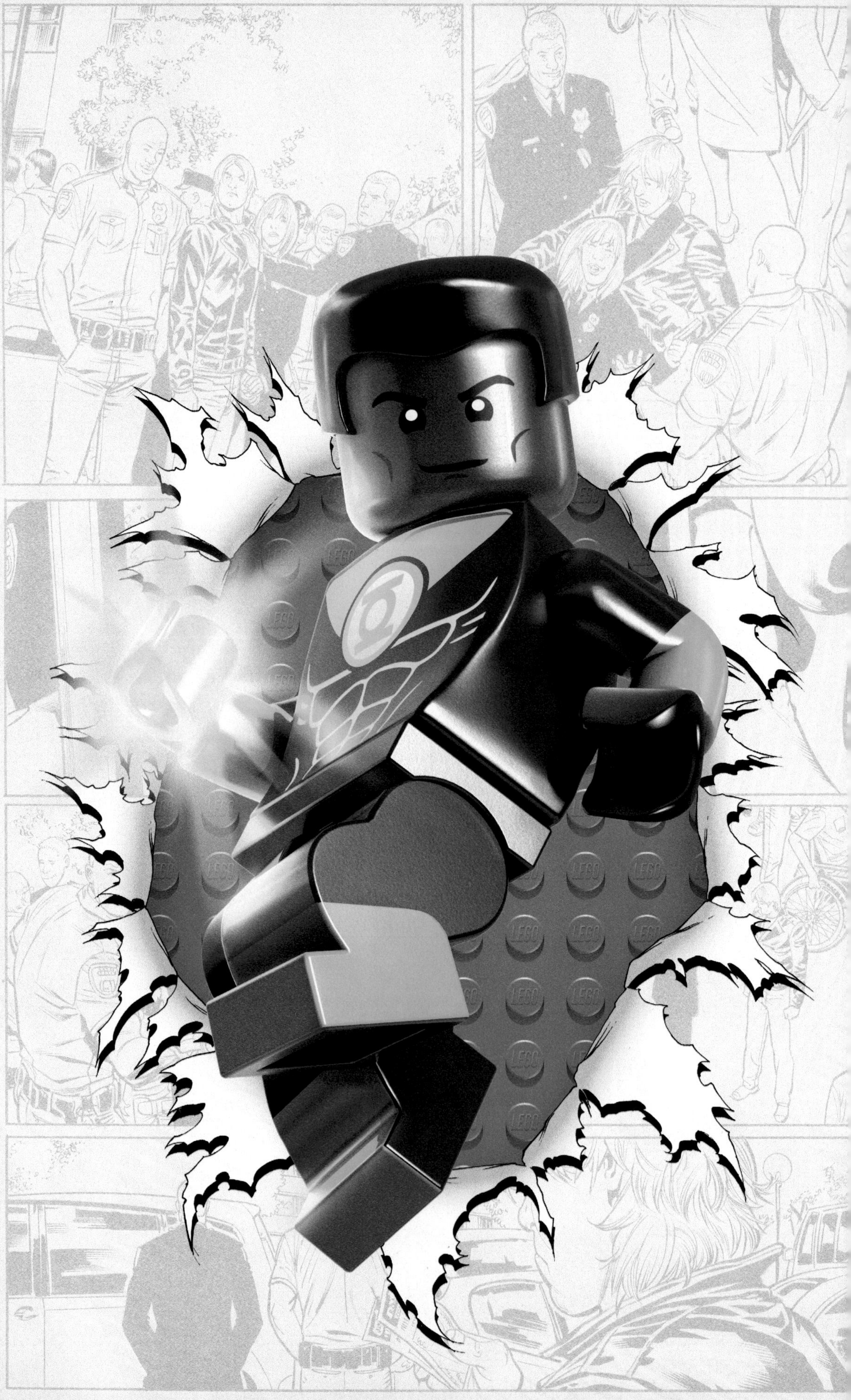

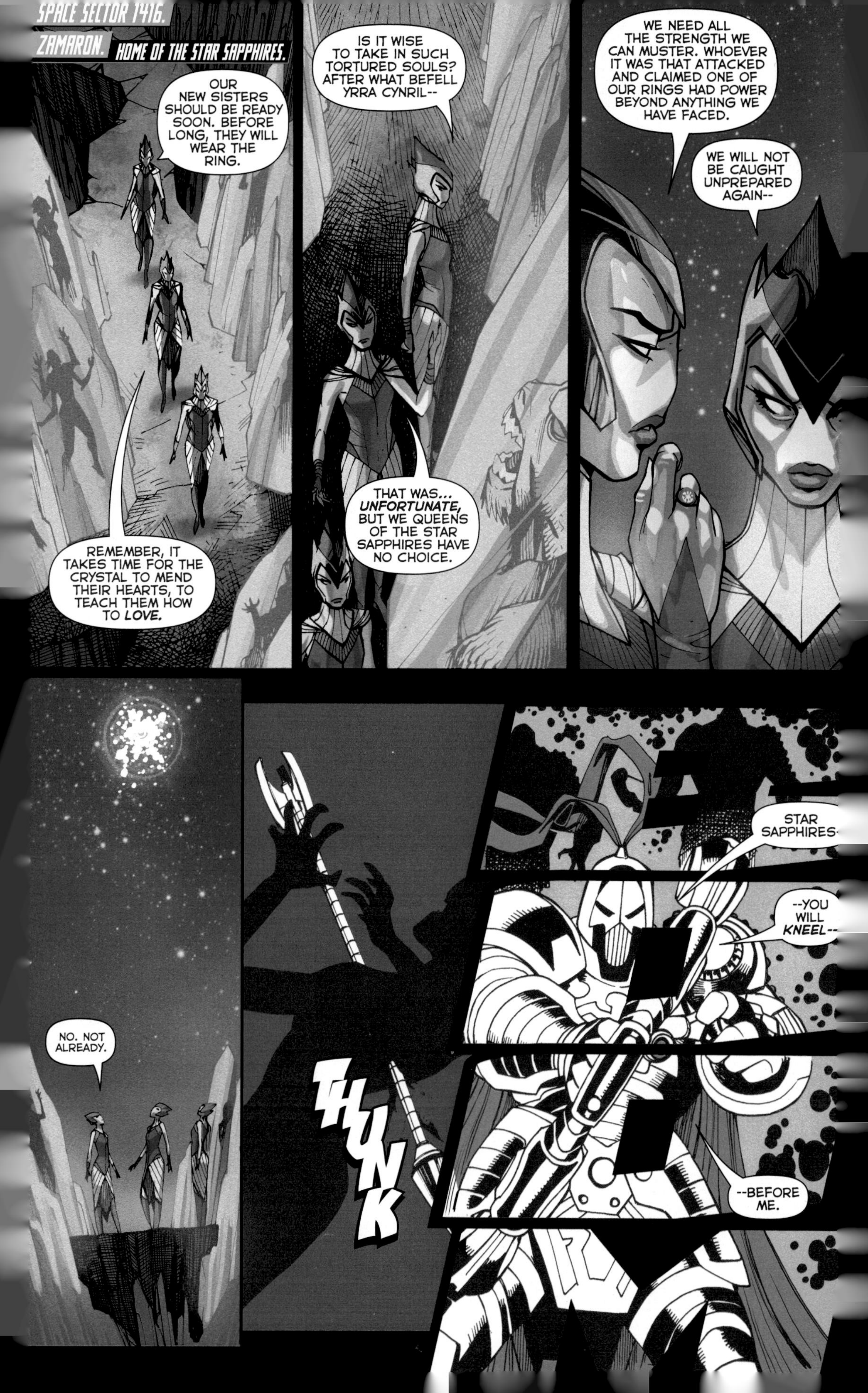
SPACE SECTOR 1416.
ZAMARON.
HOME OF THE STAR SAPPHIRES.
OUR NEW SISTERS SHOULD BE READY SOON. BEFORE LONG, THEY WILL WEAR THE RING.
REMEMBER, IT TAKES TIME FOR THE CRYSTAL TO MEND THEIR HEARTS, TO TEACH THEM HOW TO *LOVE.*
IS IT WISE TO TAKE IN SUCH TORTURED SOULS? AFTER WHAT BEFELL YRRA CYNRIL--
THAT WAS... ***UNFORTUNATE,*** BUT WE QUEENS OF THE STAR SAPPHIRES HAVE NO CHOICE.
WE NEED ALL THE STRENGTH WE CAN MUSTER. WHOEVER IT WAS THAT ATTACKED AND CLAIMED ONE OF OUR RINGS HAD POWER BEYOND ANYTHING WE HAVE FACED.
WE WILL NOT BE CAUGHT UNPREPARED AGAIN--
NO. NOT ALREADY.
THUNK
STAR SAPPHIRES-
--YOU WILL ***KNEEL***--
--BEFORE ME.

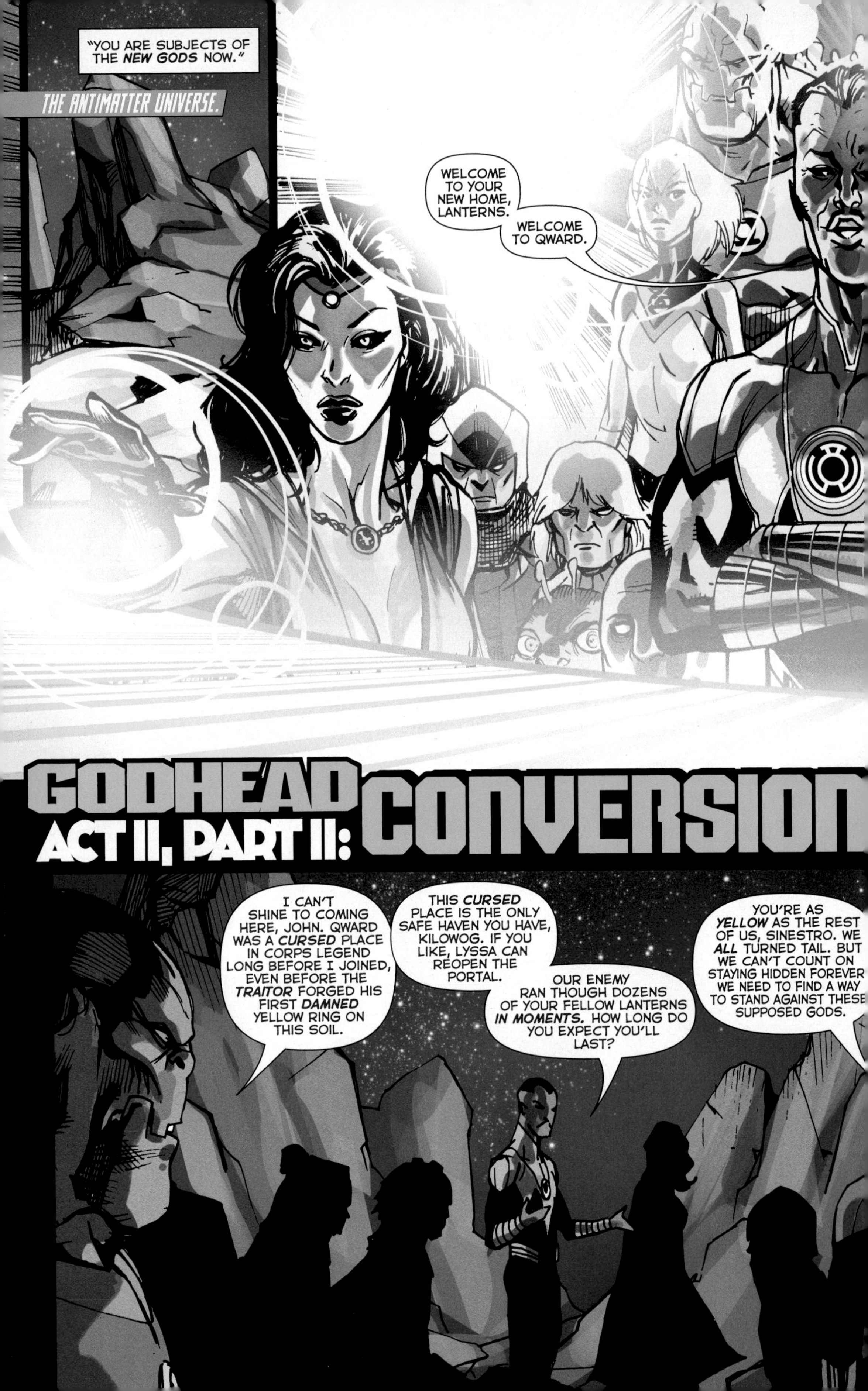
"YOU ARE SUBJECTS OF THE NEW GODS NOW."
THE ANTIMATTER UNIVERSE.
WELCOME TO YOUR NEW HOME, LANTERNS.
WELCOME TO QWARD.
GODHEAD ACT II, PART II: CONVERSION
I CAN'T SHINE TO COMING HERE, JOHN. QWARD WAS A CURSED PLACE IN CORPS LEGEND LONG BEFORE I JOINED, EVEN BEFORE THE TRAITOR FORGED HIS FIRST DAMNED YELLOW RING ON THIS SOIL.
THIS CURSED PLACE IS THE ONLY SAFE HAVEN YOU HAVE, KILOWOG. IF YOU LIKE, LYSSA CAN REOPEN THE PORTAL.
OUR ENEMY RAN THOUGH DOZENS OF YOUR FELLOW LANTERNS IN MOMENTS. HOW LONG DO YOU EXPECT YOU'LL LAST?
YOU'RE AS YELLOW AS THE REST OF US, SINESTRO. WE ALL TURNED TAIL. BUT WE CAN'T COUNT ON STAYING HIDDEN FOREVER WE NEED TO FIND A WAY TO STAND AGAINST THESE SUPPOSED GODS.

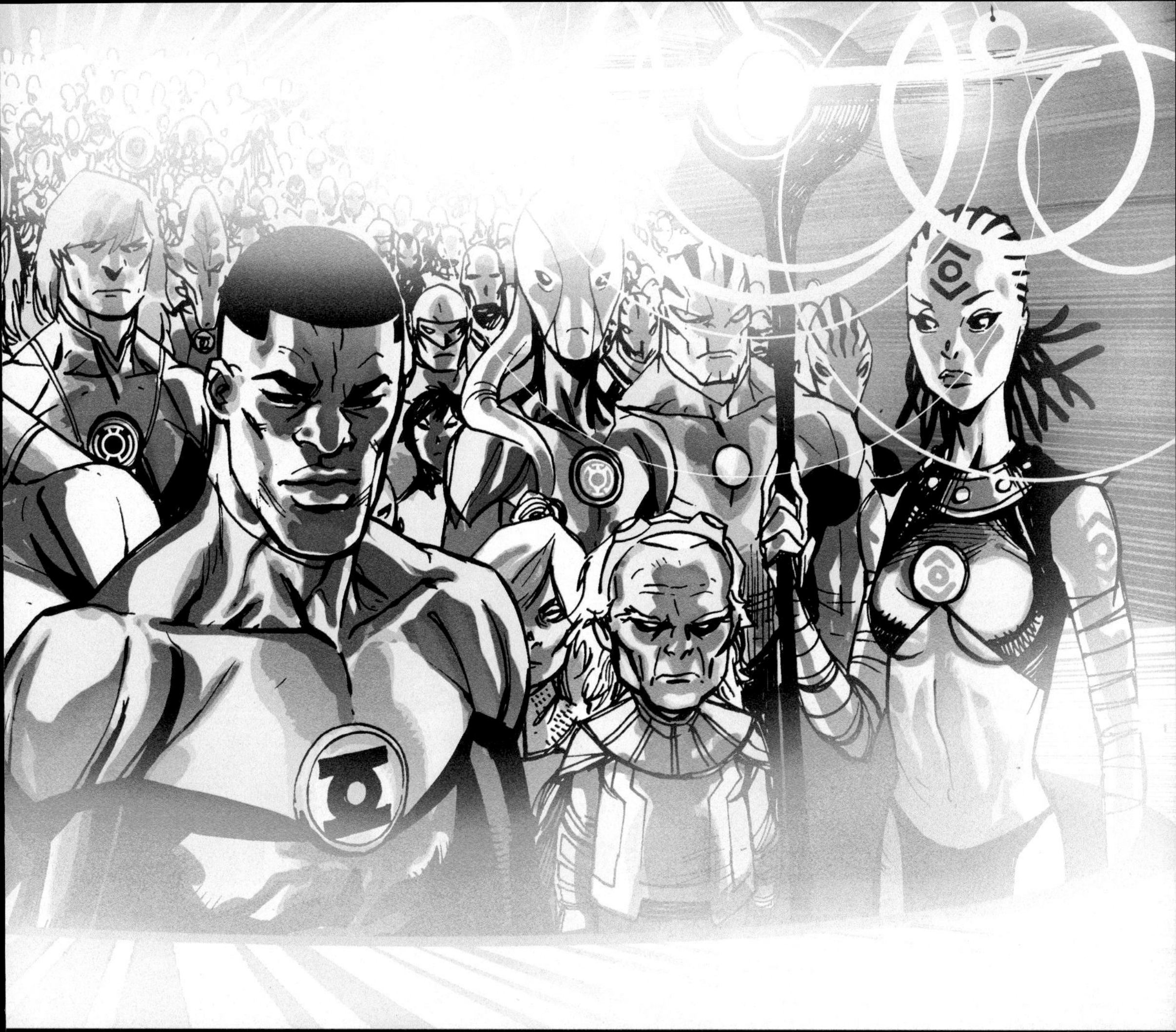

WRITER: VAN JENSEN **ARTIST:** BERNARD CHANG **COLORIST:** MARCELO MAIOLO
LETTERER: DAVE SHARPE **COVER:** BERNARD CHANG

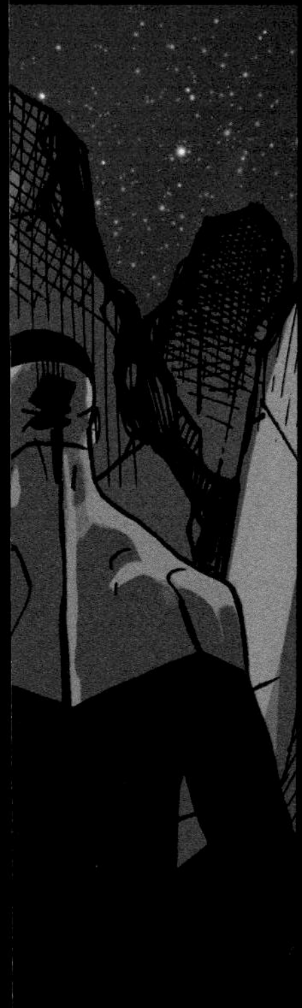

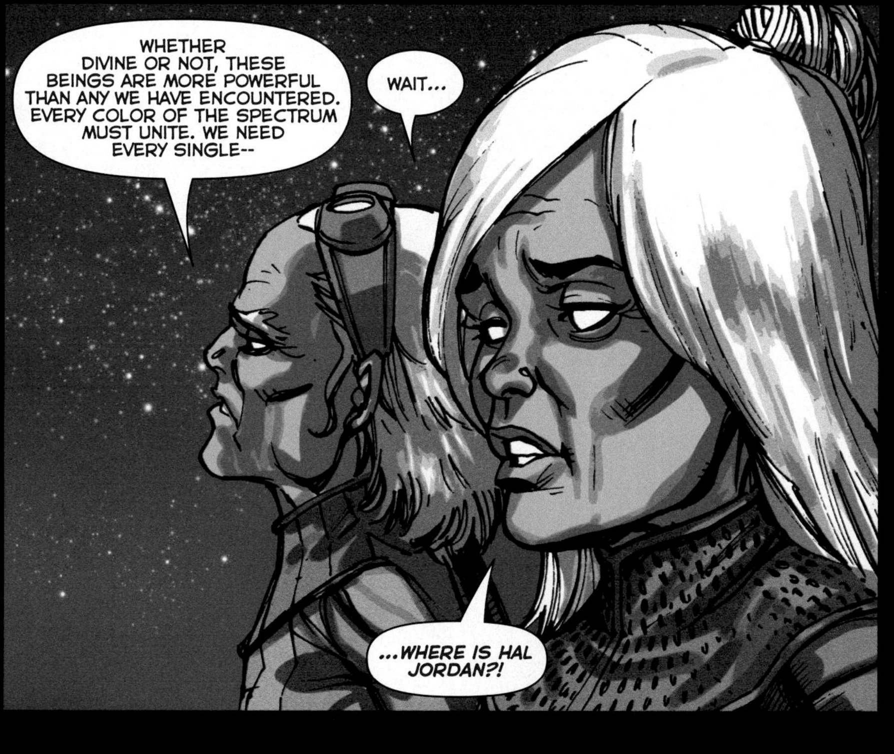
WHETHER DIVINE OR NOT, THESE BEINGS ARE MORE POWERFUL THAN ANY WE HAVE ENCOUNTERED. EVERY COLOR OF THE SPECTRUM MUST UNITE. WE NEED EVERY SINGLE--
WAIT...
...WHERE IS HAL JORDAN?!

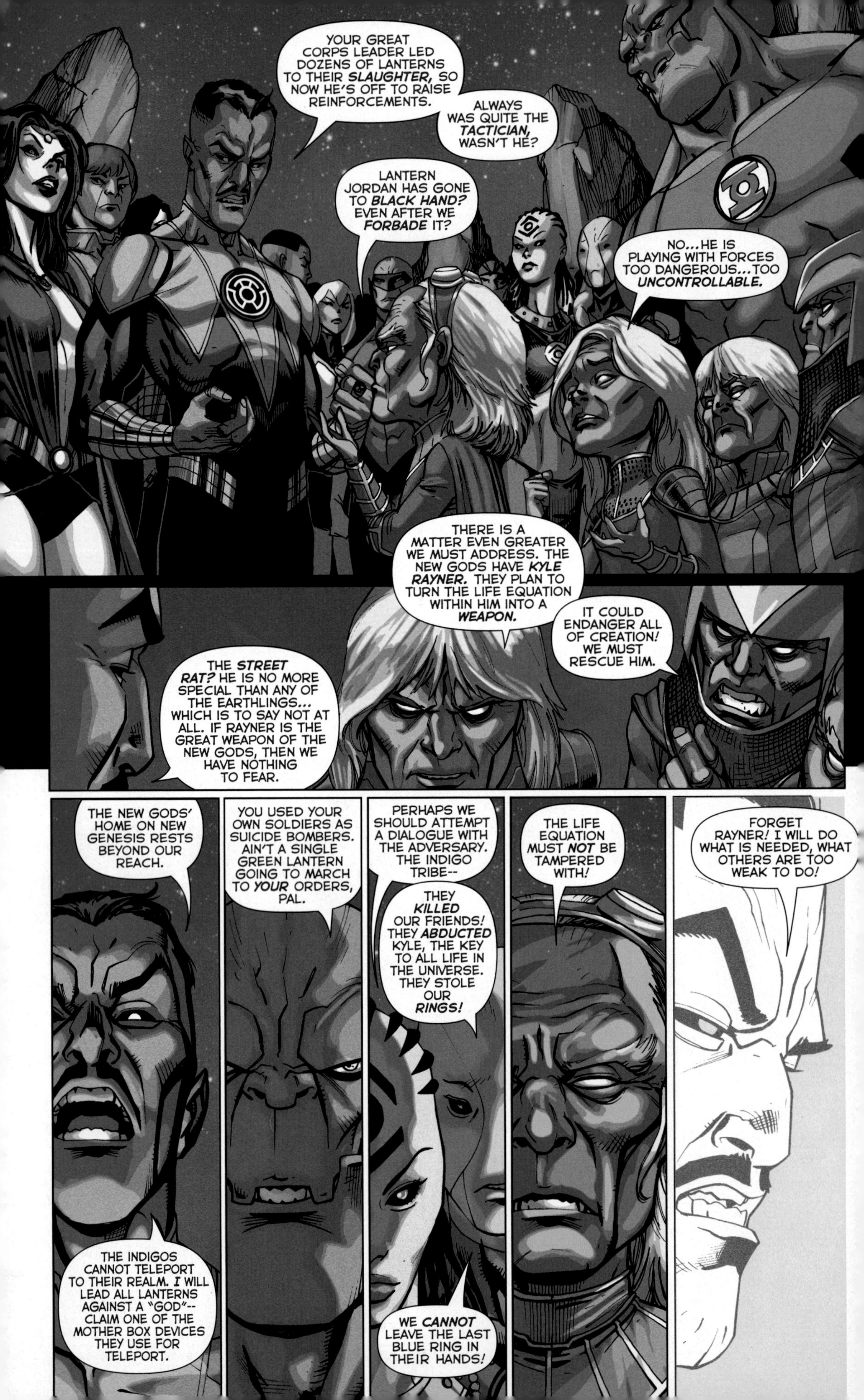
YOUR GREAT CORPS LEADER LED DOZENS OF LANTERNS TO THEIR SLAUGHTER, SO NOW HE'S OFF TO RAISE REINFORCEMENTS.
ALWAYS WAS QUITE THE TACTICIAN, WASN'T HE?
LANTERN JORDAN HAS GONE TO BLACK HAND? EVEN AFTER WE FORBADE IT?
NO...HE IS PLAYING WITH FORCES TOO DANGEROUS...TOO UNCONTROLLABLE.
THERE IS A MATTER EVEN GREATER WE MUST ADDRESS. THE NEW GODS HAVE KYLE RAYNER. THEY PLAN TO TURN THE LIFE EQUATION WITHIN HIM INTO A WEAPON.
IT COULD ENDANGER ALL OF CREATION! WE MUST RESCUE HIM.
THE STREET RAT? HE IS NO MORE SPECIAL THAN ANY OF THE EARTHLINGS... WHICH IS TO SAY NOT AT ALL. IF RAYNER IS THE GREAT WEAPON OF THE NEW GODS, THEN WE HAVE NOTHING TO FEAR.
THE NEW GODS' HOME ON NEW GENESIS RESTS BEYOND OUR REACH.
THE INDIGOS CANNOT TELEPORT TO THEIR REALM. I WILL LEAD ALL LANTERNS AGAINST A "GOD"-- CLAIM ONE OF THE MOTHER BOX DEVICES THEY USE FOR TELEPORT.
YOU USED YOUR OWN SOLDIERS AS SUICIDE BOMBERS. AIN'T A SINGLE GREEN LANTERN GOING TO MARCH TO YOUR ORDERS, PAL.
PERHAPS WE SHOULD ATTEMPT A DIALOGUE WITH THE ADVERSARY. THE INDIGO TRIBE--
THEY KILLED OUR FRIENDS! THEY ABDUCTED KYLE, THE KEY TO ALL LIFE IN THE UNIVERSE. THEY STOLE OUR RINGS!
WE CANNOT LEAVE THE LAST BLUE RING IN THEIR HANDS!
THE LIFE EQUATION MUST NOT BE TAMPERED WITH!
FORGET RAYNER! I WILL DO WHAT IS NEEDED, WHAT OTHERS ARE TOO WEAK TO DO!

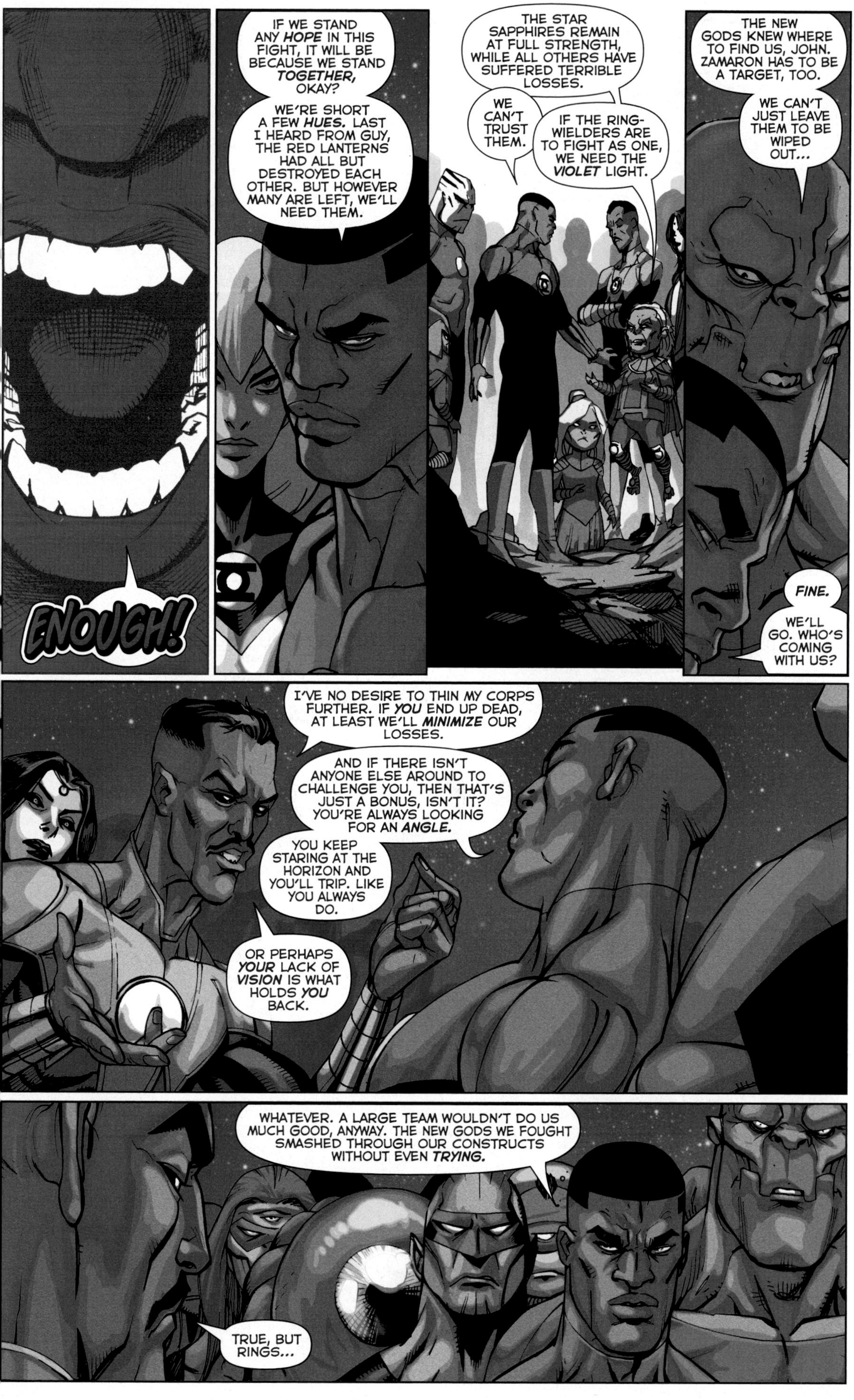
ENOUGH!
IF WE STAND ANY HOPE IN THIS FIGHT, IT WILL BE BECAUSE WE STAND TOGETHER, OKAY?
WE'RE SHORT A FEW HUES. LAST I HEARD FROM GUY, THE RED LANTERNS HAD ALL BUT DESTROYED EACH OTHER. BUT HOWEVER MANY ARE LEFT, WE'LL NEED THEM.
THE STAR SAPPHIRES REMAIN AT FULL STRENGTH, WHILE ALL OTHERS HAVE SUFFERED TERRIBLE LOSSES.
WE CAN'T TRUST THEM.
IF THE RING-WIELDERS ARE TO FIGHT AS ONE, WE NEED THE VIOLET LIGHT.
THE NEW GODS KNEW WHERE TO FIND US, JOHN. ZAMARON HAS TO BE A TARGET, TOO.
WE CAN'T JUST LEAVE THEM TO BE WIPED OUT...
FINE.
WE'LL GO. WHO'S COMING WITH US?
I'VE NO DESIRE TO THIN MY CORPS FURTHER. IF YOU END UP DEAD, AT LEAST WE'LL MINIMIZE OUR LOSSES.
AND IF THERE ISN'T ANYONE ELSE AROUND TO CHALLENGE YOU, THEN THAT'S JUST A BONUS, ISN'T IT? YOU'RE ALWAYS LOOKING FOR AN ANGLE.
YOU KEEP STARING AT THE HORIZON AND YOU'LL TRIP. LIKE YOU ALWAYS DO.
OR PERHAPS YOUR LACK OF VISION IS WHAT HOLDS YOU BACK.
WHATEVER. A LARGE TEAM WOULDN'T DO US MUCH GOOD, ANYWAY. THE NEW GODS WE FOUGHT SMASHED THROUGH OUR CONSTRUCTS WITHOUT EVEN TRYING.
TRUE, BUT RINGS...

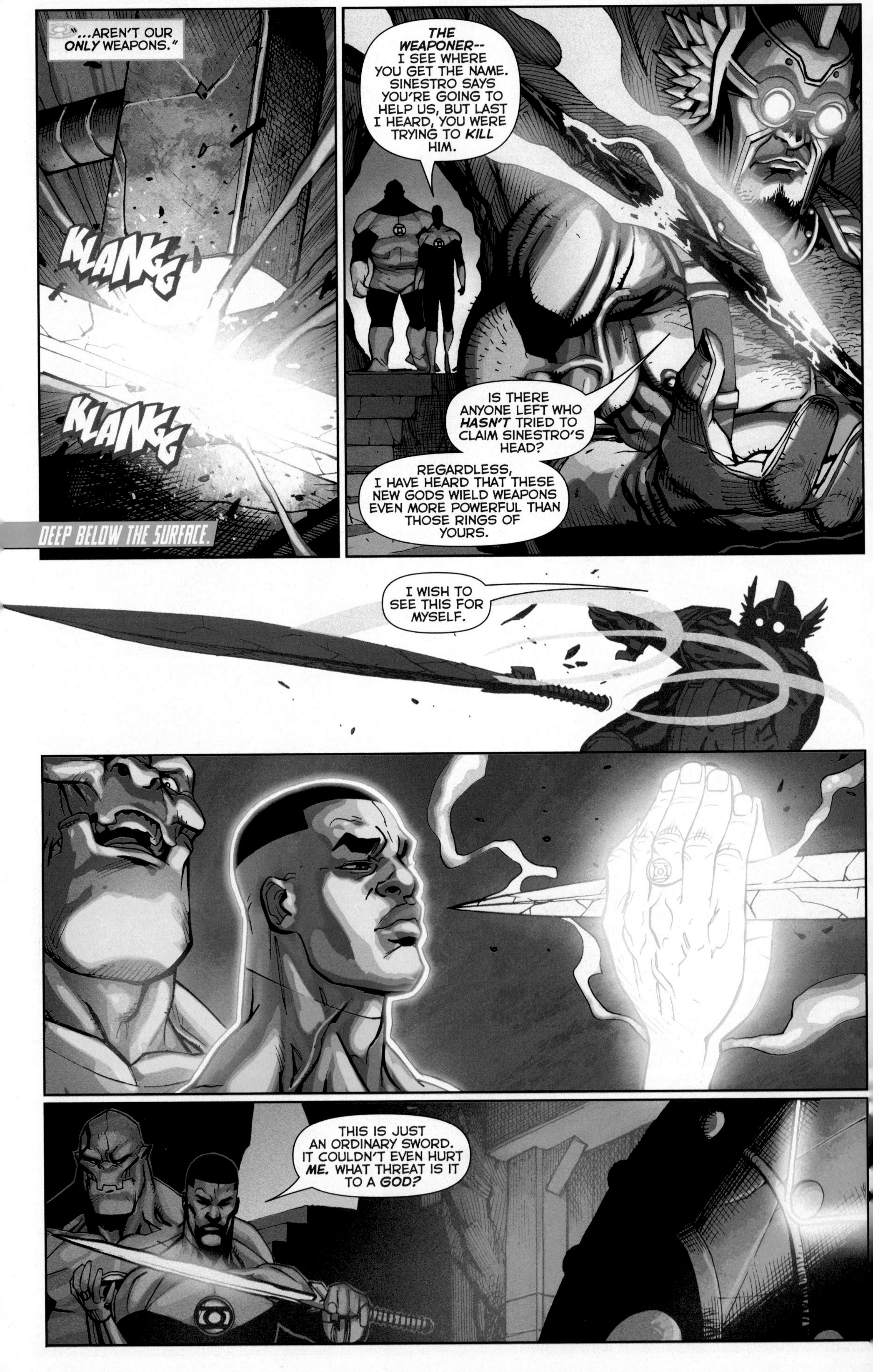
"...AREN'T OUR ONLY WEAPONS."
KLANGG
KLANGG
DEEP BELOW THE SURFACE.
THE WEAPONER-- I SEE WHERE YOU GET THE NAME. SINESTRO SAYS YOU'RE GOING TO HELP US, BUT LAST I HEARD, YOU WERE TRYING TO KILL HIM.
IS THERE ANYONE LEFT WHO HASN'T TRIED TO CLAIM SINESTRO'S HEAD?
REGARDLESS, I HAVE HEARD THAT THESE NEW GODS WIELD WEAPONS EVEN MORE POWERFUL THAN THOSE RINGS OF YOURS.
I WISH TO SEE THIS FOR MYSELF.
THIS IS JUST AN ORDINARY SWORD. IT COULDN'T EVEN HURT ME. WHAT THREAT IS IT TO A GOD?

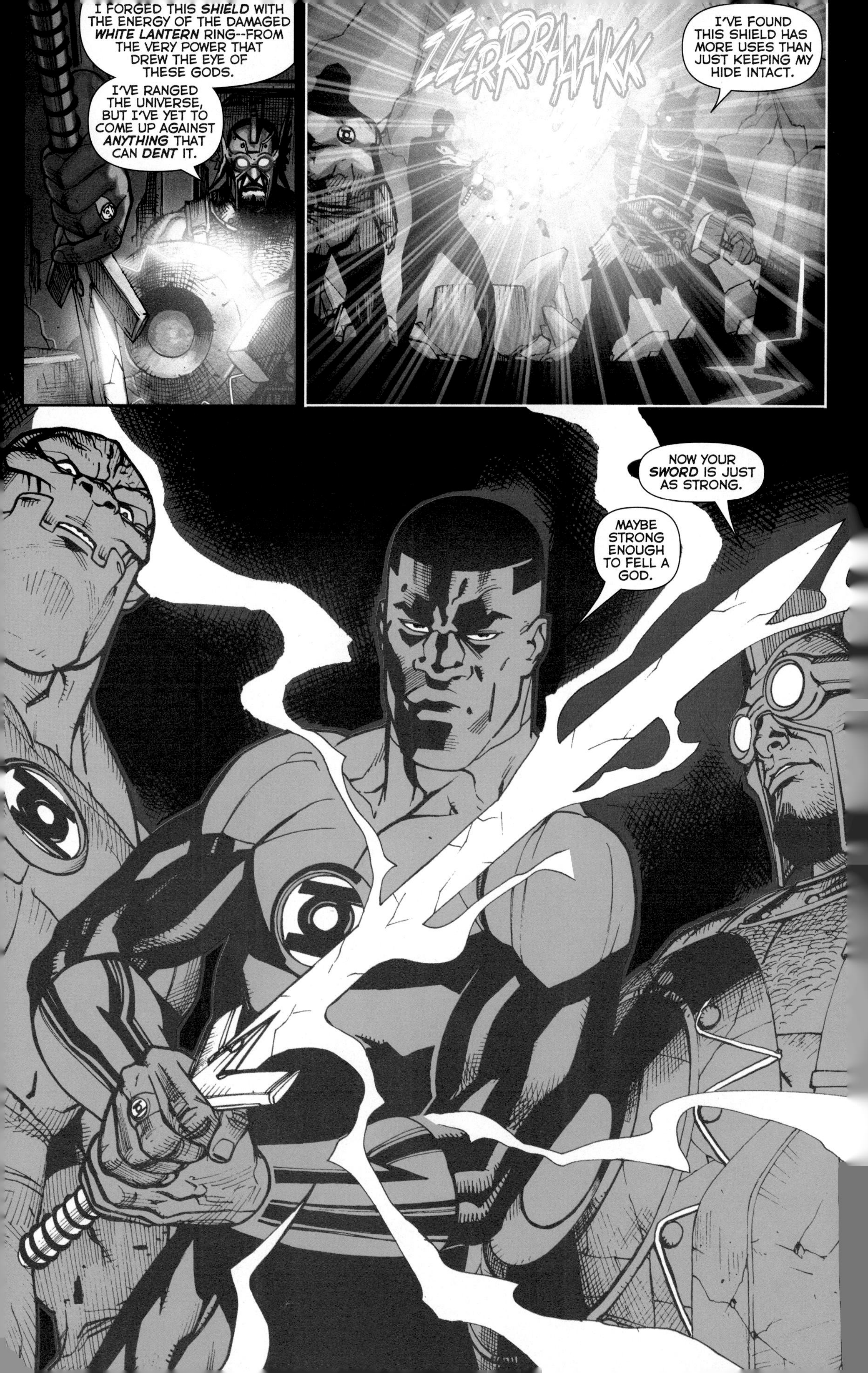
I FORGED THIS SHIELD WITH THE ENERGY OF THE DAMAGED WHITE LANTERN RING--FROM THE VERY POWER THAT DREW THE EYE OF THESE GODS.
I'VE RANGED THE UNIVERSE, BUT I'VE YET TO COME UP AGAINST ANYTHING THAT CAN DENT IT.
ZZZRRRAAAKK
I'VE FOUND THIS SHIELD HAS MORE USES THAN JUST KEEPING MY HIDE INTACT.
NOW YOUR SWORD IS JUST AS STRONG.
MAYBE STRONG ENOUGH TO FELL A GOD.

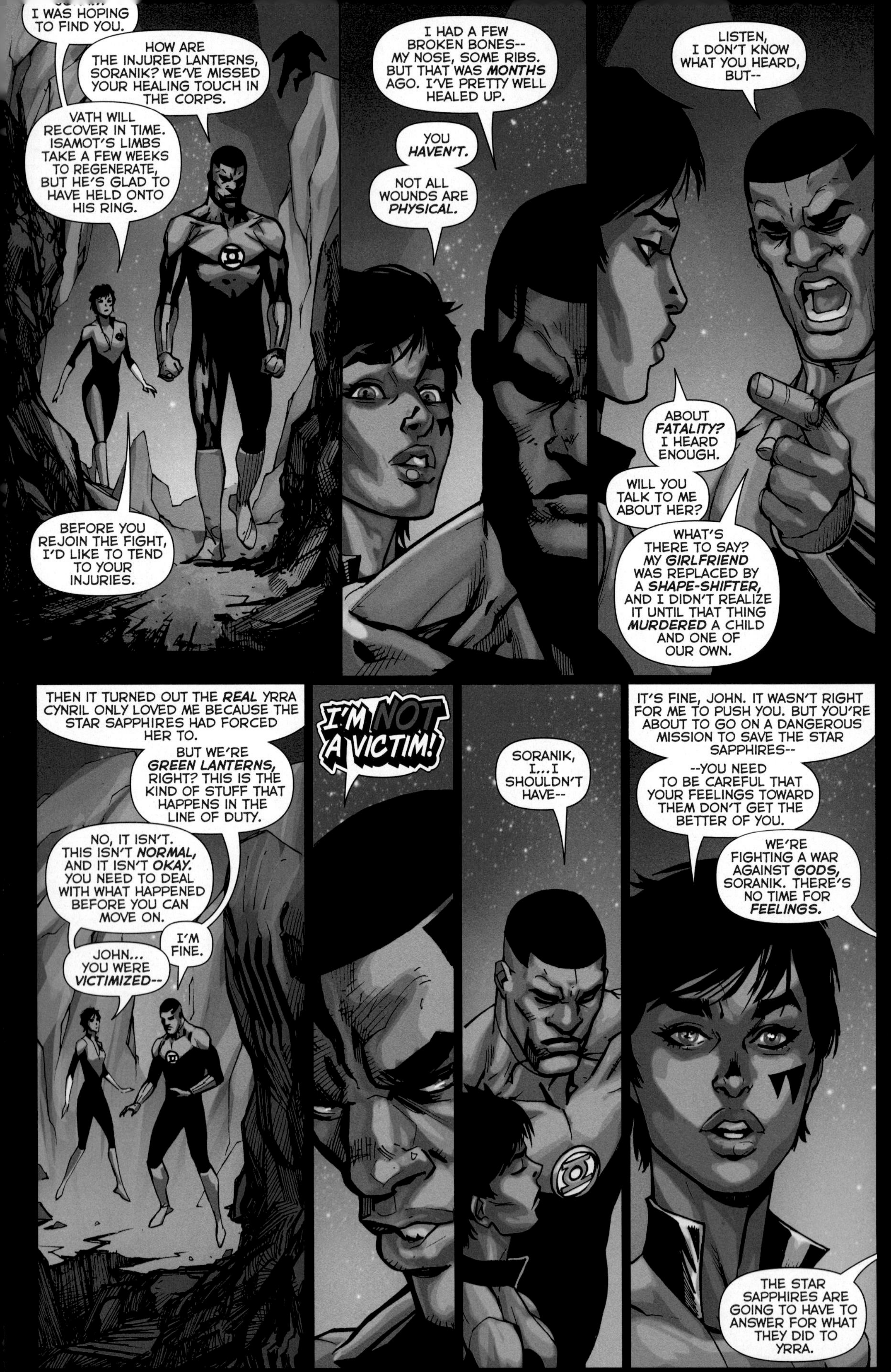
I WAS HOPING TO FIND YOU.
HOW ARE THE INJURED LANTERNS, SORANIK? WE'VE MISSED YOUR HEALING TOUCH IN THE CORPS.
VATH WILL RECOVER IN TIME. ISAMOT'S LIMBS TAKE A FEW WEEKS TO REGENERATE, BUT HE'S GLAD TO HAVE HELD ONTO HIS RING.
BEFORE YOU REJOIN THE FIGHT, I'D LIKE TO TEND TO YOUR INJURIES.
I HAD A FEW BROKEN BONES-- MY NOSE, SOME RIBS. BUT THAT WAS MONTHS AGO. I'VE PRETTY WELL HEALED UP.
YOU HAVEN'T.
NOT ALL WOUNDS ARE PHYSICAL.
LISTEN, I DON'T KNOW WHAT YOU HEARD, BUT--
ABOUT FATALITY? I HEARD ENOUGH.
WILL YOU TALK TO ME ABOUT HER?
WHAT'S THERE TO SAY? MY GIRLFRIEND WAS REPLACED BY A SHAPE-SHIFTER, AND I DIDN'T REALIZE IT UNTIL THAT THING MURDERED A CHILD AND ONE OF OUR OWN.
THEN IT TURNED OUT THE REAL YRRA CYNRIL ONLY LOVED ME BECAUSE THE STAR SAPPHIRES HAD FORCED HER TO.
BUT WE'RE GREEN LANTERNS, RIGHT? THIS IS THE KIND OF STUFF THAT HAPPENS IN THE LINE OF DUTY.
NO, IT ISN'T. THIS ISN'T NORMAL, AND IT ISN'T OKAY. YOU NEED TO DEAL WITH WHAT HAPPENED BEFORE YOU CAN MOVE ON.
I'M FINE.
JOHN... YOU WERE VICTIMIZED--
I'M NOT A VICTIM!
SORANIK, I...I SHOULDN'T HAVE--
IT'S FINE, JOHN. IT WASN'T RIGHT FOR ME TO PUSH YOU. BUT YOU'RE ABOUT TO GO ON A DANGEROUS MISSION TO SAVE THE STAR SAPPHIRES--
--YOU NEED TO BE CAREFUL THAT YOUR FEELINGS TOWARD THEM DON'T GET THE BETTER OF YOU.
WE'RE FIGHTING A WAR AGAINST GODS, SORANIK. THERE'S NO TIME FOR FEELINGS.
THE STAR SAPPHIRES ARE GOING TO HAVE TO ANSWER FOR WHAT THEY DID TO YRRA.

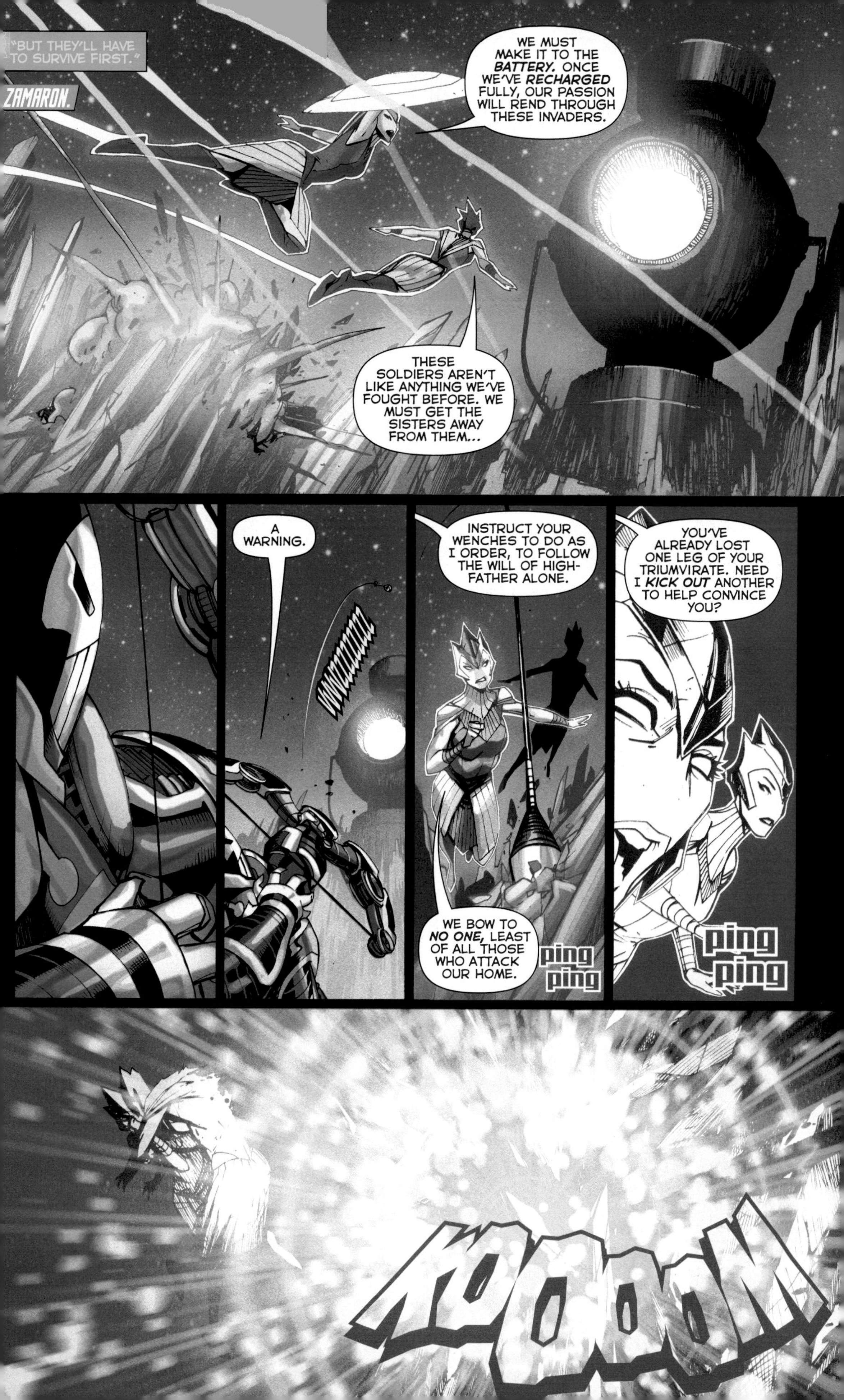
"BUT THEY'LL HAVE TO SURVIVE FIRST."
ZAMARON.
WE MUST MAKE IT TO THE BATTERY. ONCE WE'VE RECHARGED FULLY, OUR PASSION WILL REND THROUGH THESE INVADERS.
THESE SOLDIERS AREN'T LIKE ANYTHING WE'VE FOUGHT BEFORE. WE MUST GET THE SISTERS AWAY FROM THEM...
A WARNING.
INSTRUCT YOUR WENCHES TO DO AS I ORDER, TO FOLLOW THE WILL OF HIGH-FATHER ALONE.
WE BOW TO NO ONE, LEAST OF ALL THOSE WHO ATTACK OUR HOME.
ping ping
YOU'VE ALREADY LOST ONE LEG OF YOUR TRIUMVIRATE. NEED I KICK OUT ANOTHER TO HELP CONVINCE YOU?
ping ping
KOOOOM

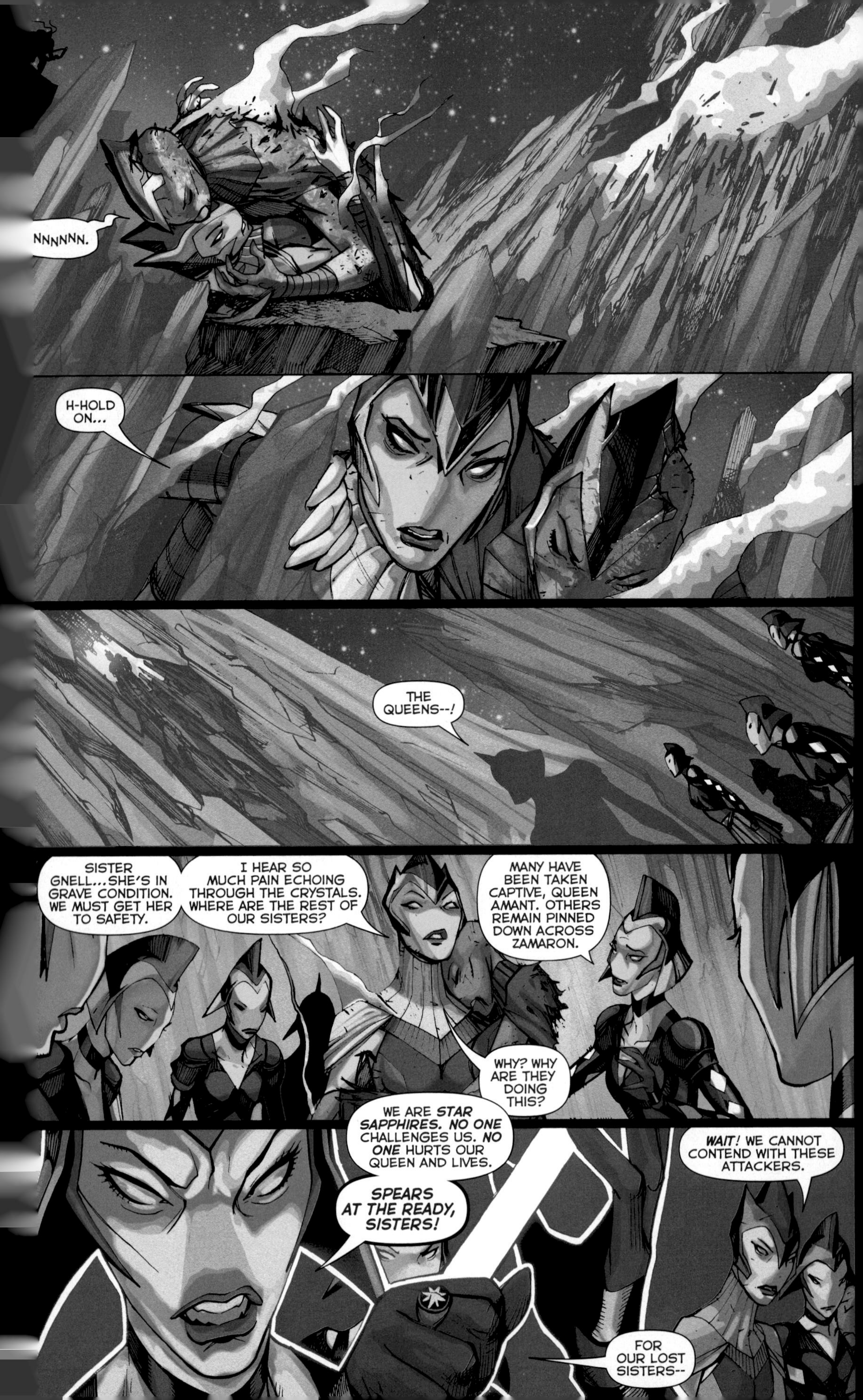
NNNNNN.
H-HOLD ON...
THE QUEENS--!
SISTER GNELL...SHE'S IN GRAVE CONDITION. WE MUST GET HER TO SAFETY.
I HEAR SO MUCH PAIN ECHOING THROUGH THE CRYSTALS. WHERE ARE THE REST OF OUR SISTERS?
MANY HAVE BEEN TAKEN CAPTIVE, QUEEN AMANT. OTHERS REMAIN PINNED DOWN ACROSS ZAMARON.
WHY? WHY ARE THEY DOING THIS?
WE ARE STAR SAPPHIRES. NO ONE CHALLENGES US. NO ONE HURTS OUR QUEEN AND LIVES.
SPEARS AT THE READY, SISTERS!
WAIT! WE CANNOT CONTEND WITH THESE ATTACKERS.
FOR OUR LOST SISTERS--

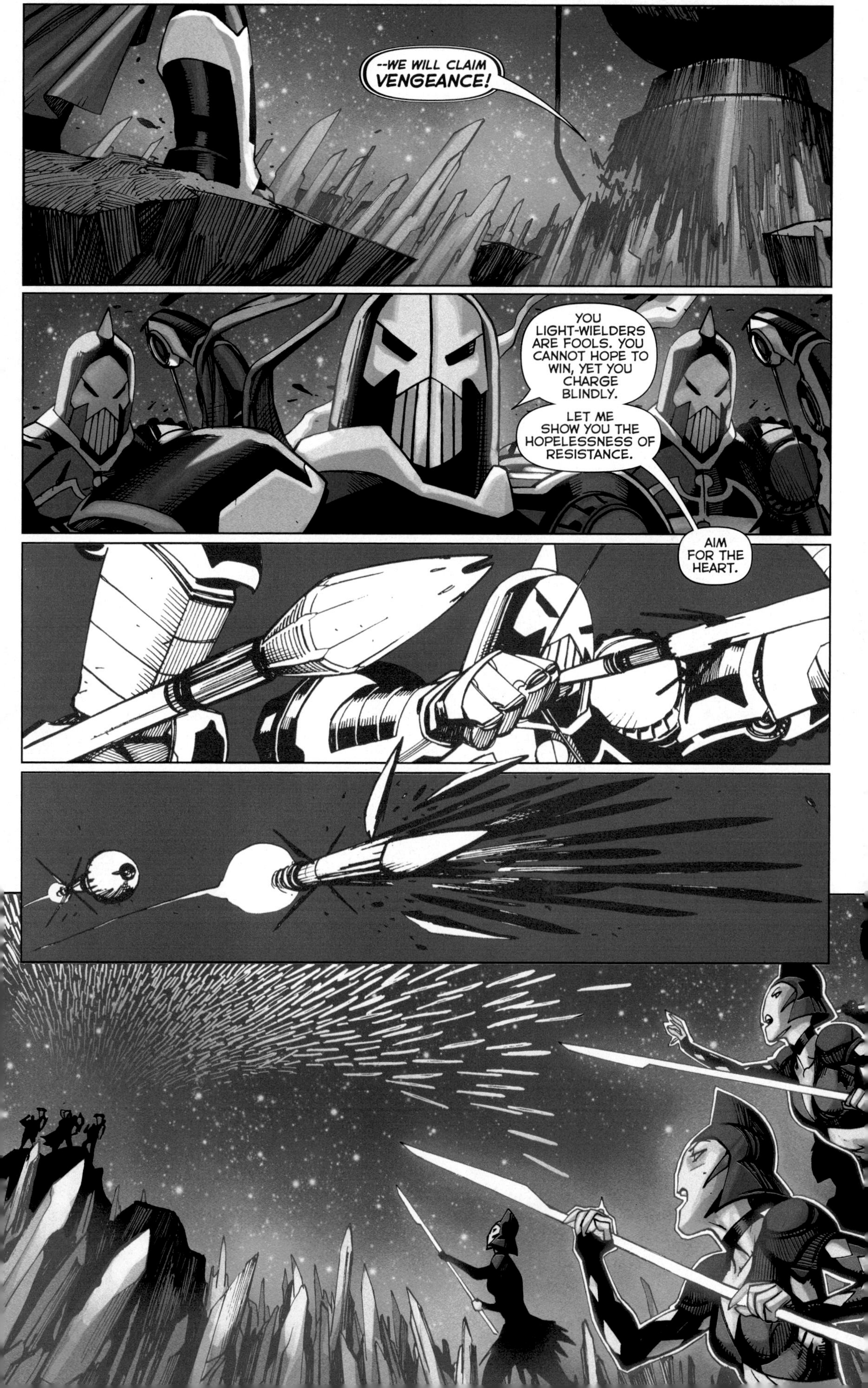
--WE WILL CLAIM VENGEANCE!
YOU LIGHT-WIELDERS ARE FOOLS. YOU CANNOT HOPE TO WIN, YET YOU CHARGE BLINDLY.
LET ME SHOW YOU THE HOPELESSNESS OF RESISTANCE.
AIM FOR THE HEART.

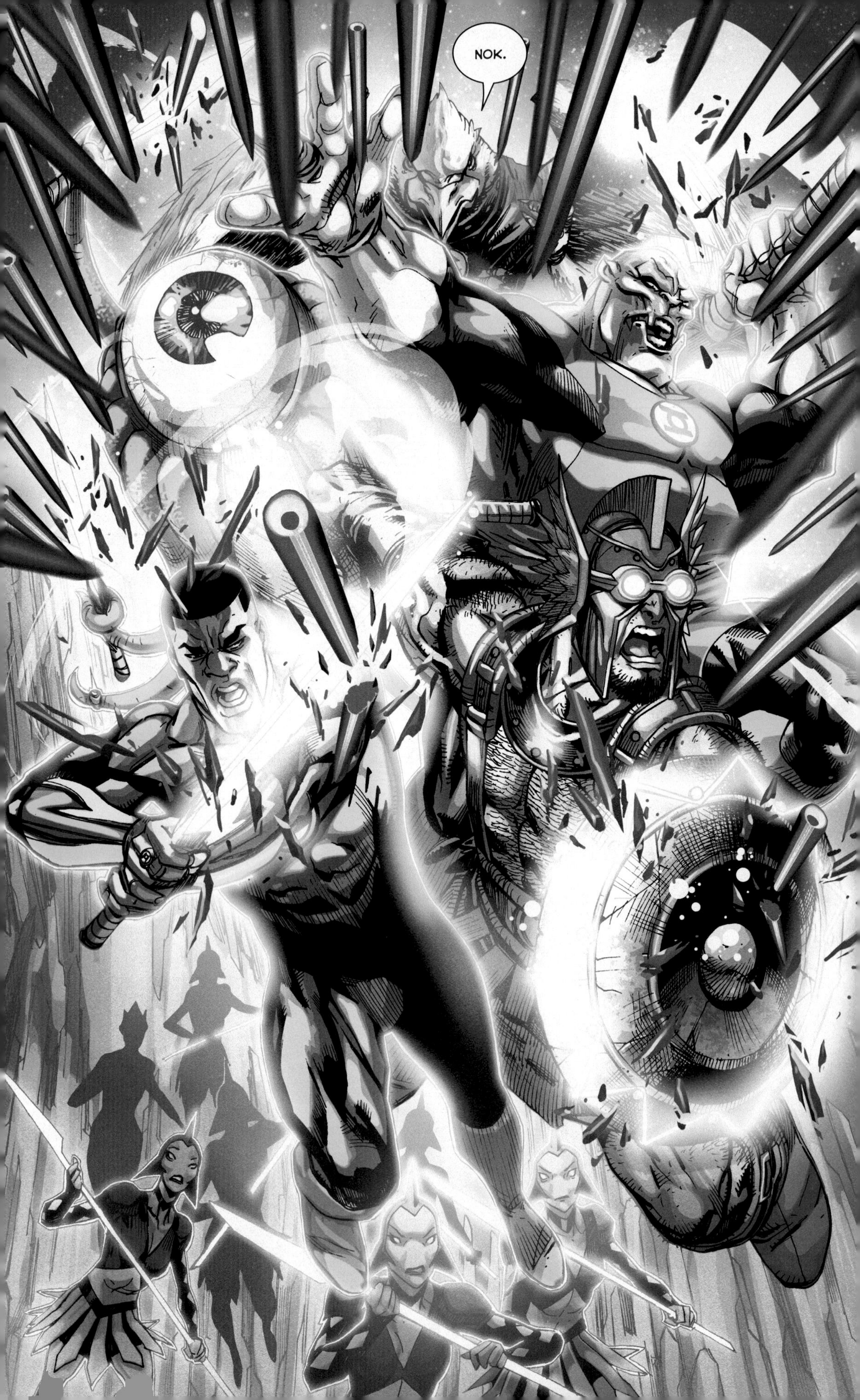
NOK.

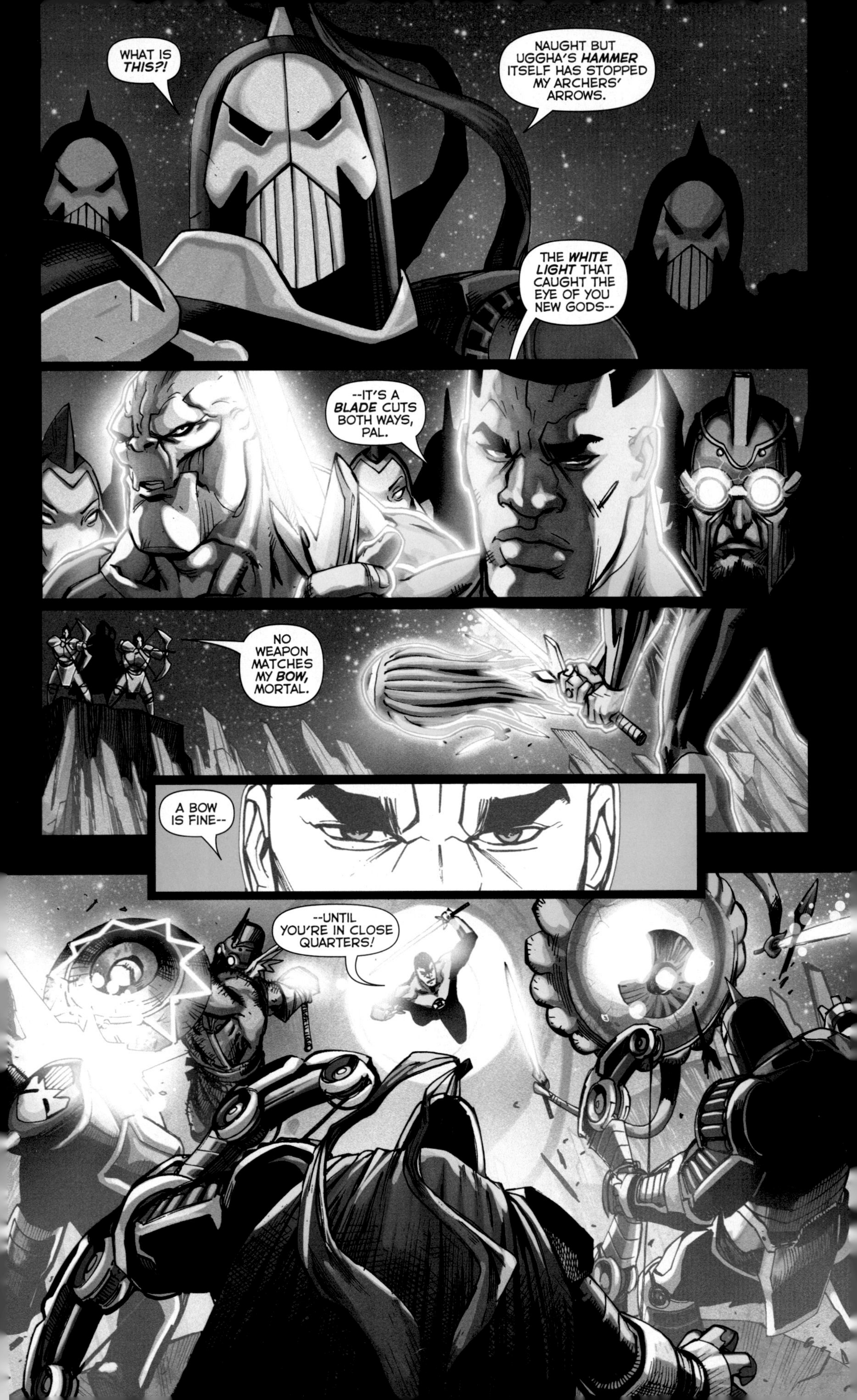
WHAT IS THIS?!
NAUGHT BUT UGGHA'S HAMMER ITSELF HAS STOPPED MY ARCHERS' ARROWS.
THE WHITE LIGHT THAT CAUGHT THE EYE OF YOU NEW GODS--
--IT'S A BLADE CUTS BOTH WAYS, PAL.
NO WEAPON MATCHES MY BOW, MORTAL.
A BOW IS FINE--
--UNTIL YOU'RE IN CLOSE QUARTERS!

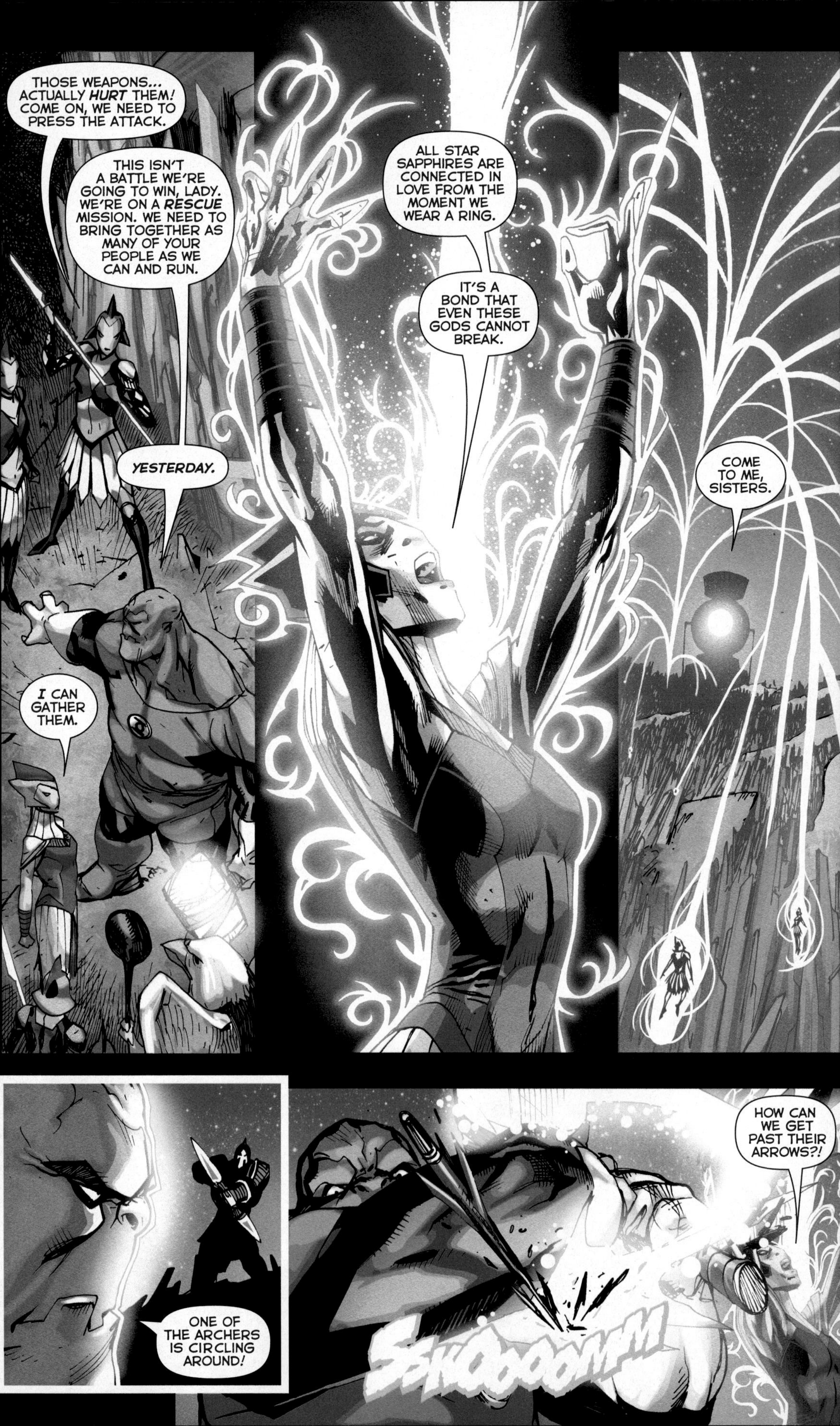
THOSE WEAPONS... ACTUALLY *HURT* THEM! COME ON, WE NEED TO PRESS THE ATTACK.
THIS ISN'T A BATTLE WE'RE GOING TO WIN, LADY. WE'RE ON A *RESCUE* MISSION. WE NEED TO BRING TOGETHER AS MANY OF YOUR PEOPLE AS WE CAN AND RUN.
YESTERDAY.
I CAN GATHER THEM.
ALL STAR SAPPHIRES ARE CONNECTED IN LOVE FROM THE MOMENT WE WEAR A RING.
IT'S A BOND THAT EVEN THESE GODS CANNOT BREAK.
COME TO ME, SISTERS.
ONE OF THE ARCHERS IS CIRCLING AROUND!
HOW CAN WE GET PAST THEIR ARROWS?!
SSHOOOOOM

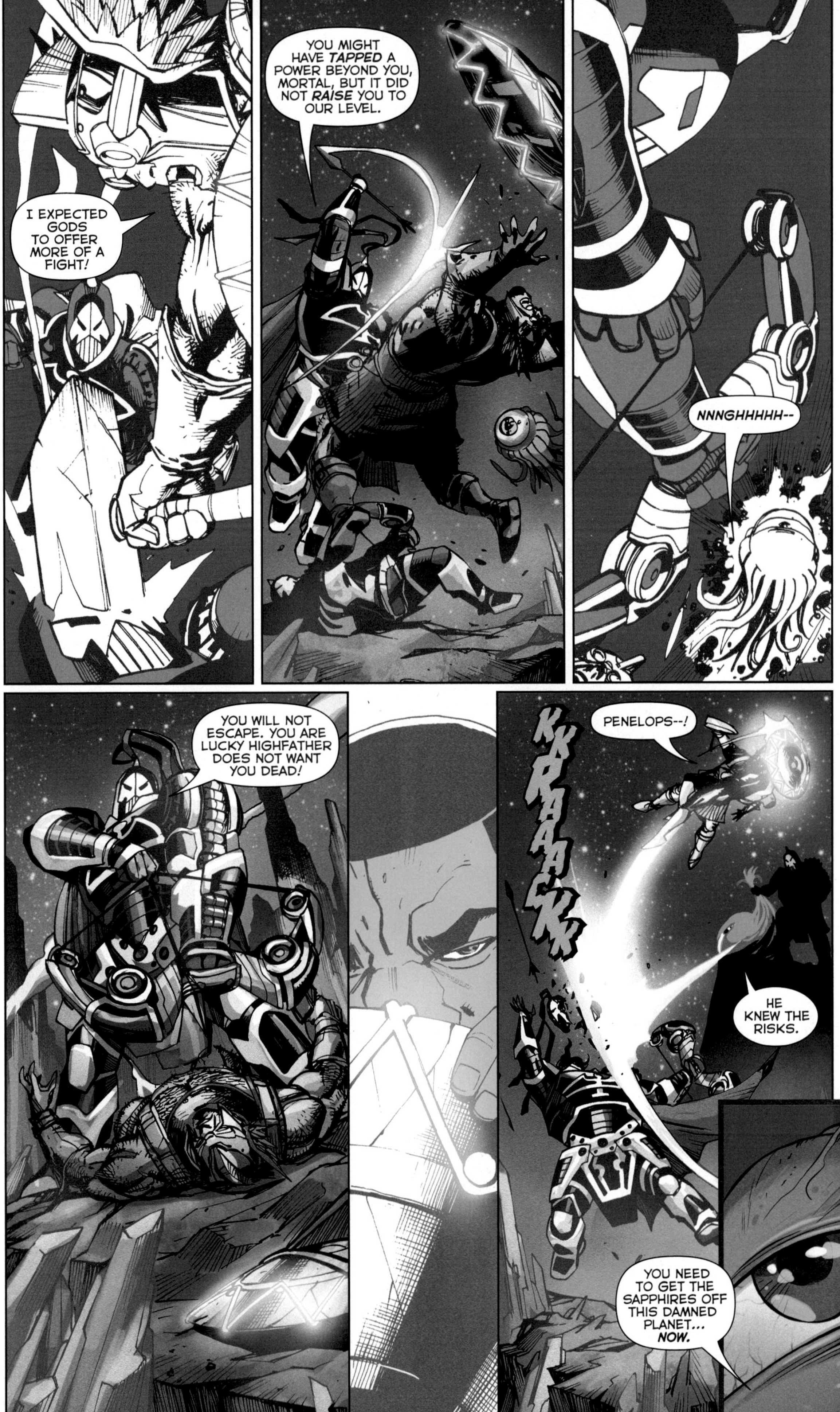
I EXPECTED GODS TO OFFER MORE OF A FIGHT!
YOU MIGHT HAVE TAPPED A POWER BEYOND YOU, MORTAL, BUT IT DID NOT RAISE YOU TO OUR LEVEL.
NNNGHHHHH--
YOU WILL NOT ESCAPE. YOU ARE LUCKY HIGHFATHER DOES NOT WANT YOU DEAD!
KKRAAASKK
PENELOPS--!
HE KNEW THE RISKS.
YOU NEED TO GET THE SAPPHIRES OFF THIS DAMNED PLANET... NOW.

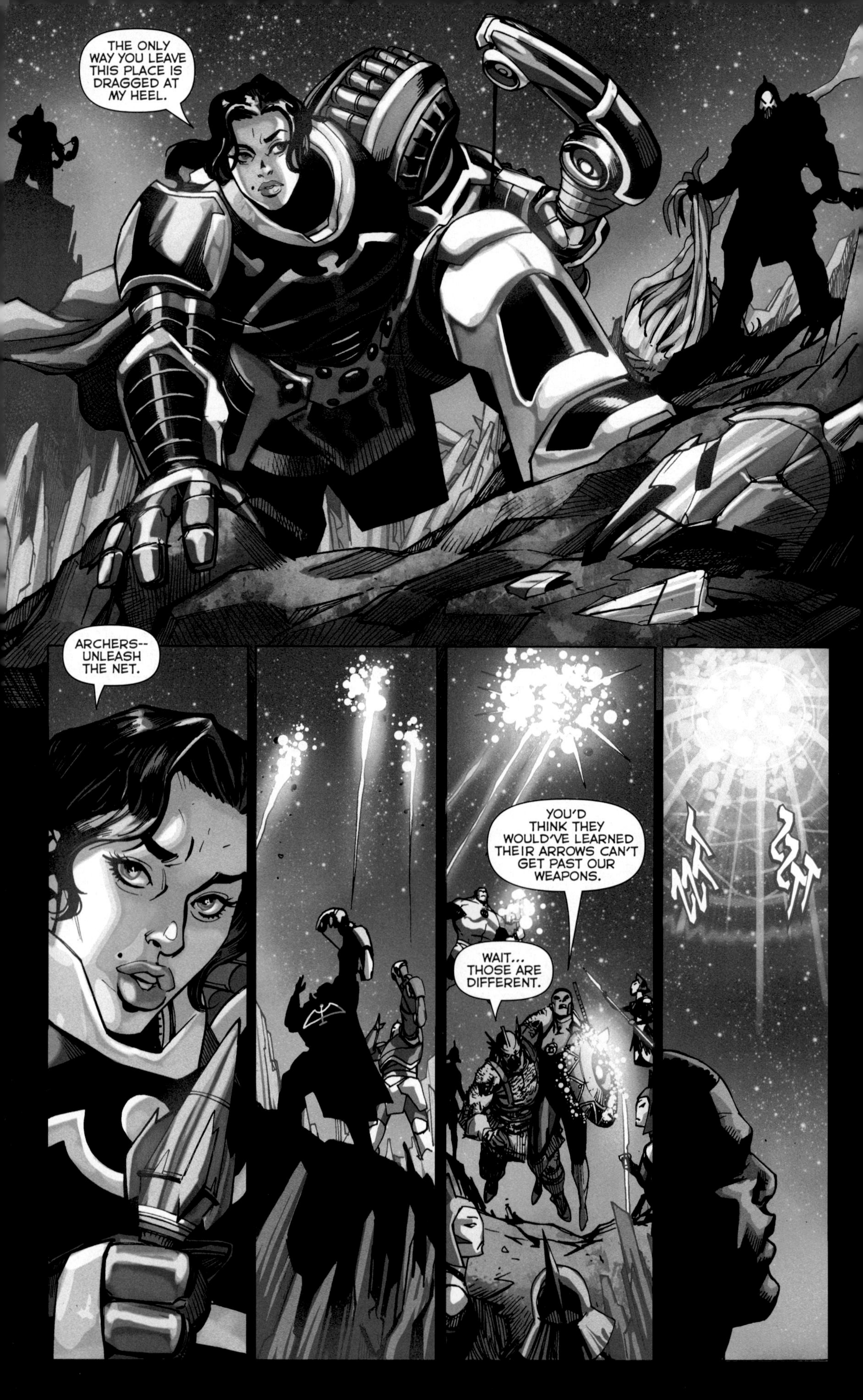
THE ONLY WAY YOU LEAVE THIS PLACE IS DRAGGED AT MY HEEL.
ARCHERS-- UNLEASH THE NET.
YOU'D THINK THEY WOULD'VE LEARNED THEIR ARROWS CAN'T GET PAST OUR WEAPONS.
WAIT... THOSE ARE DIFFERENT.
ZZT
ZZT

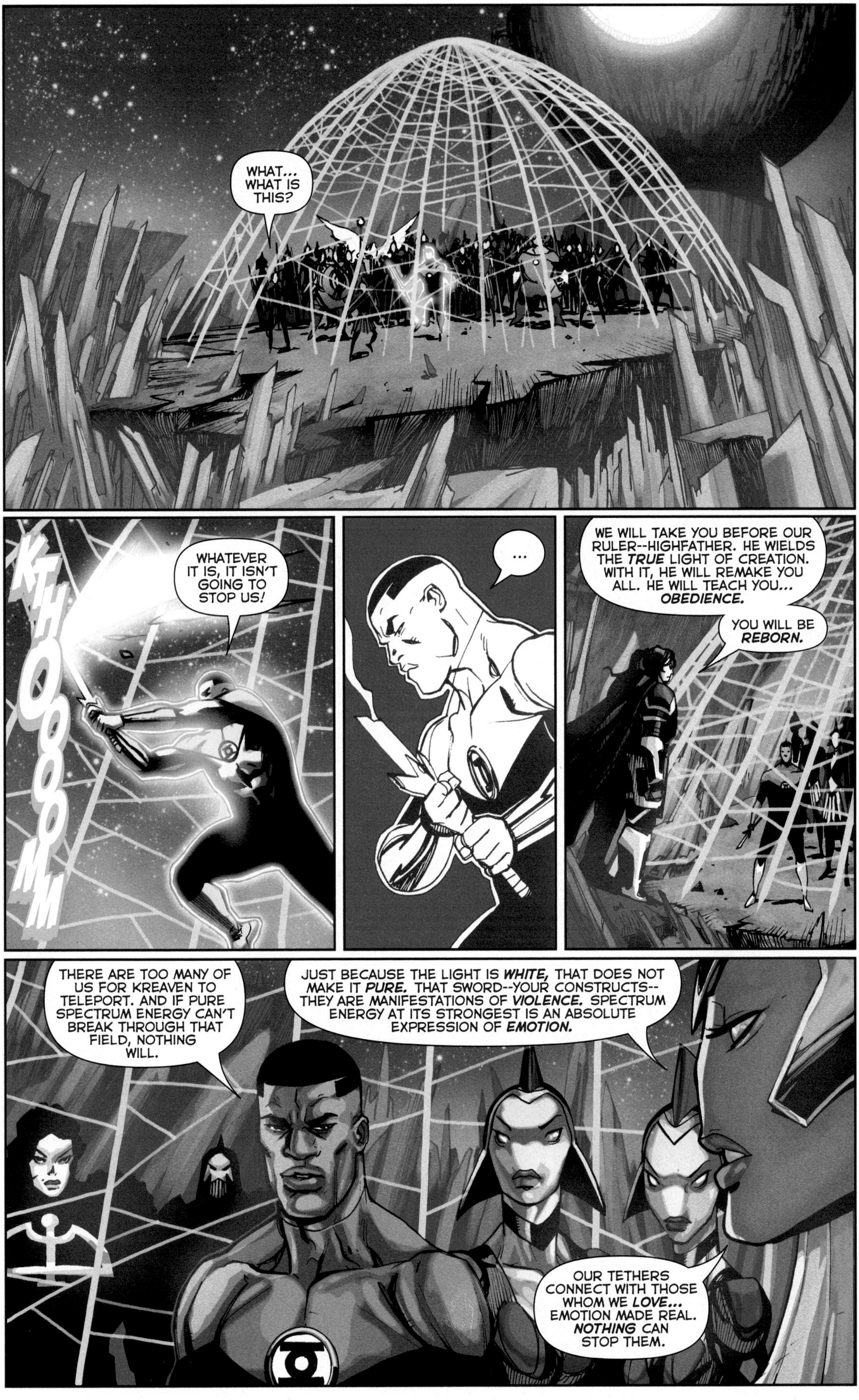
WHAT... WHAT IS THIS?
WHATEVER IT IS, IT ISN'T GOING TO STOP US!
KTHOOOOOOMM
...
WE WILL TAKE YOU BEFORE OUR RULER--HIGHFATHER. HE WIELDS THE TRUE LIGHT OF CREATION. WITH IT, HE WILL REMAKE YOU ALL. HE WILL TEACH YOU... OBEDIENCE.
YOU WILL BE REBORN.
THERE ARE TOO MANY OF US FOR KREAVEN TO TELEPORT. AND IF PURE SPECTRUM ENERGY CAN'T BREAK THROUGH THAT FIELD, NOTHING WILL.
JUST BECAUSE THE LIGHT IS WHITE, THAT DOES NOT MAKE IT PURE. THAT SWORD--YOUR CONSTRUCTS--THEY ARE MANIFESTATIONS OF VIOLENCE. SPECTRUM ENERGY AT ITS STRONGEST IS AN ABSOLUTE EXPRESSION OF EMOTION.
OUR TETHERS CONNECT WITH THOSE WHOM WE LOVE... EMOTION MADE REAL. NOTHING CAN STOP THEM.

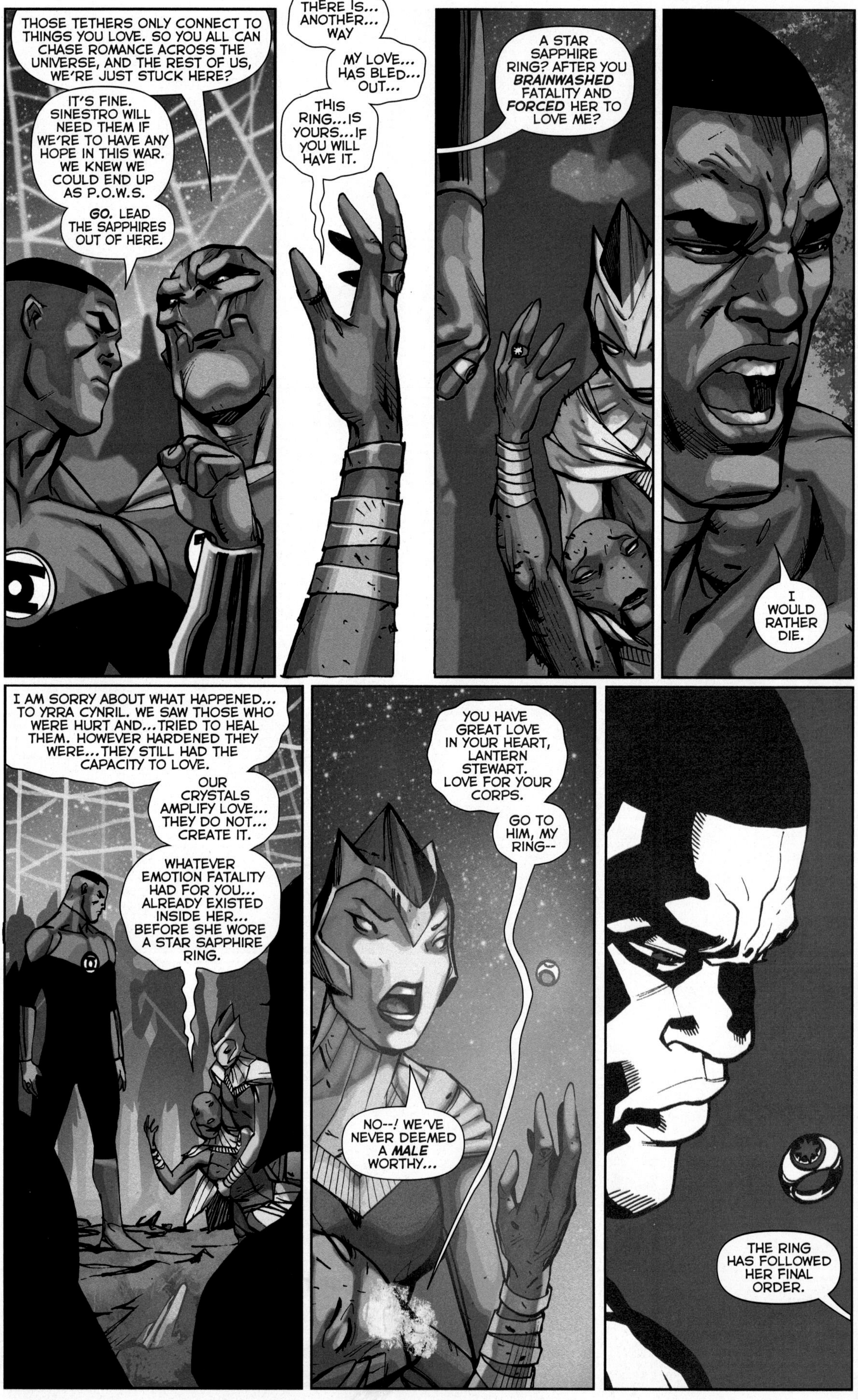
THOSE TETHERS ONLY CONNECT TO THINGS YOU LOVE. SO YOU ALL CAN CHASE ROMANCE ACROSS THE UNIVERSE, AND THE REST OF US, WE'RE JUST STUCK HERE?
IT'S FINE. SINESTRO WILL NEED THEM IF WE'RE TO HAVE ANY HOPE IN THIS WAR. WE KNEW WE COULD END UP AS P.O.W.S.
GO. LEAD THE SAPPHIRES OUT OF HERE.
THERE IS... ANOTHER... WAY
MY LOVE... HAS BLED... OUT...
THIS RING...IS YOURS...IF YOU WILL HAVE IT.
A STAR SAPPHIRE RING? AFTER YOU BRAINWASHED FATALITY AND FORCED HER TO LOVE ME?
I WOULD RATHER DIE.
I AM SORRY ABOUT WHAT HAPPENED... TO YRRA CYNRIL. WE SAW THOSE WHO WERE HURT AND...TRIED TO HEAL THEM. HOWEVER HARDENED THEY WERE...THEY STILL HAD THE CAPACITY TO LOVE.
OUR CRYSTALS AMPLIFY LOVE... THEY DO NOT... CREATE IT.
WHATEVER EMOTION FATALITY HAD FOR YOU... ALREADY EXISTED INSIDE HER... BEFORE SHE WORE A STAR SAPPHIRE RING.
YOU HAVE GREAT LOVE IN YOUR HEART, LANTERN STEWART. LOVE FOR YOUR CORPS.
GO TO HIM, MY RING--
NO--! WE'VE NEVER DEEMED A MALE WORTHY...
THE RING HAS FOLLOWED HER FINAL ORDER.

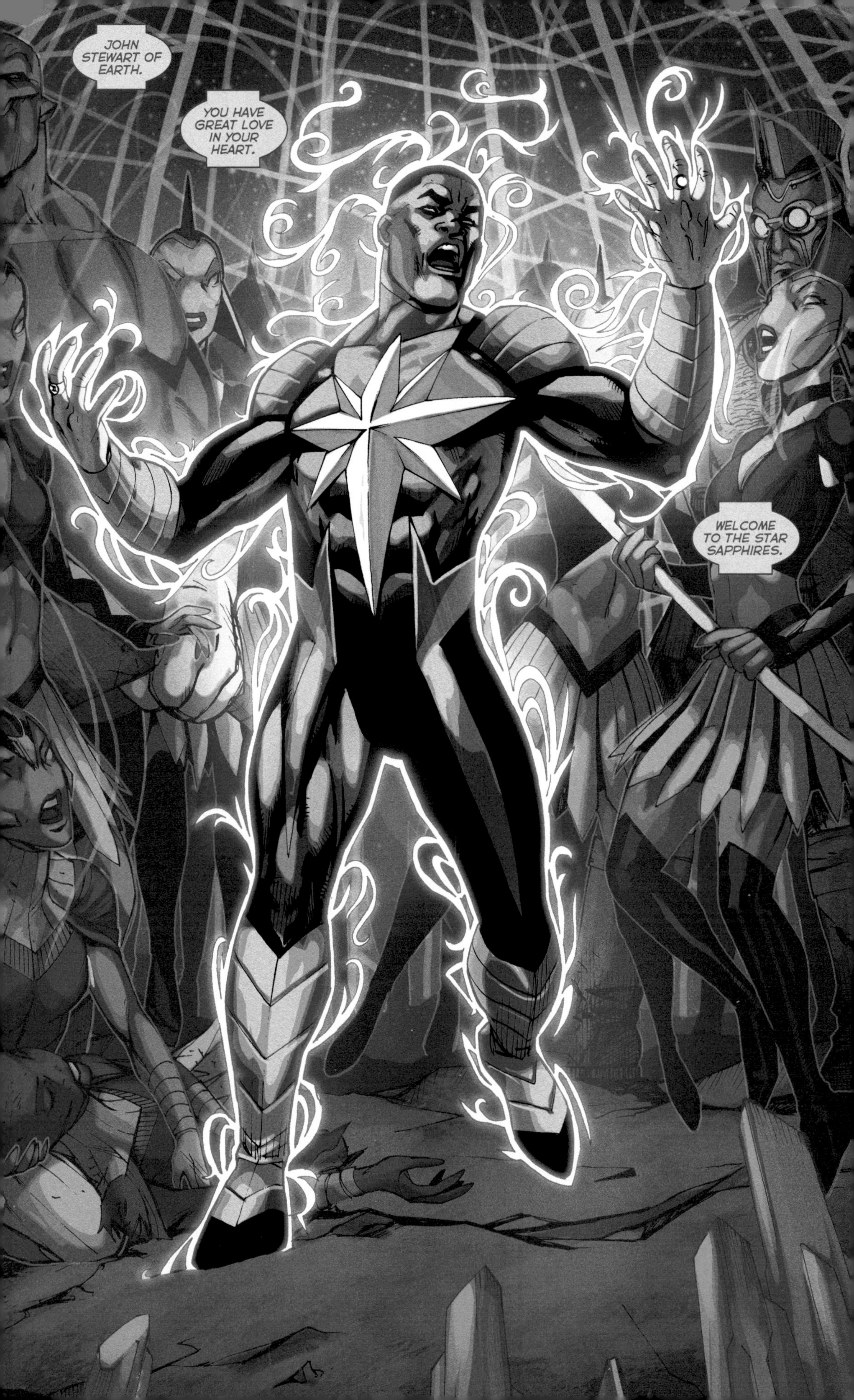
JOHN STEWART OF EARTH.
YOU HAVE GREAT LOVE IN YOUR HEART.
WELCOME TO THE STAR SAPPHIRES.

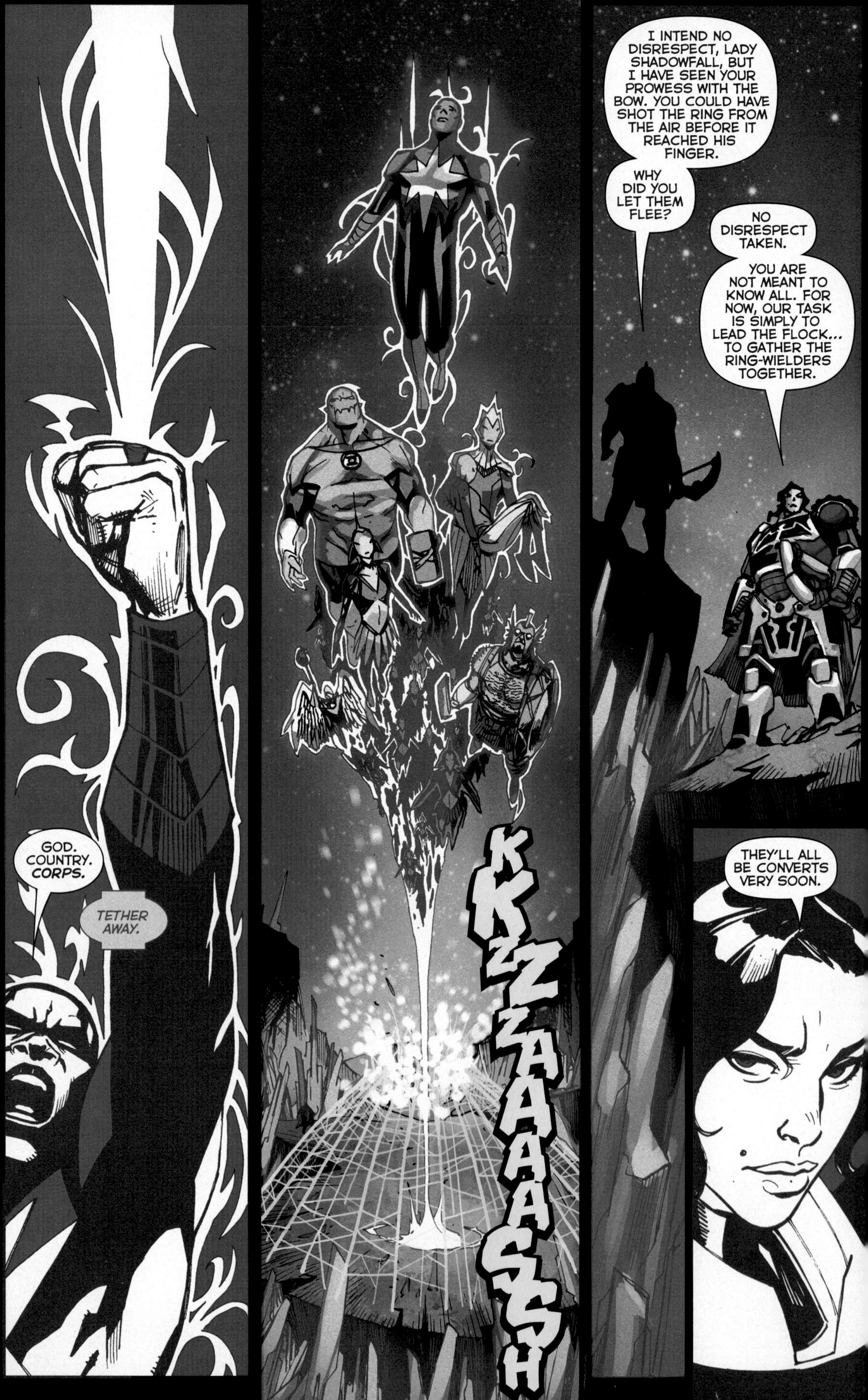
GOD. COUNTRY. *CORPS.*
TETHER AWAY.
KKZZZAAAAASSH
I INTEND NO DISRESPECT, LADY SHADOWFALL, BUT I HAVE SEEN YOUR PROWESS WITH THE BOW. YOU COULD HAVE SHOT THE RING FROM THE AIR BEFORE IT REACHED HIS FINGER.
WHY DID YOU LET THEM FLEE?
NO DISRESPECT TAKEN.
YOU ARE NOT MEANT TO KNOW ALL. FOR NOW, OUR TASK IS SIMPLY TO LEAD THE FLOCK... TO GATHER THE RING-WIELDERS TOGETHER.
THEY'LL ALL BE CONVERTS VERY SOON.

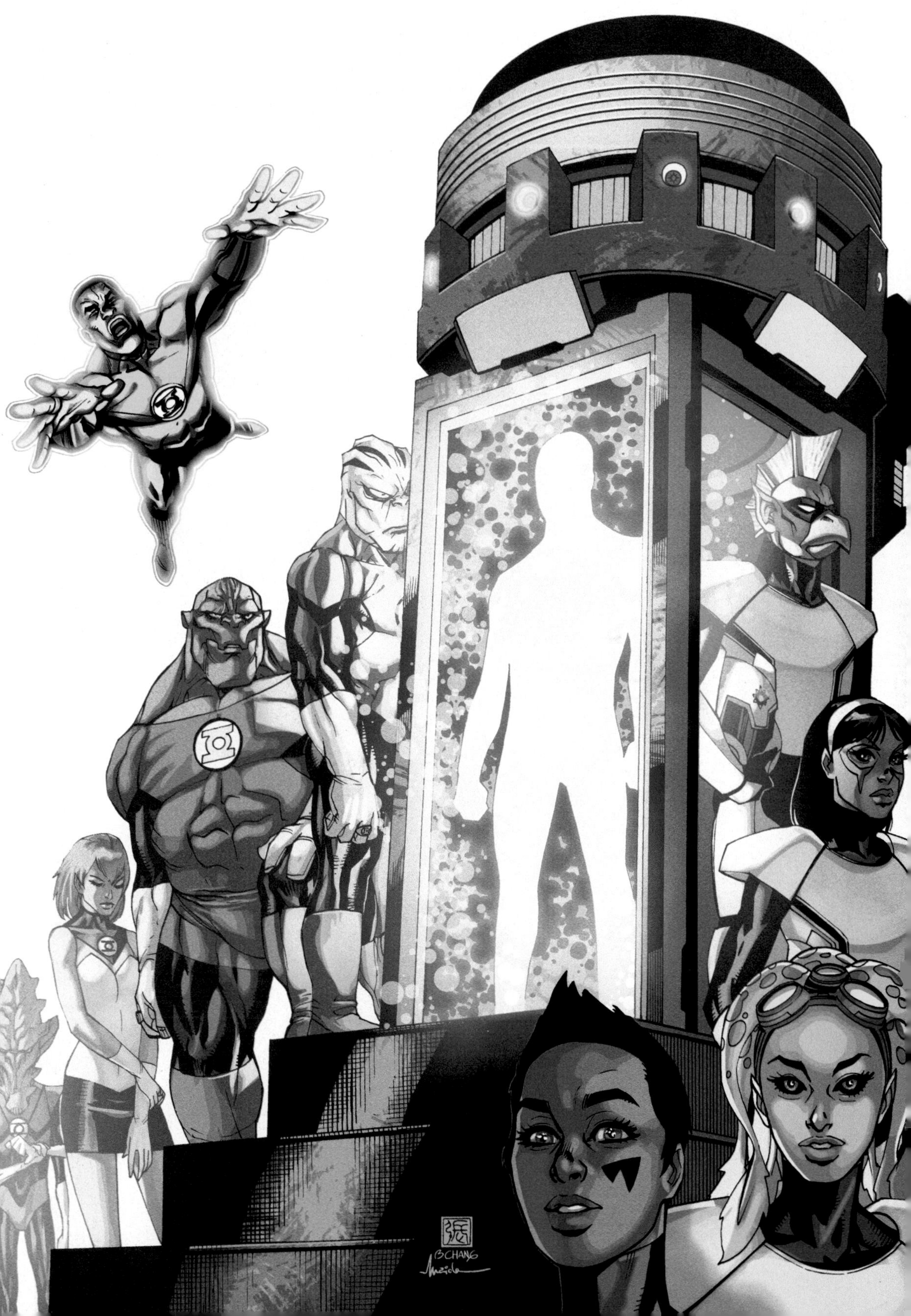
BCHANG

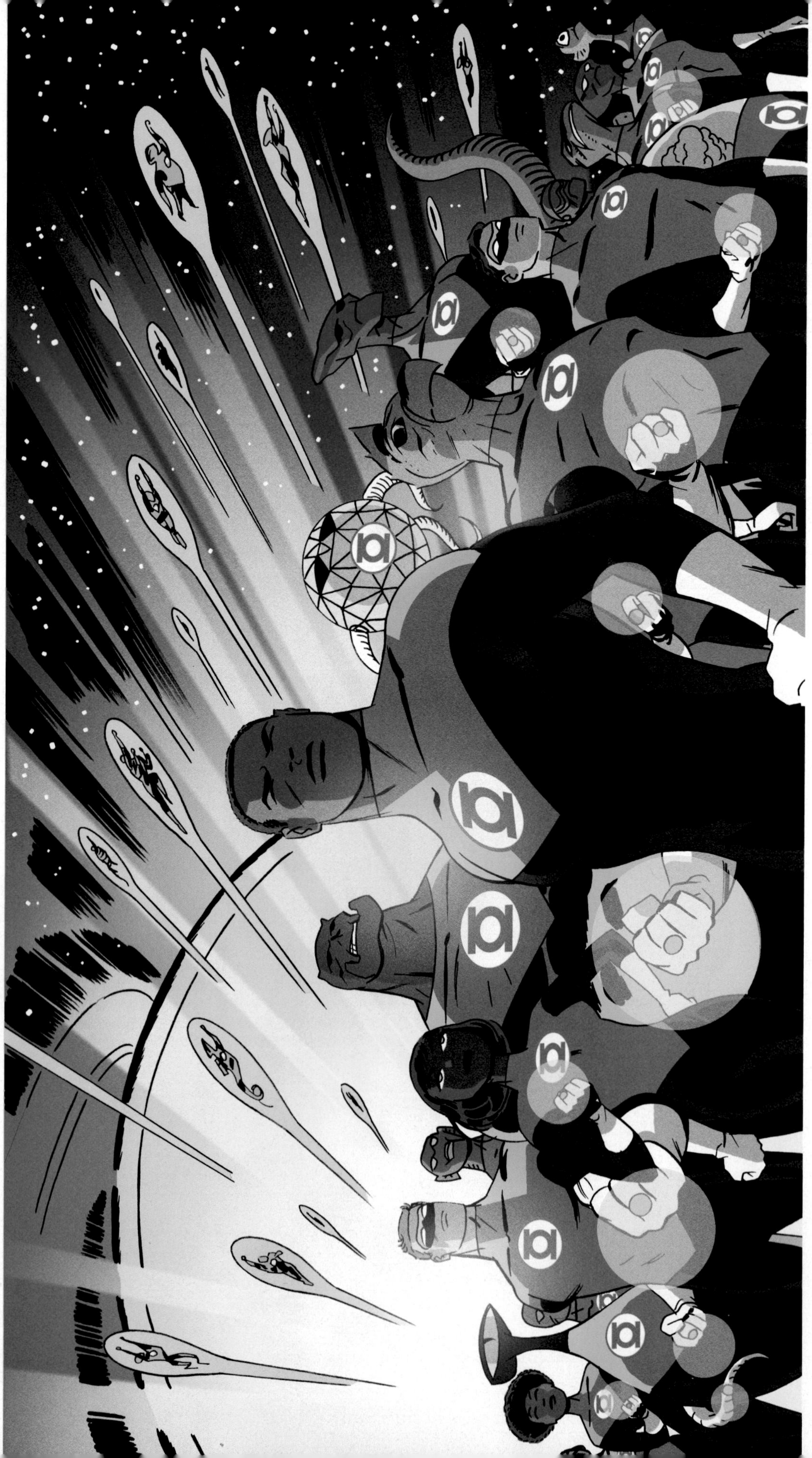

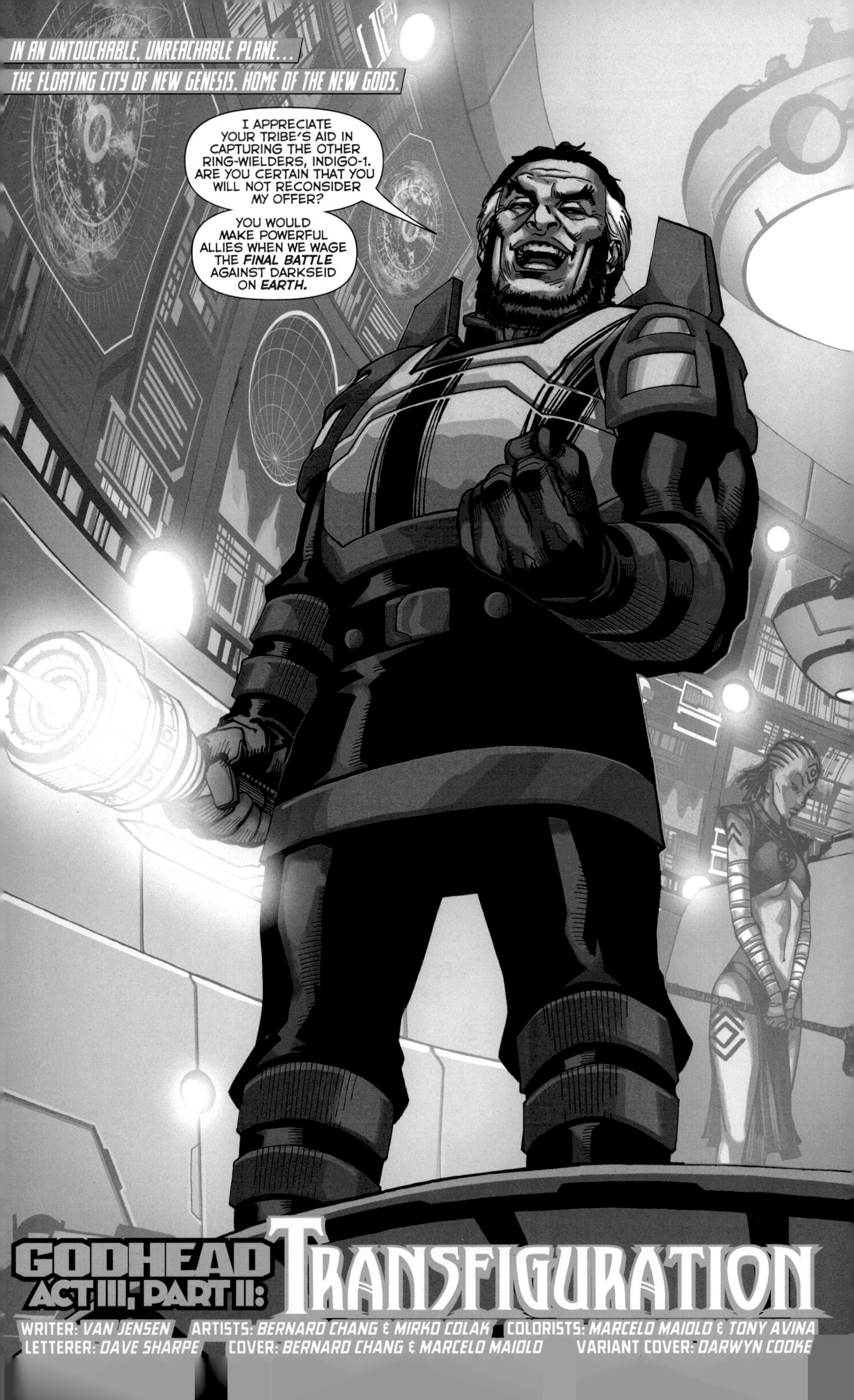
IN AN UNTOUCHABLE, UNREACHABLE PLANE...
THE FLOATING CITY OF NEW GENESIS. HOME OF THE NEW GODS.
I APPRECIATE YOUR TRIBE'S AID IN CAPTURING THE OTHER RING-WIELDERS, INDIGO-1. ARE YOU CERTAIN THAT YOU WILL NOT RECONSIDER MY OFFER?
YOU WOULD MAKE POWERFUL ALLIES WHEN WE WAGE THE FINAL BATTLE AGAINST DARKSEID ON EARTH.
GODHEAD ACT III, PART II: TRANSFIGURATION
WRITER: VAN JENSEN ARTISTS: BERNARD CHANG & MIRKO COLAK COLORISTS: MARCELO MAIOLO & TONY AVINA
LETTERER: DAVE SHARPE COVER: BERNARD CHANG & MARCELO MAIOLO VARIANT COVER: DARWYN COOKE

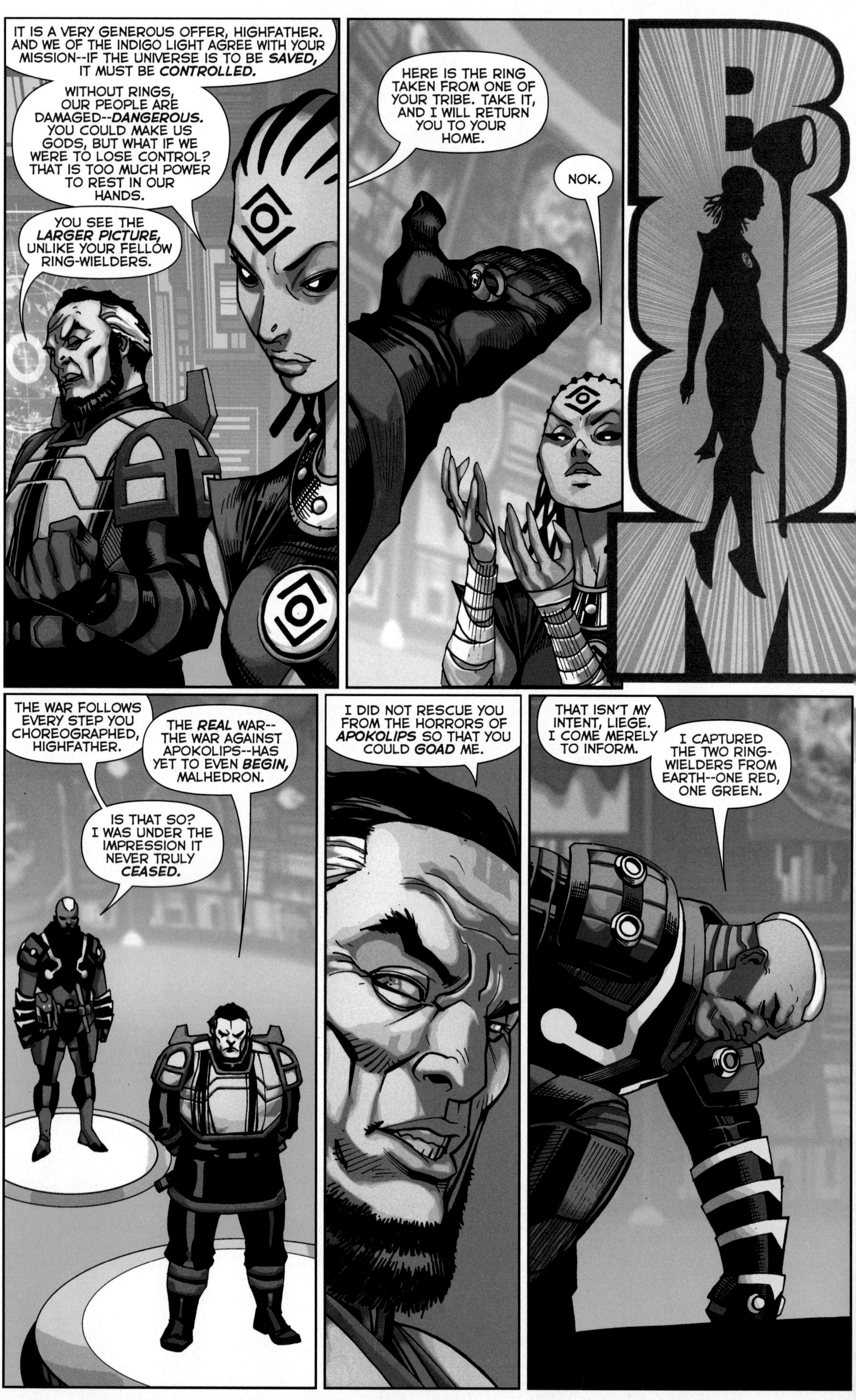
IT IS A VERY GENEROUS OFFER, HIGHFATHER. AND WE OF THE INDIGO LIGHT AGREE WITH YOUR MISSION--IF THE UNIVERSE IS TO BE SAVED, IT MUST BE CONTROLLED.
WITHOUT RINGS, OUR PEOPLE ARE DAMAGED--DANGEROUS. YOU COULD MAKE US GODS, BUT WHAT IF WE WERE TO LOSE CONTROL? THAT IS TOO MUCH POWER TO REST IN OUR HANDS.
YOU SEE THE LARGER PICTURE, UNLIKE YOUR FELLOW RING-WIELDERS.
HERE IS THE RING TAKEN FROM ONE OF YOUR TRIBE. TAKE IT, AND I WILL RETURN YOU TO YOUR HOME.
NOK.
BOOM
THE WAR FOLLOWS EVERY STEP YOU CHOREOGRAPHED, HIGHFATHER.
THE REAL WAR--THE WAR AGAINST APOKOLIPS--HAS YET TO EVEN BEGIN, MALHEDRON.
IS THAT SO? I WAS UNDER THE IMPRESSION IT NEVER TRULY CEASED.
I DID NOT RESCUE YOU FROM THE HORRORS OF APOKOLIPS SO THAT YOU COULD GOAD ME.
THAT ISN'T MY INTENT, LIEGE. I COME MERELY TO INFORM.
I CAPTURED THE TWO RING-WIELDERS FROM EARTH--ONE RED, ONE GREEN.

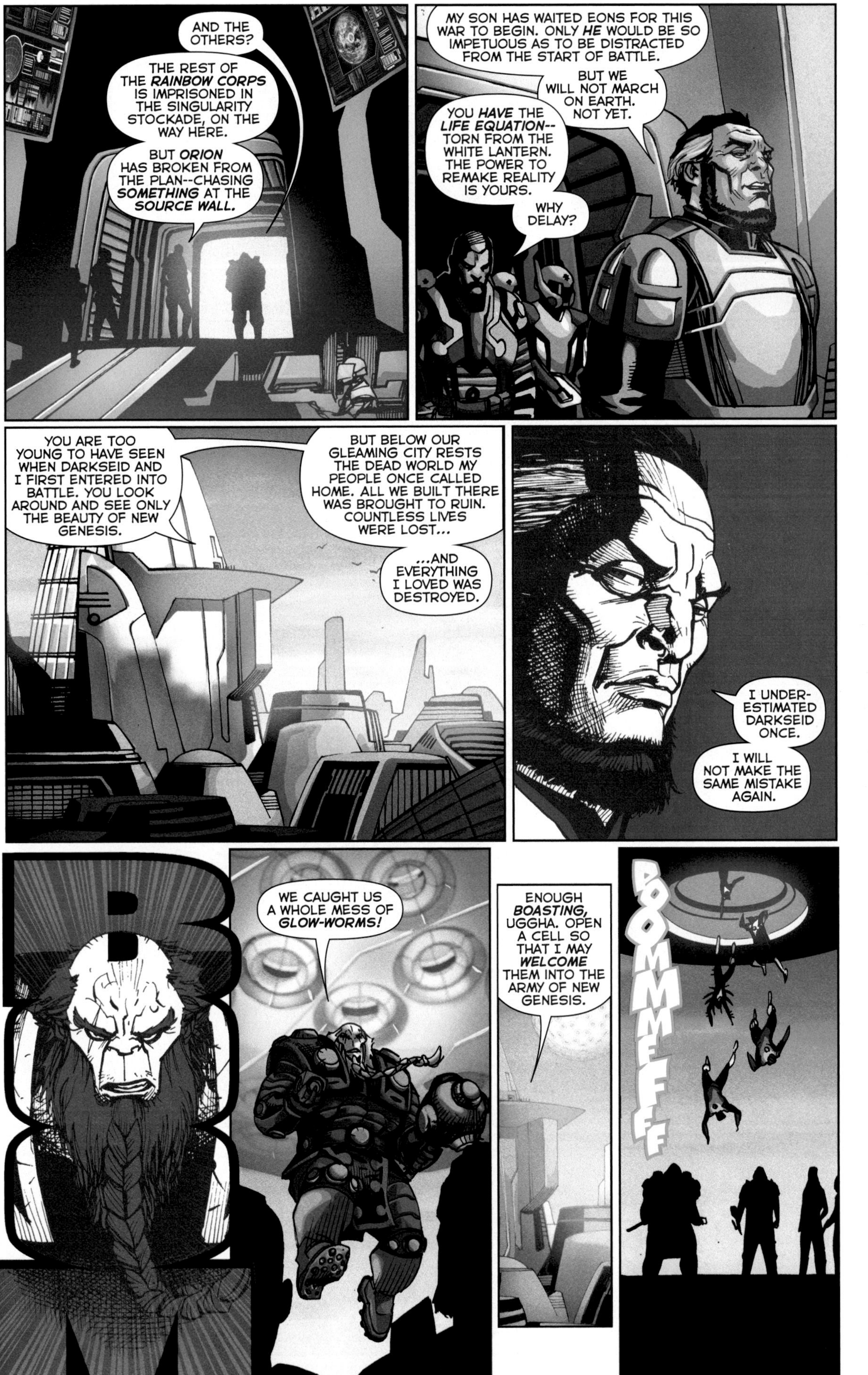

AND THE OTHERS?
THE REST OF THE *RAINBOW CORPS* IS IMPRISONED IN THE SINGULARITY STOCKADE, ON THE WAY HERE.
BUT *ORION* HAS BROKEN FROM THE PLAN--CHASING *SOMETHING* AT THE *SOURCE WALL.*
MY SON HAS WAITED EONS FOR THIS WAR TO BEGIN. ONLY *HE* WOULD BE SO IMPETUOUS AS TO BE DISTRACTED FROM THE START OF BATTLE.
BUT WE WILL NOT MARCH ON EARTH. NOT YET.
YOU *HAVE* THE *LIFE EQUATION*--TORN FROM THE WHITE LANTERN. THE POWER TO REMAKE REALITY IS YOURS.
WHY DELAY?
YOU ARE TOO YOUNG TO HAVE SEEN WHEN DARKSEID AND I FIRST ENTERED INTO BATTLE. YOU LOOK AROUND AND SEE ONLY THE BEAUTY OF NEW GENESIS.
BUT BELOW OUR GLEAMING CITY RESTS THE DEAD WORLD MY PEOPLE ONCE CALLED HOME. ALL WE BUILT THERE WAS BROUGHT TO RUIN. COUNTLESS LIVES WERE LOST...
...AND EVERYTHING I LOVED WAS DESTROYED.
I UNDER-ESTIMATED DARKSEID ONCE.
I WILL NOT MAKE THE SAME MISTAKE AGAIN.
BOOM
WE CAUGHT US A WHOLE MESS OF *GLOW-WORMS!*
ENOUGH *BOASTING,* UGGHA. OPEN A CELL SO THAT I MAY *WELCOME* THEM INTO THE ARMY OF NEW GENESIS.
DOOMMMEFF

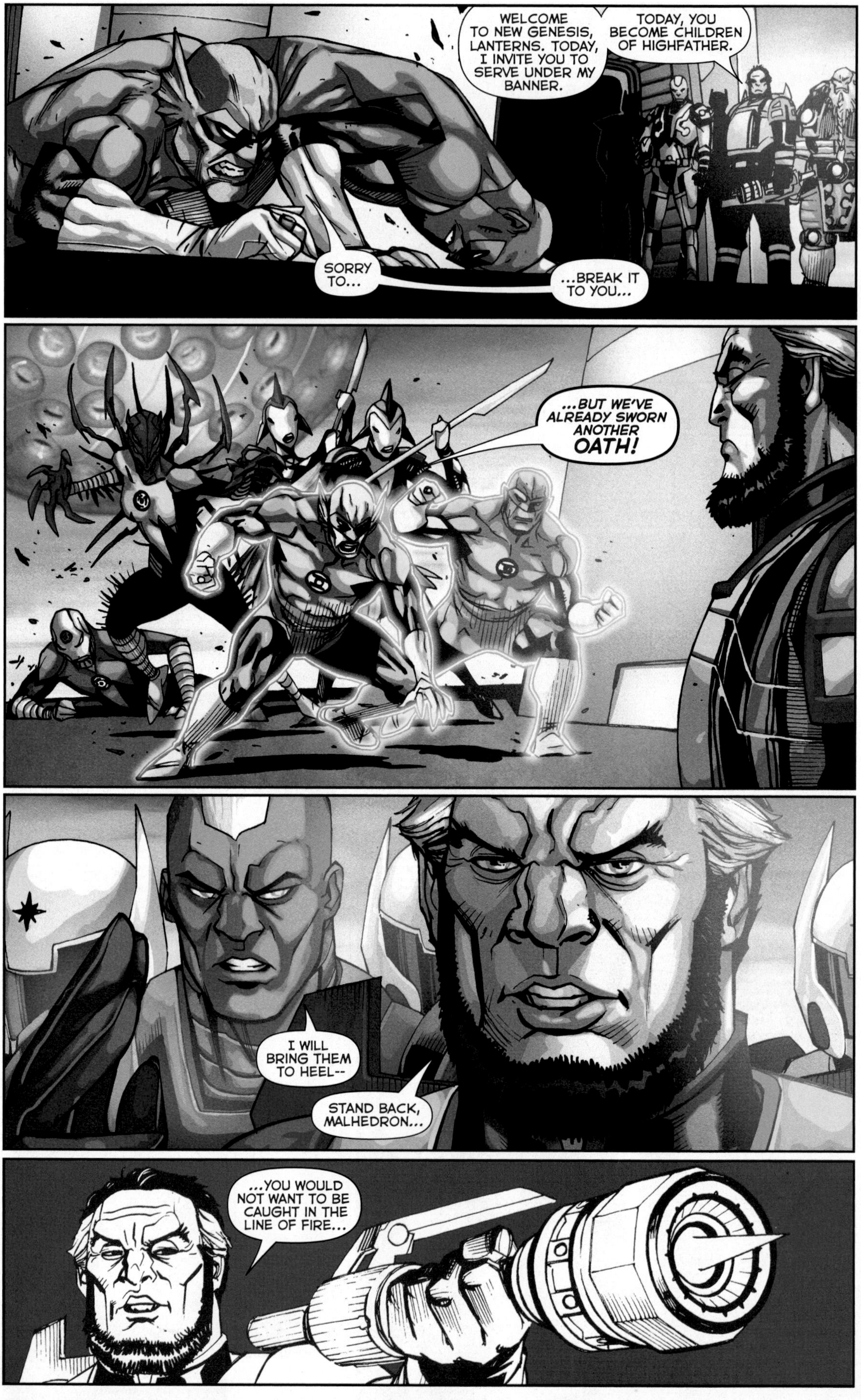
WELCOME TO NEW GENESIS, LANTERNS. TODAY, I INVITE YOU TO SERVE UNDER MY BANNER.
TODAY, YOU BECOME CHILDREN OF HIGHFATHER.
SORRY TO...
...BREAK IT TO YOU...
...BUT WE'VE ALREADY SWORN ANOTHER OATH!
I WILL BRING THEM TO HEEL--
STAND BACK, MALHEDRON...
...YOU WOULD NOT WANT TO BE CAUGHT IN THE LINE OF FIRE...

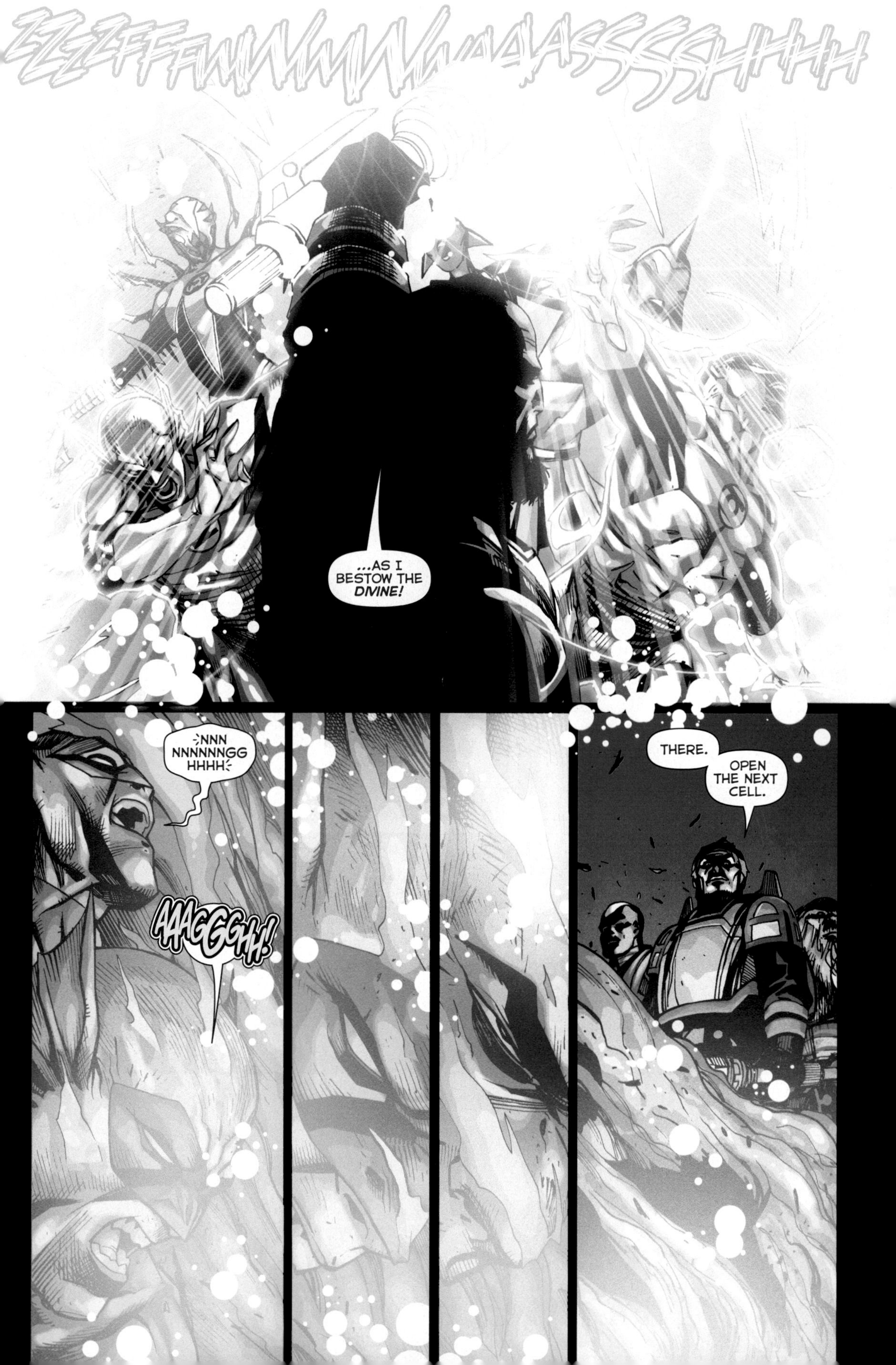
ZZZZFFFWWWWWWWWAAAASSSSSHHHH
...AS I BESTOW THE DIVINE!
-NNN NNNNNNGG HHHH-
AAAGGGHH!
THERE.
OPEN THE NEXT CELL.

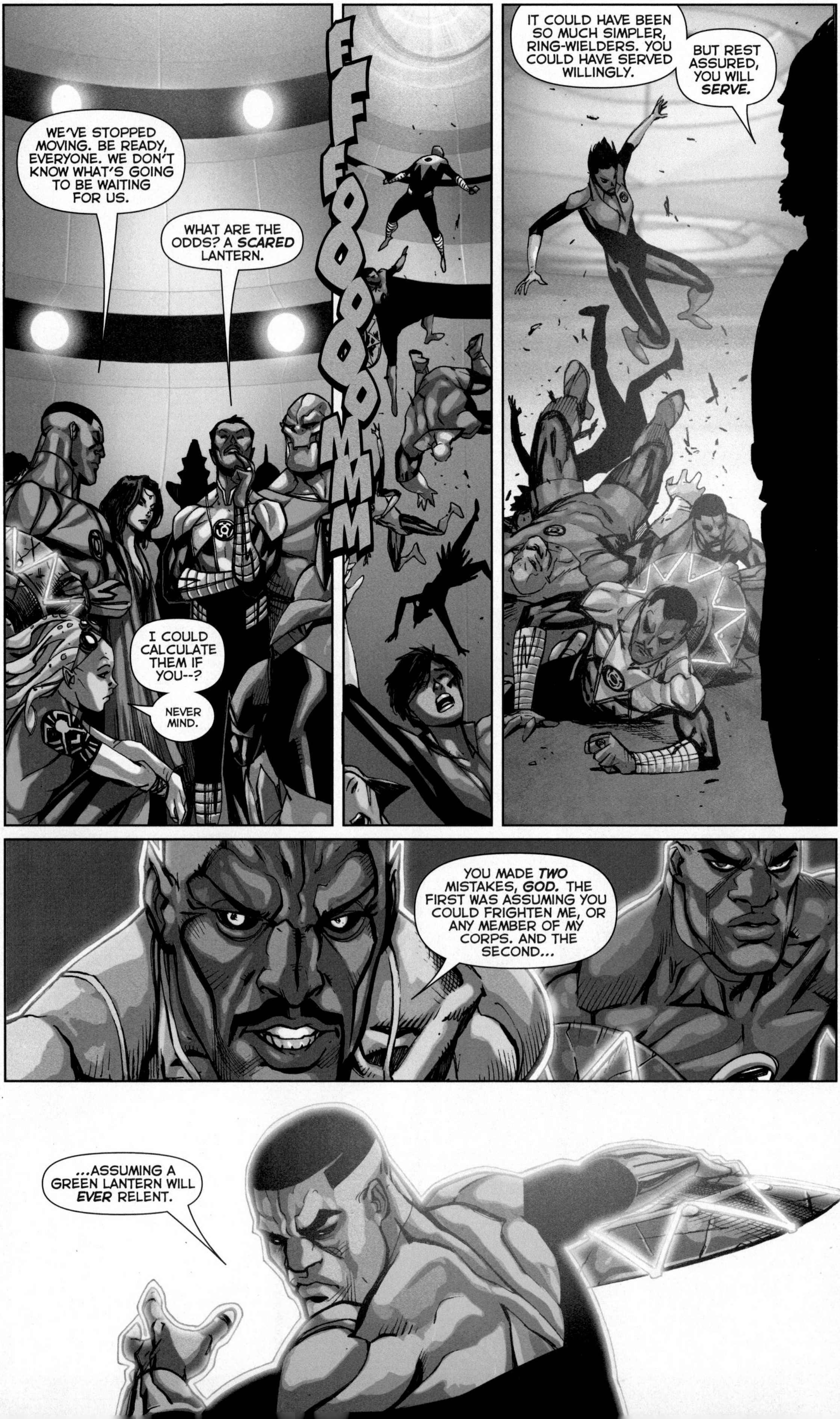

WE'VE STOPPED MOVING. BE READY, EVERYONE. WE DON'T KNOW WHAT'S GOING TO BE WAITING FOR US.
WHAT ARE THE ODDS? A SCARED LANTERN.
I COULD CALCULATE THEM IF YOU--?
NEVER MIND.
FFOOOOOOMMM
IT COULD HAVE BEEN SO MUCH SIMPLER, RING-WIELDERS. YOU COULD HAVE SERVED WILLINGLY.
BUT REST ASSURED, YOU WILL SERVE.
YOU MADE TWO MISTAKES, GOD. THE FIRST WAS ASSUMING YOU COULD FRIGHTEN ME, OR ANY MEMBER OF MY CORPS. AND THE SECOND...
...ASSUMING A GREEN LANTERN WILL EVER RELENT.

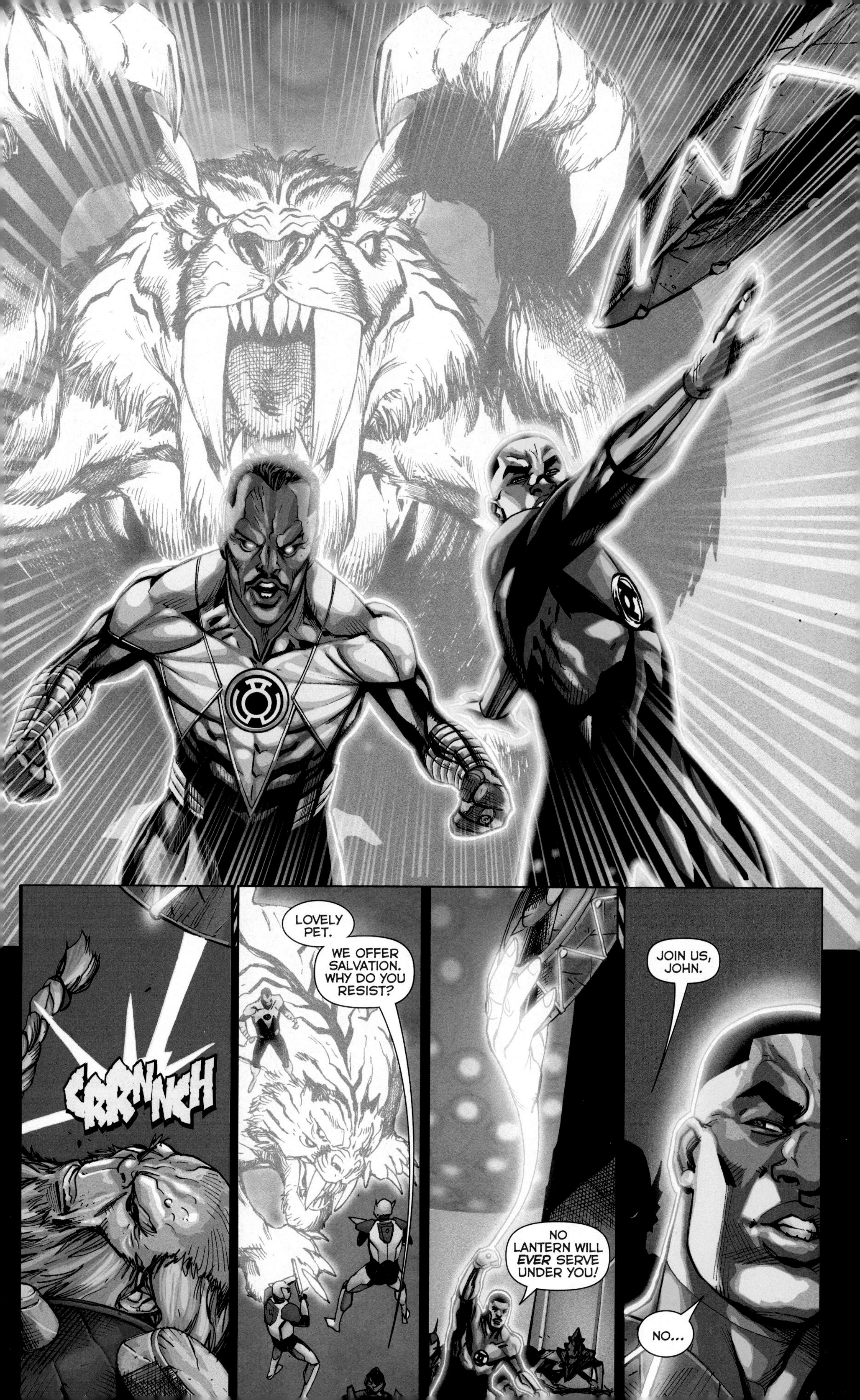
CRRNNCH
LOVELY PET.
WE OFFER SALVATION. WHY DO YOU RESIST?
NO LANTERN WILL *EVER* SERVE UNDER YOU!
JOIN US, JOHN.
NO...

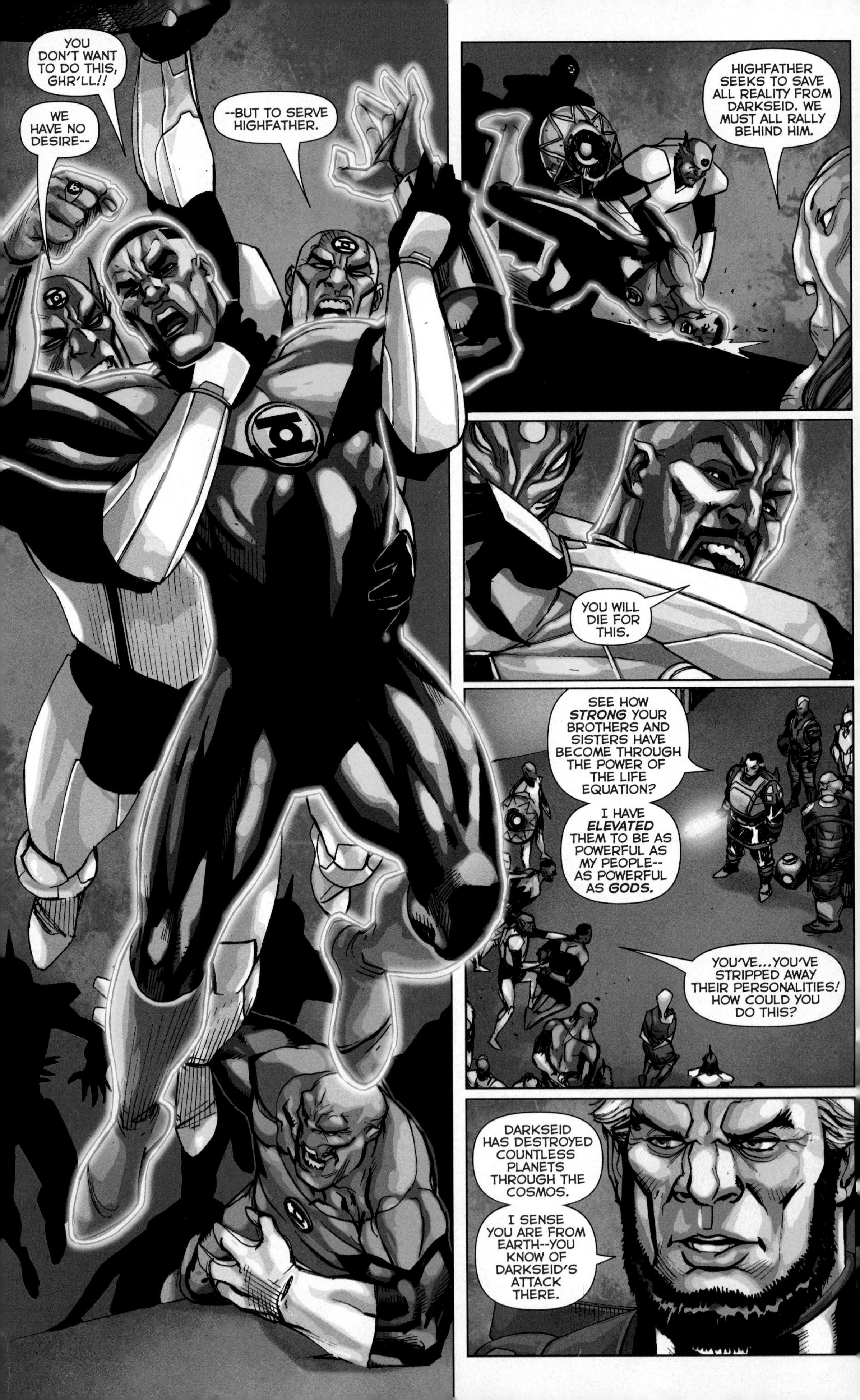
YOU DON'T WANT TO DO THIS, GHR'LL!!
WE HAVE NO DESIRE--
--BUT TO SERVE HIGHFATHER.
HIGHFATHER SEEKS TO SAVE ALL REALITY FROM DARKSEID. WE MUST ALL RALLY BEHIND HIM.
YOU WILL DIE FOR THIS.
SEE HOW STRONG YOUR BROTHERS AND SISTERS HAVE BECOME THROUGH THE POWER OF THE LIFE EQUATION?
I HAVE ELEVATED THEM TO BE AS POWERFUL AS MY PEOPLE-- AS POWERFUL AS GODS.
YOU'VE...YOU'VE STRIPPED AWAY THEIR PERSONALITIES! HOW COULD YOU DO THIS?
DARKSEID HAS DESTROYED COUNTLESS PLANETS THROUGH THE COSMOS.
I SENSE YOU ARE FROM EARTH--YOU KNOW OF DARKSEID'S ATTACK THERE.

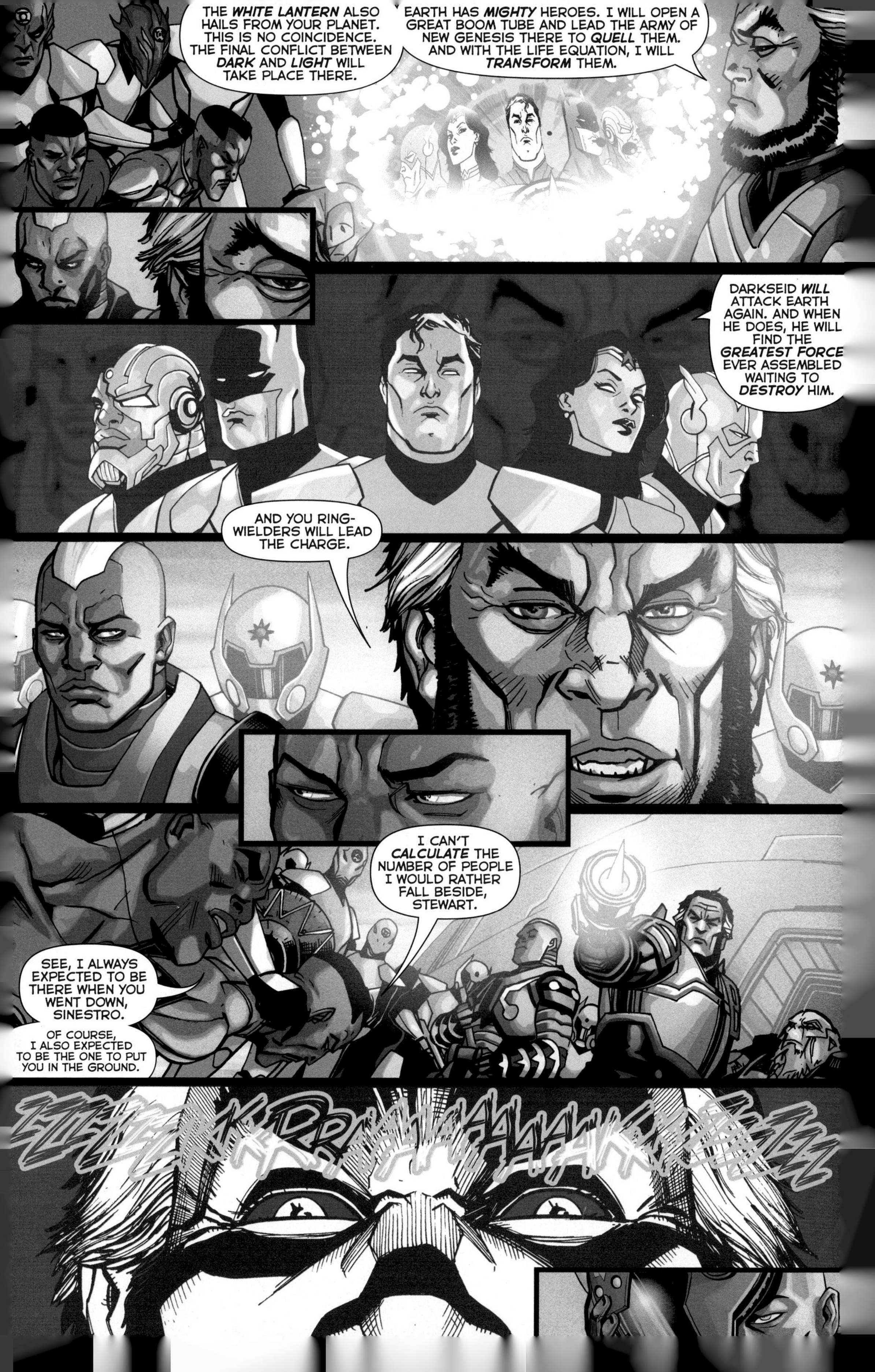
THE WHITE LANTERN ALSO HAILS FROM YOUR PLANET. THIS IS NO COINCIDENCE. THE FINAL CONFLICT BETWEEN DARK AND LIGHT WILL TAKE PLACE THERE.
EARTH HAS MIGHTY HEROES. I WILL OPEN A GREAT BOOM TUBE AND LEAD THE ARMY OF NEW GENESIS THERE TO QUELL THEM. AND WITH THE LIFE EQUATION, I WILL TRANSFORM THEM.
DARKSEID WILL ATTACK EARTH AGAIN. AND WHEN HE DOES, HE WILL FIND THE GREATEST FORCE EVER ASSEMBLED WAITING TO DESTROY HIM.
AND YOU RING-WIELDERS WILL LEAD THE CHARGE.
I CAN'T CALCULATE THE NUMBER OF PEOPLE I WOULD RATHER FALL BESIDE, STEWART.
SEE, I ALWAYS EXPECTED TO BE THERE WHEN YOU WENT DOWN, SINESTRO.
OF COURSE, I ALSO EXPECTED TO BE THE ONE TO PUT YOU IN THE GROUND.

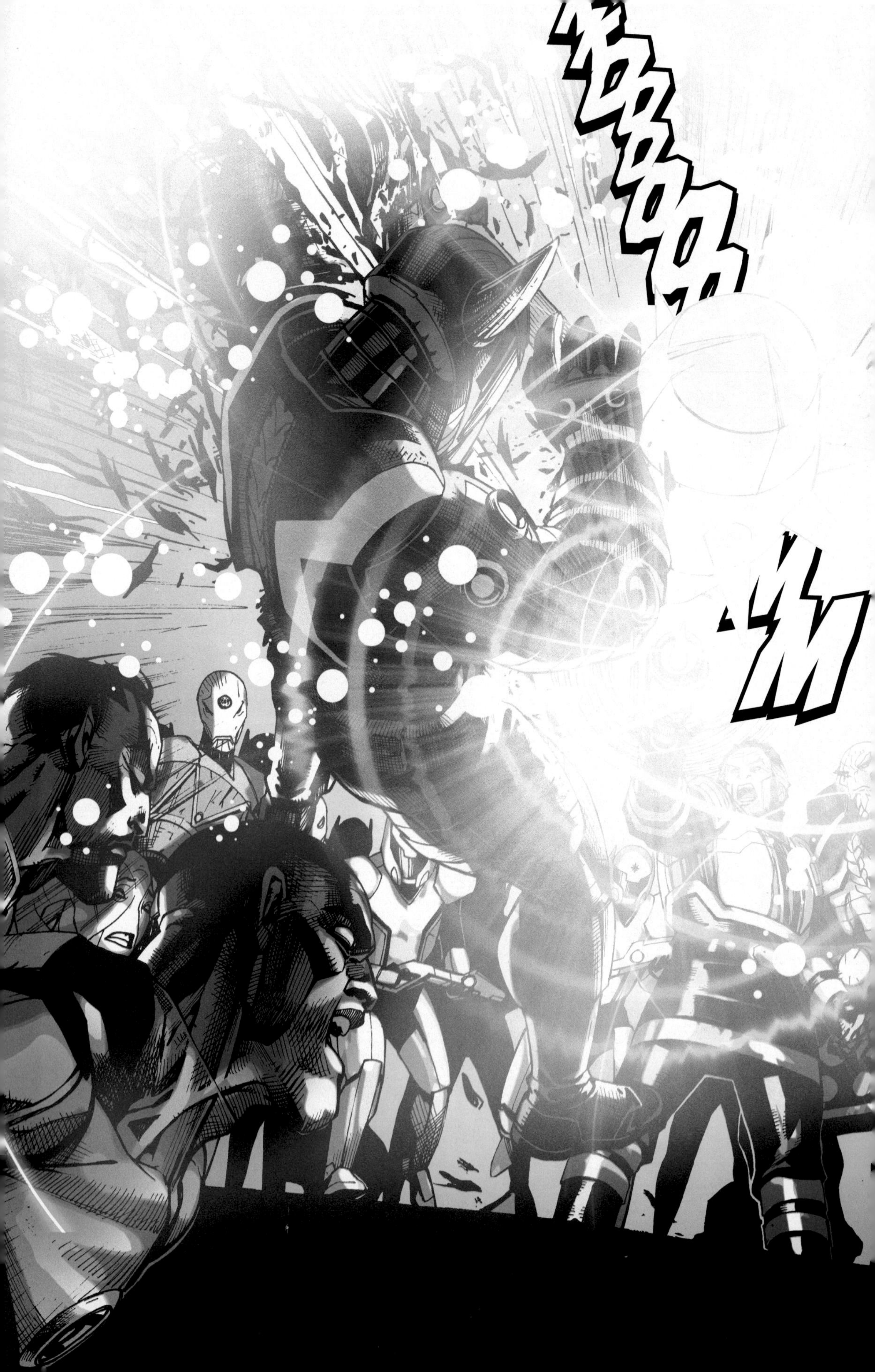

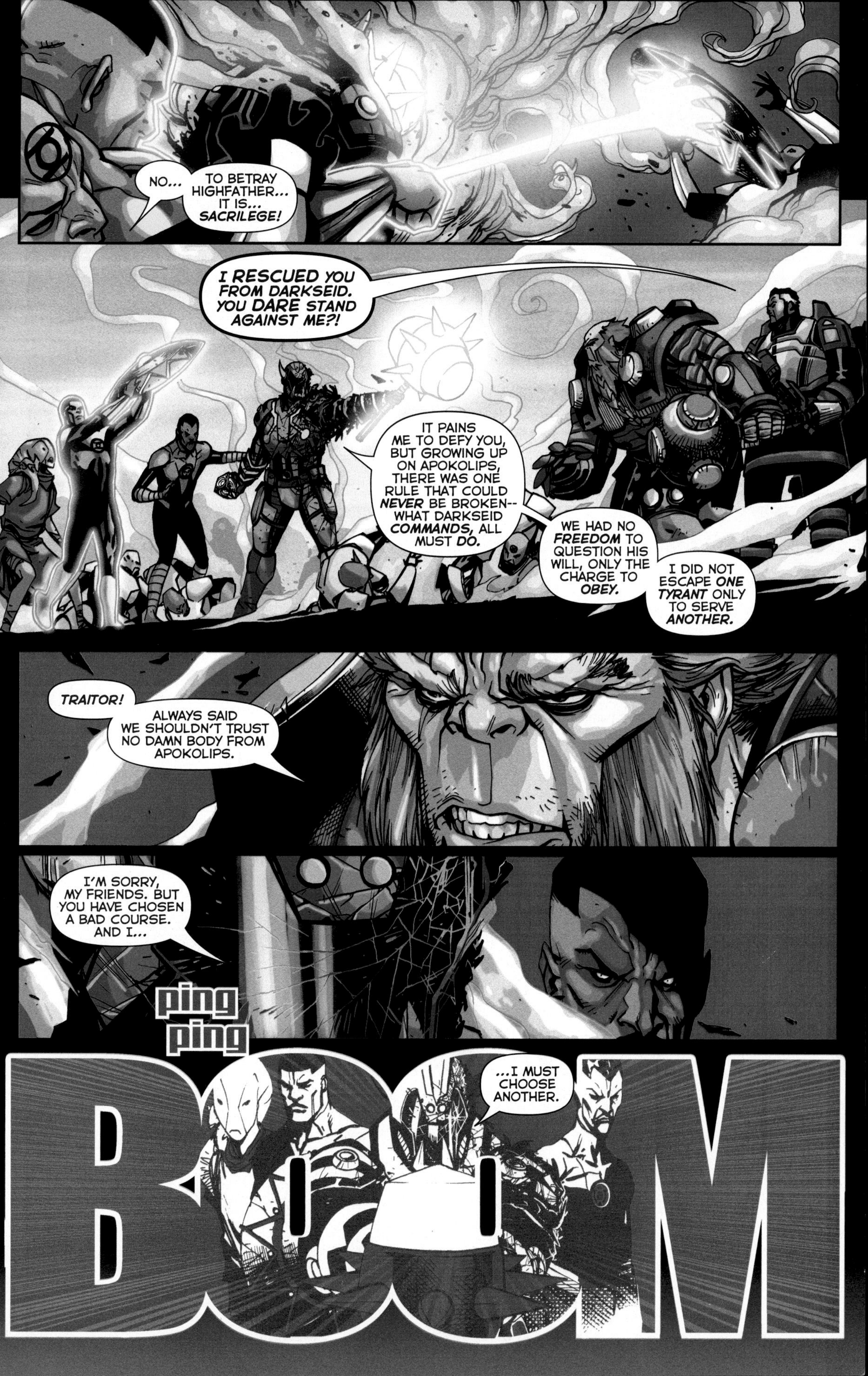
NO...
TO BETRAY HIGHFATHER... IT IS... SACRILEGE!
I RESCUED YOU FROM DARKSEID. YOU DARE STAND AGAINST ME?!
IT PAINS ME TO DEFY YOU, BUT GROWING UP ON APOKOLIPS, THERE WAS ONE RULE THAT COULD NEVER BE BROKEN--WHAT DARKSEID COMMANDS, ALL MUST DO.
WE HAD NO FREEDOM TO QUESTION HIS WILL, ONLY THE CHARGE TO OBEY.
I DID NOT ESCAPE ONE TYRANT ONLY TO SERVE ANOTHER.
TRAITOR!
ALWAYS SAID WE SHOULDN'T TRUST NO DAMN BODY FROM APOKOLIPS.
I'M SORRY, MY FRIENDS. BUT YOU HAVE CHOSEN A BAD COURSE. AND I...
ping ping
BOOM
...I MUST CHOOSE ANOTHER.

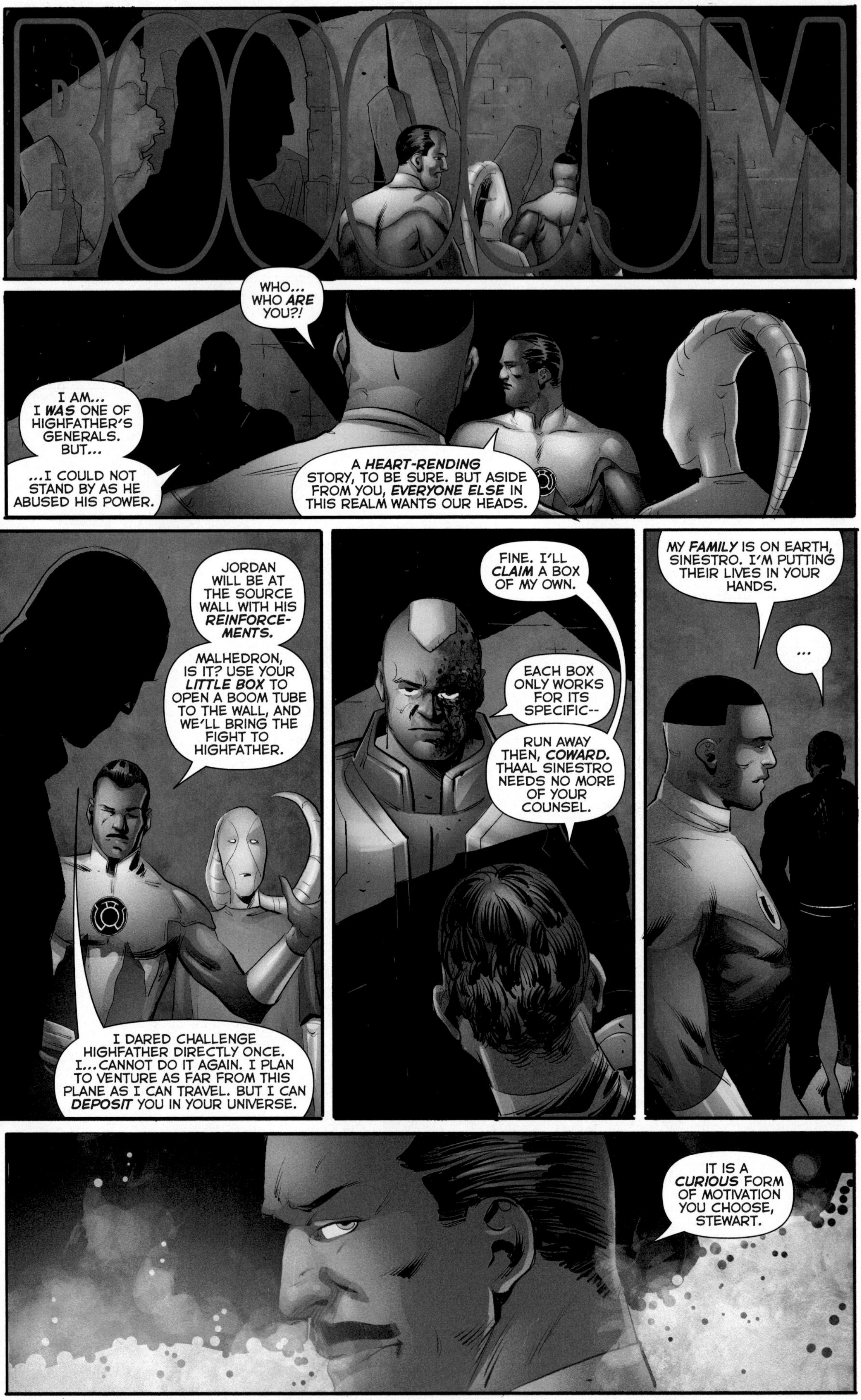
BOOOOOM
WHO... WHO ARE YOU?!
I AM... I WAS ONE OF HIGHFATHER'S GENERALS. BUT...
...I COULD NOT STAND BY AS HE ABUSED HIS POWER.
A HEART-RENDING STORY, TO BE SURE. BUT ASIDE FROM YOU, EVERYONE ELSE IN THIS REALM WANTS OUR HEADS.
JORDAN WILL BE AT THE SOURCE WALL WITH HIS REINFORCE-MENTS.
MALHEDRON, IS IT? USE YOUR LITTLE BOX TO OPEN A BOOM TUBE TO THE WALL, AND WE'LL BRING THE FIGHT TO HIGHFATHER.
I DARED CHALLENGE HIGHFATHER DIRECTLY ONCE. I...CANNOT DO IT AGAIN. I PLAN TO VENTURE AS FAR FROM THIS PLANE AS I CAN TRAVEL. BUT I CAN DEPOSIT YOU IN YOUR UNIVERSE.
FINE. I'LL CLAIM A BOX OF MY OWN.
EACH BOX ONLY WORKS FOR ITS SPECIFIC--
RUN AWAY THEN, COWARD. THAAL SINESTRO NEEDS NO MORE OF YOUR COUNSEL.
MY FAMILY IS ON EARTH, SINESTRO. I'M PUTTING THEIR LIVES IN YOUR HANDS.
...
IT IS A CURIOUS FORM OF MOTIVATION YOU CHOOSE, STEWART.

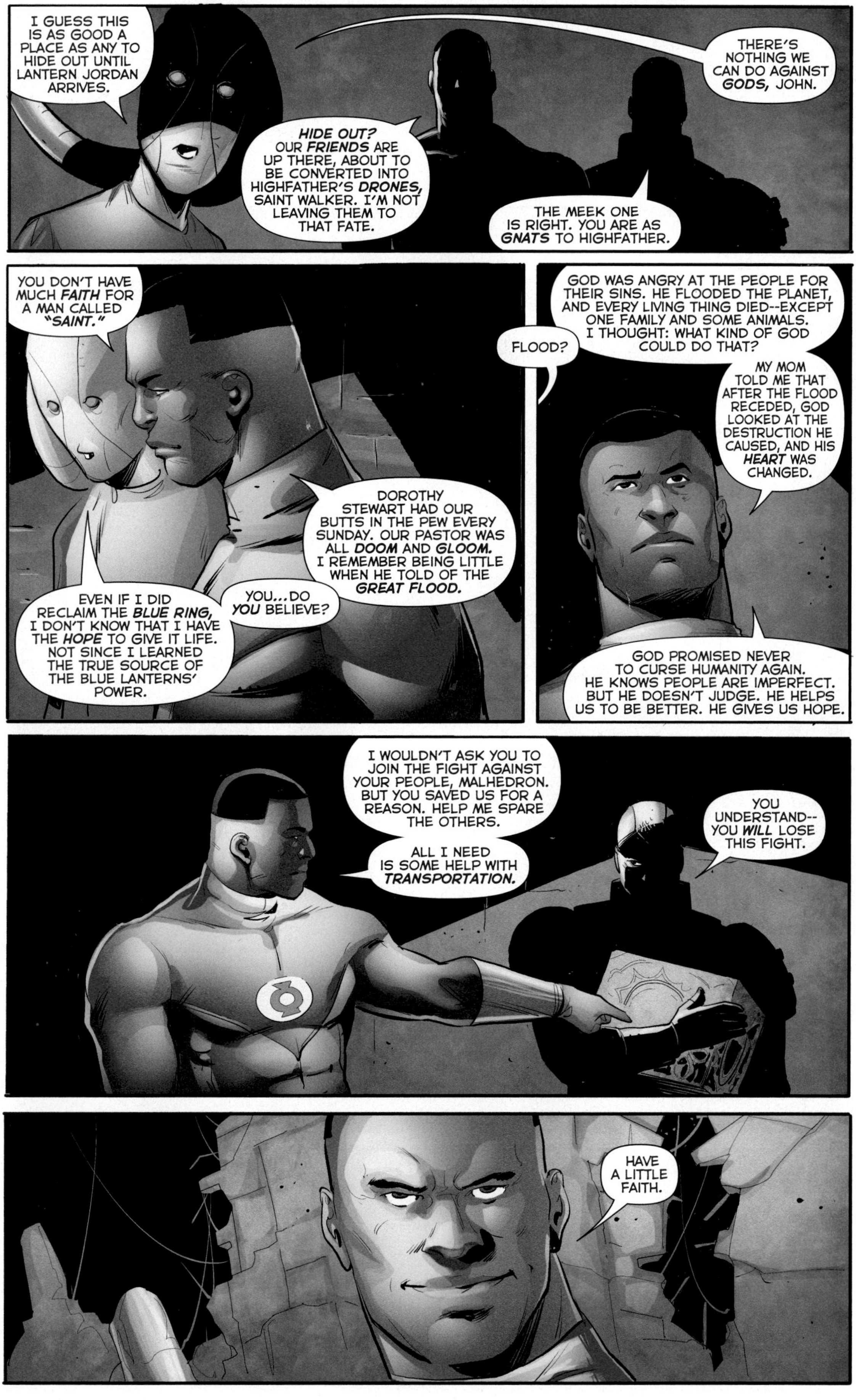
I GUESS THIS IS AS GOOD A PLACE AS ANY TO HIDE OUT UNTIL LANTERN JORDAN ARRIVES.
THERE'S NOTHING WE CAN DO AGAINST GODS, JOHN.
HIDE OUT? OUR FRIENDS ARE UP THERE, ABOUT TO BE CONVERTED INTO HIGHFATHER'S DRONES, SAINT WALKER. I'M NOT LEAVING THEM TO THAT FATE.
THE MEEK ONE IS RIGHT. YOU ARE AS GNATS TO HIGHFATHER.
YOU DON'T HAVE MUCH FAITH FOR A MAN CALLED "SAINT."
EVEN IF I DID RECLAIM THE BLUE RING, I DON'T KNOW THAT I HAVE THE HOPE TO GIVE IT LIFE. NOT SINCE I LEARNED THE TRUE SOURCE OF THE BLUE LANTERNS' POWER.
YOU...DO YOU BELIEVE?
DOROTHY STEWART HAD OUR BUTTS IN THE PEW EVERY SUNDAY. OUR PASTOR WAS ALL DOOM AND GLOOM. I REMEMBER BEING LITTLE WHEN HE TOLD OF THE GREAT FLOOD.
FLOOD?
GOD WAS ANGRY AT THE PEOPLE FOR THEIR SINS. HE FLOODED THE PLANET, AND EVERY LIVING THING DIED--EXCEPT ONE FAMILY AND SOME ANIMALS. I THOUGHT: WHAT KIND OF GOD COULD DO THAT?
MY MOM TOLD ME THAT AFTER THE FLOOD RECEDED, GOD LOOKED AT THE DESTRUCTION HE CAUSED, AND HIS HEART WAS CHANGED.
GOD PROMISED NEVER TO CURSE HUMANITY AGAIN. HE KNOWS PEOPLE ARE IMPERFECT. BUT HE DOESN'T JUDGE. HE HELPS US TO BE BETTER. HE GIVES US HOPE.
I WOULDN'T ASK YOU TO JOIN THE FIGHT AGAINST YOUR PEOPLE, MALHEDRON. BUT YOU SAVED US FOR A REASON. HELP ME SPARE THE OTHERS.
ALL I NEED IS SOME HELP WITH TRANSPORTATION.
YOU UNDERSTAND-- YOU WILL LOSE THIS FIGHT.
HAVE A LITTLE FAITH.

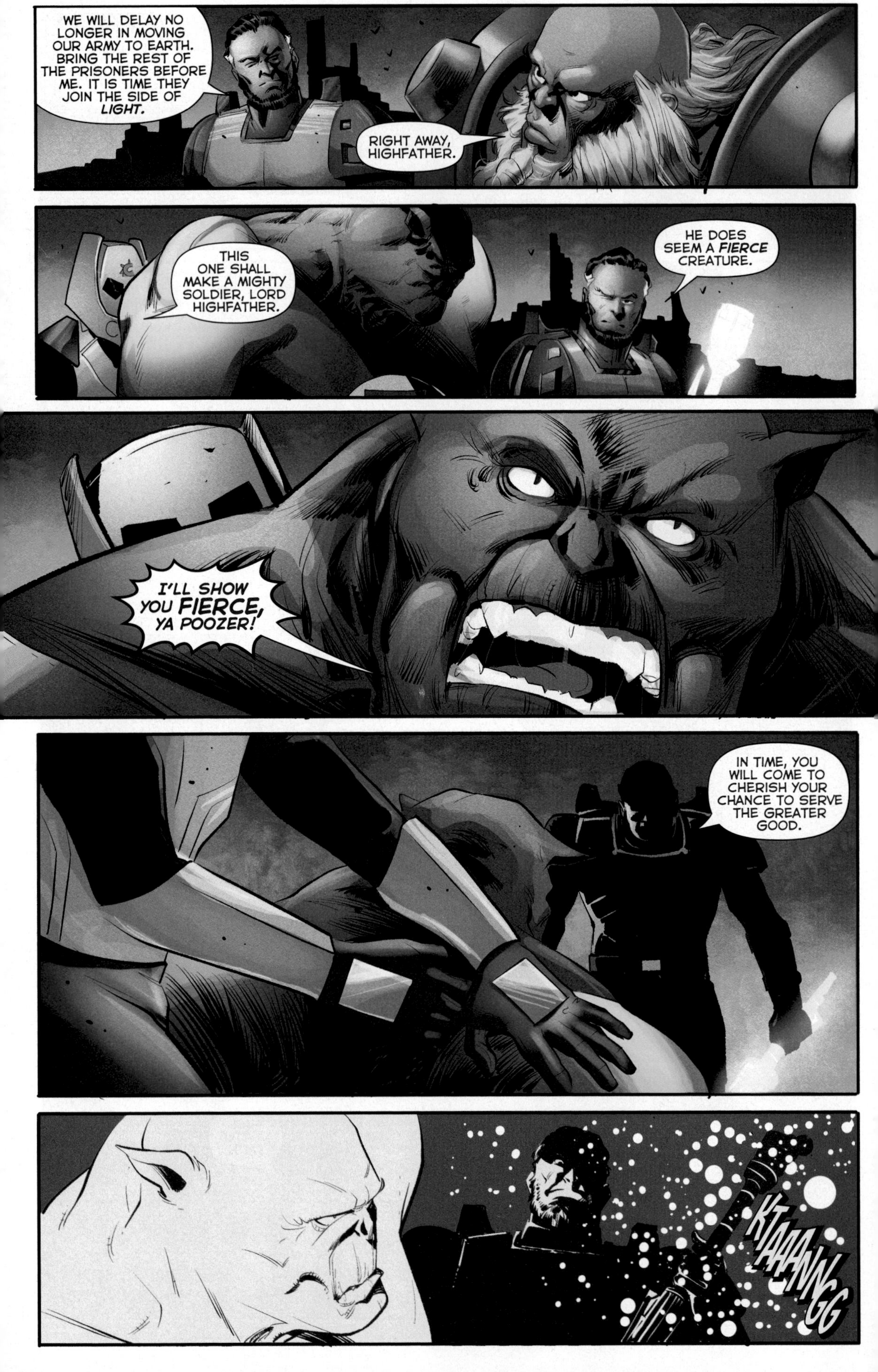

WE WILL DELAY NO LONGER IN MOVING OUR ARMY TO EARTH. BRING THE REST OF THE PRISONERS BEFORE ME. IT IS TIME THEY JOIN THE SIDE OF *LIGHT.*
RIGHT AWAY, HIGHFATHER.
THIS ONE SHALL MAKE A MIGHTY SOLDIER, LORD HIGHFATHER.
HE DOES SEEM A *FIERCE* CREATURE.
I'LL SHOW YOU **FIERCE,** YA POOZER!
IN TIME, YOU WILL COME TO CHERISH YOUR CHANCE TO SERVE THE GREATER GOOD.
KTAAANNGG

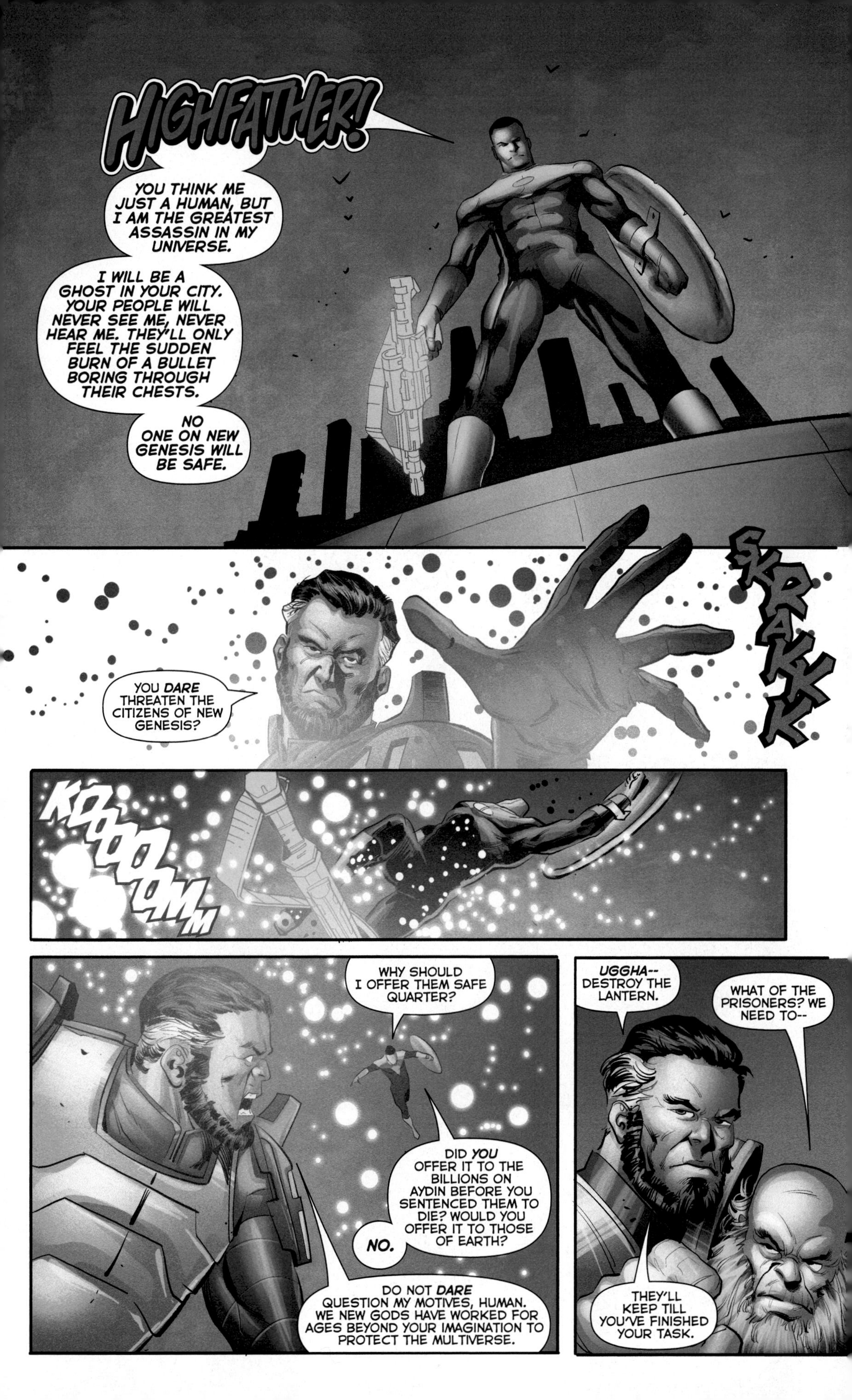
HIGHFATHER!
YOU THINK ME JUST A HUMAN, BUT I AM THE GREATEST ASSASSIN IN MY UNIVERSE.
I WILL BE A GHOST IN YOUR CITY. YOUR PEOPLE WILL NEVER SEE ME, NEVER HEAR ME. THEY'LL ONLY FEEL THE SUDDEN BURN OF A BULLET BORING THROUGH THEIR CHESTS.
NO ONE ON NEW GENESIS WILL BE SAFE.
SKRAKK
YOU DARE THREATEN THE CITIZENS OF NEW GENESIS?
KOOOOOMM
WHY SHOULD I OFFER THEM SAFE QUARTER?
DID YOU OFFER IT TO THE BILLIONS ON AYDIN BEFORE YOU SENTENCED THEM TO DIE? WOULD YOU OFFER IT TO THOSE OF EARTH?
NO.
DO NOT DARE QUESTION MY MOTIVES, HUMAN. WE NEW GODS HAVE WORKED FOR AGES BEYOND YOUR IMAGINATION TO PROTECT THE MULTIVERSE.
UGGHA-- DESTROY THE LANTERN.
WHAT OF THE PRISONERS? WE NEED TO--
THEY'LL KEEP TILL YOU'VE FINISHED YOUR TASK.

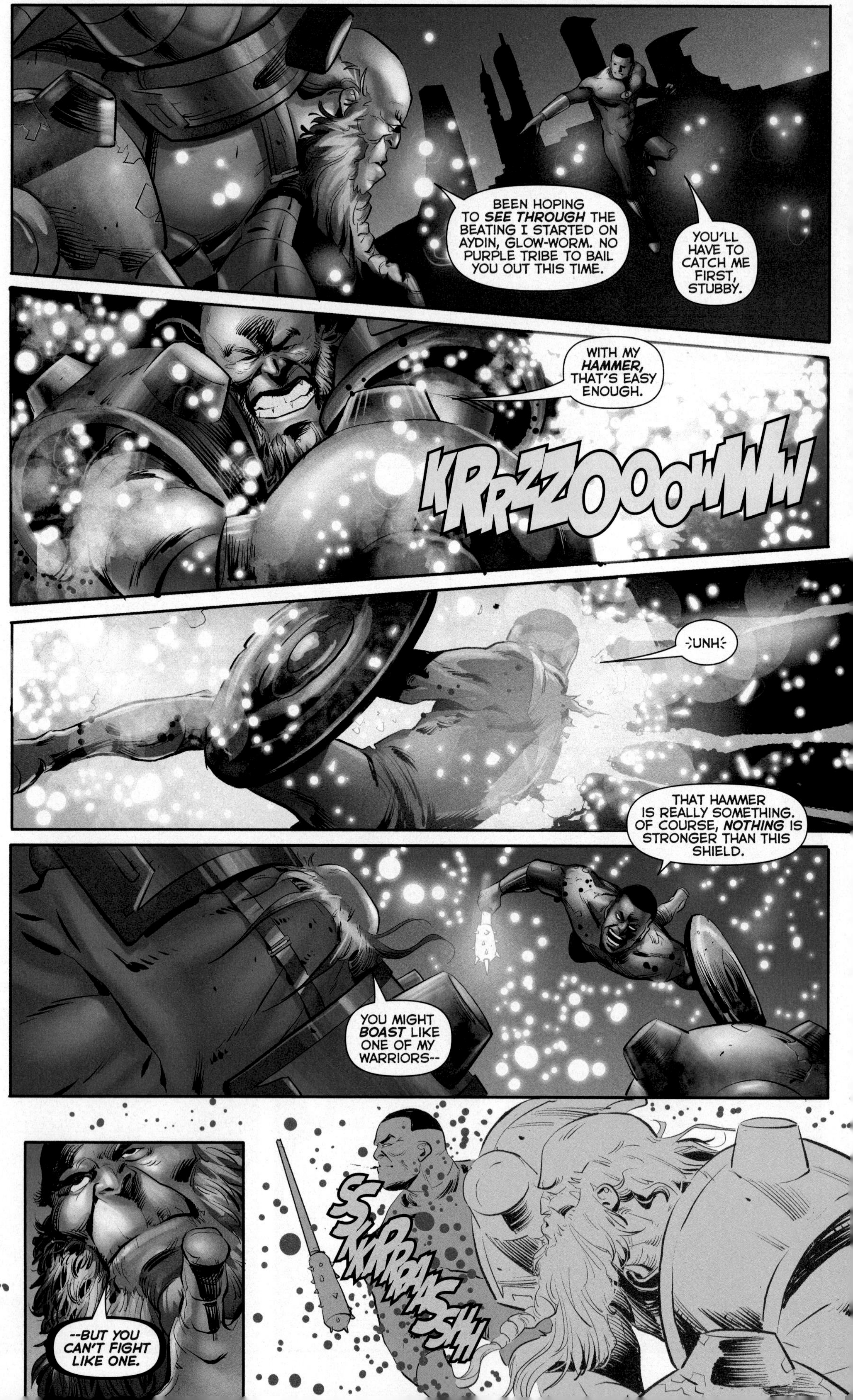
BEEN HOPING TO SEE THROUGH THE BEATING I STARTED ON AYDIN, GLOW-WORM. NO PURPLE TRIBE TO BAIL YOU OUT THIS TIME.
YOU'LL HAVE TO CATCH ME FIRST, STUBBY.
WITH MY HAMMER, THAT'S EASY ENOUGH.
KRRZZOOOWWW
UNH
THAT HAMMER IS REALLY SOMETHING. OF COURSE, NOTHING IS STRONGER THAN THIS SHIELD.
YOU MIGHT BOAST LIKE ONE OF MY WARRIORS--
--BUT YOU CAN'T FIGHT LIKE ONE.
SSHKRRAASHH

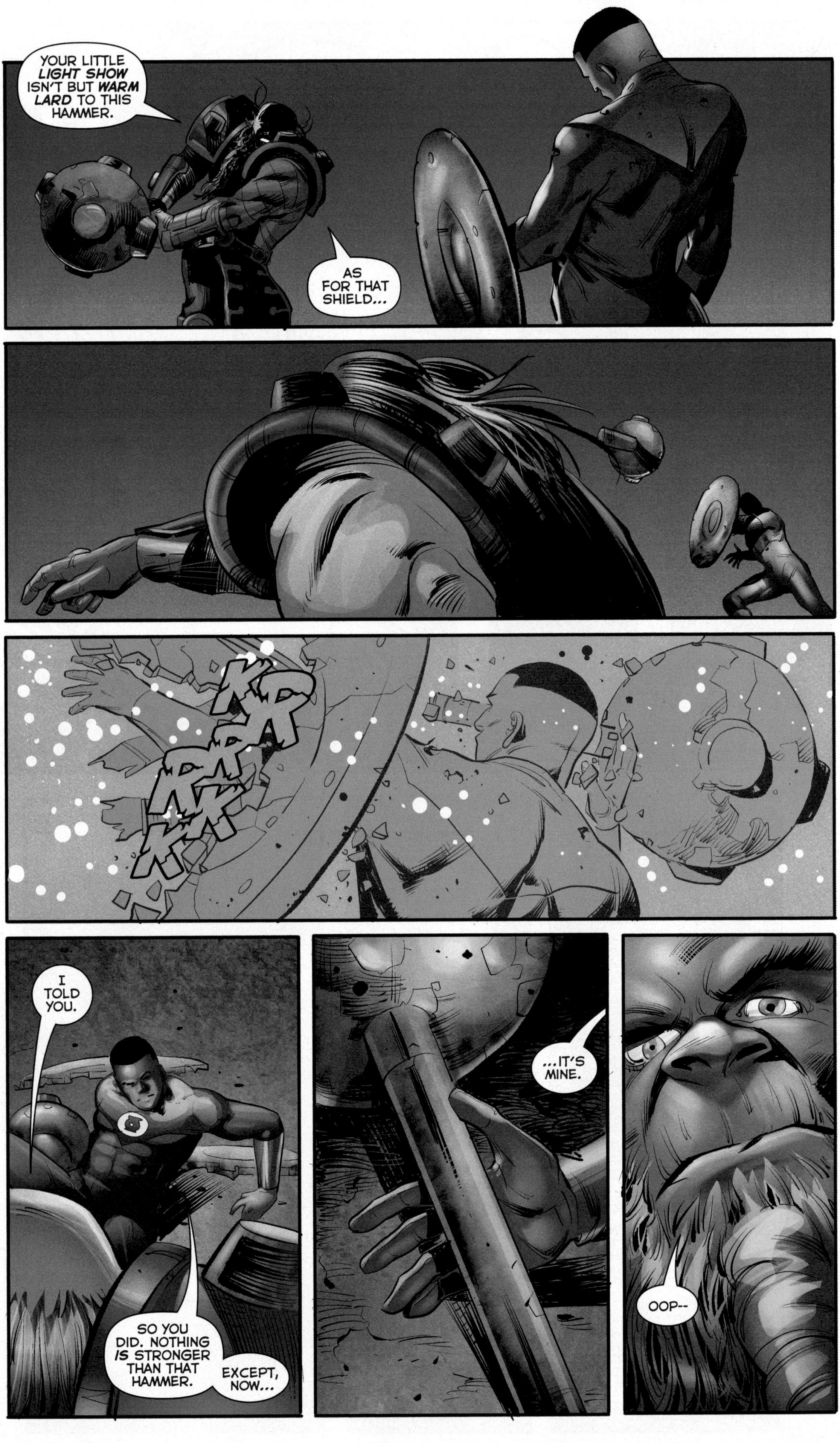
YOUR LITTLE LIGHT SHOW ISN'T BUT WARM LARD TO THIS HAMMER.
AS FOR THAT SHIELD...
KRRRAKK
I TOLD YOU.
SO YOU DID. NOTHING IS STRONGER THAN THAT HAMMER.
EXCEPT, NOW...
...IT'S MINE.
OOP--

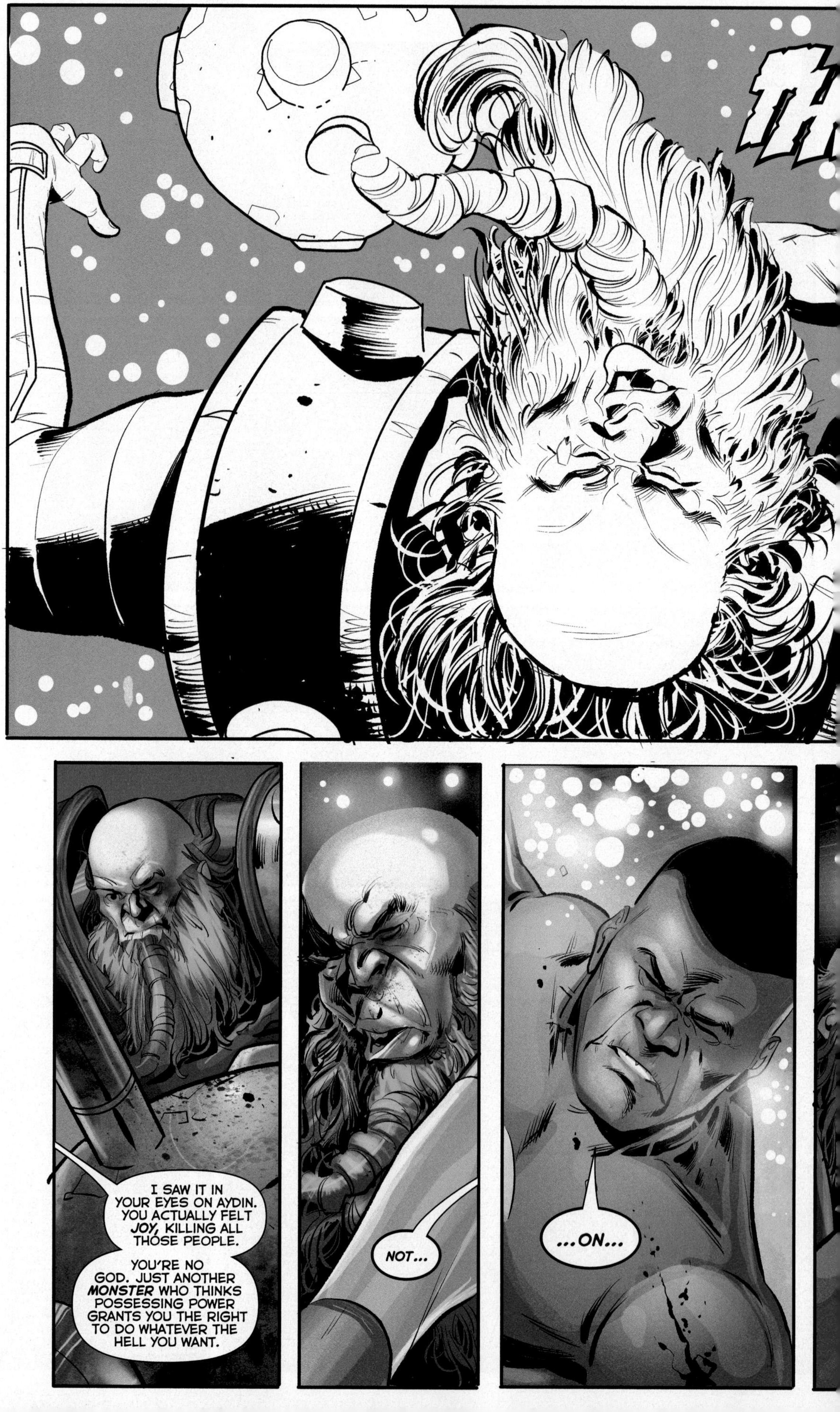
I SAW IT IN YOUR EYES ON AYDIN. YOU ACTUALLY FELT JOY, KILLING ALL THOSE PEOPLE.
YOU'RE NO GOD. JUST ANOTHER MONSTER WHO THINKS POSSESSING POWER GRANTS YOU THE RIGHT TO DO WHATEVER THE HELL YOU WANT.
NOT...
...ON...

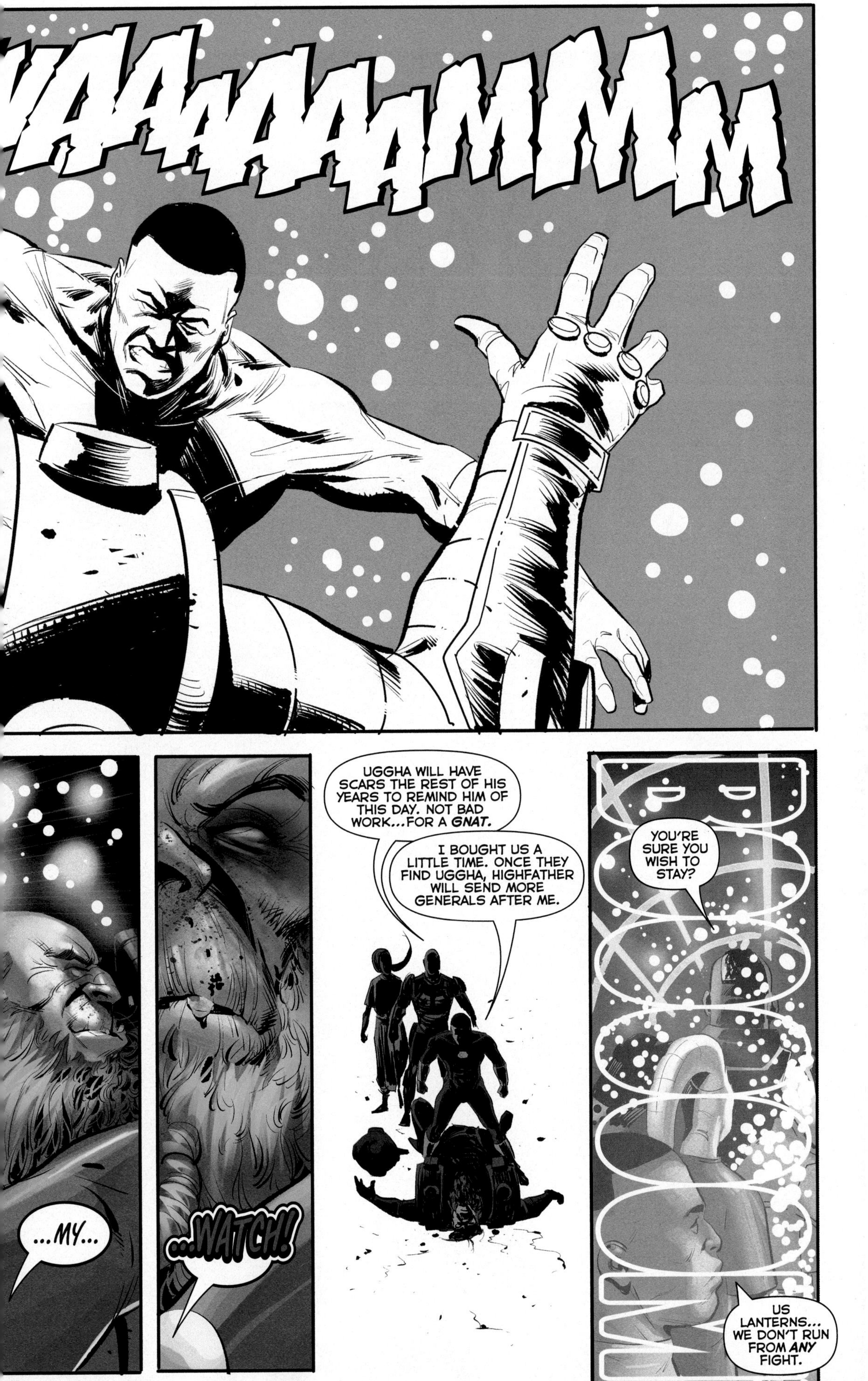
...MY...
...WATCH!
UGGHA WILL HAVE SCARS THE REST OF HIS YEARS TO REMIND HIM OF THIS DAY. NOT BAD WORK...FOR A GNAT.
I BOUGHT US A LITTLE TIME. ONCE THEY FIND UGGHA, HIGHFATHER WILL SEND MORE GENERALS AFTER ME.
YOU'RE SURE YOU WISH TO STAY?
US LANTERNS... WE DON'T RUN FROM ANY FIGHT.

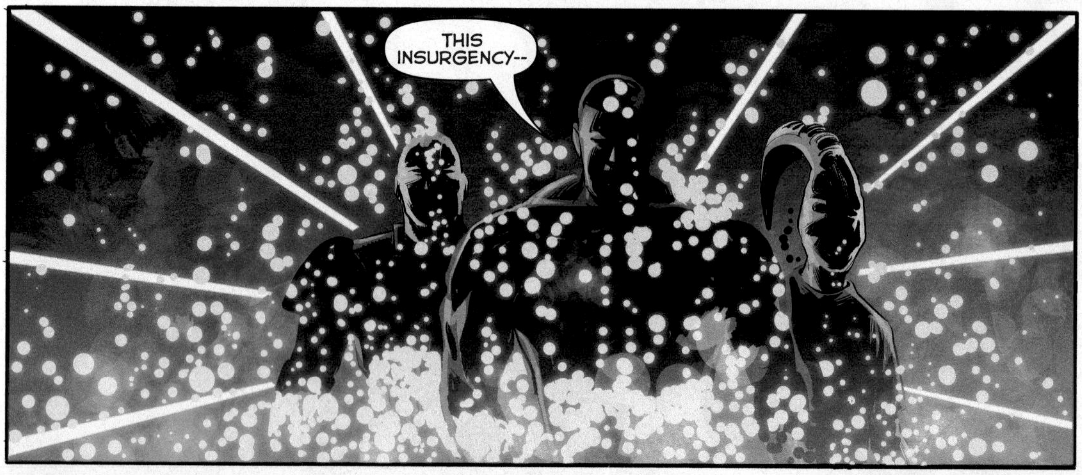
THIS INSURGENCY--

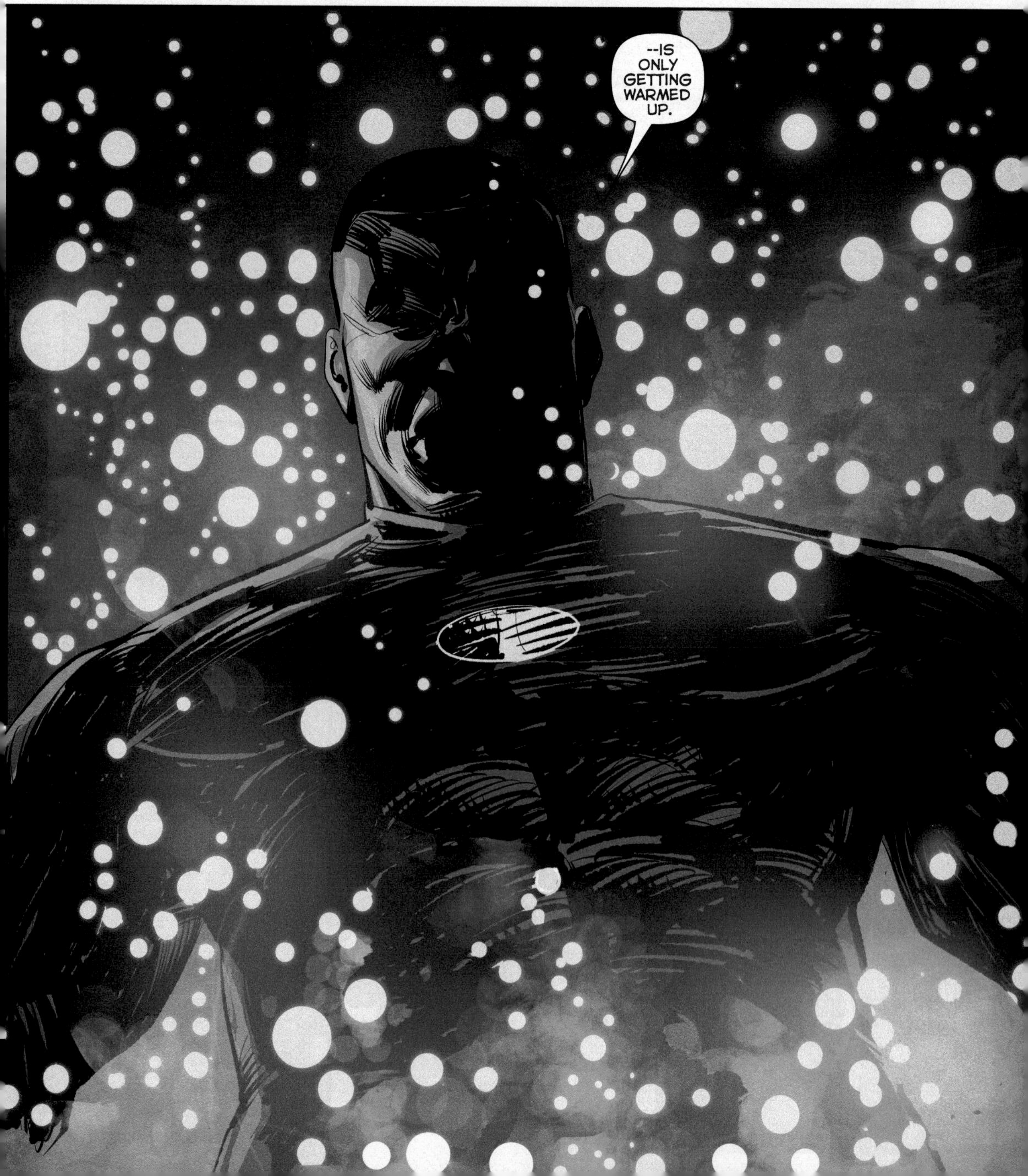
--IS ONLY GETTING WARMED UP.

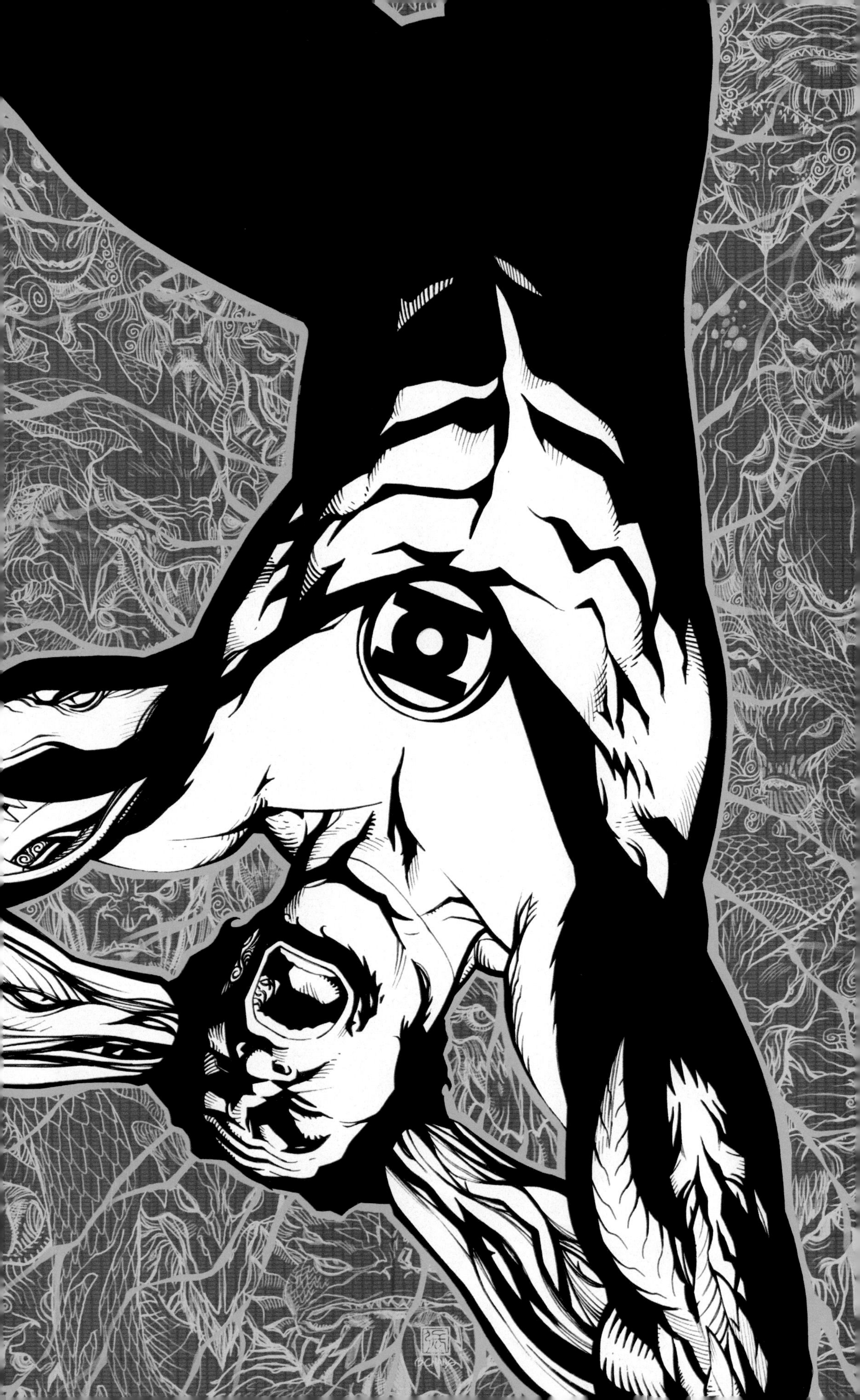

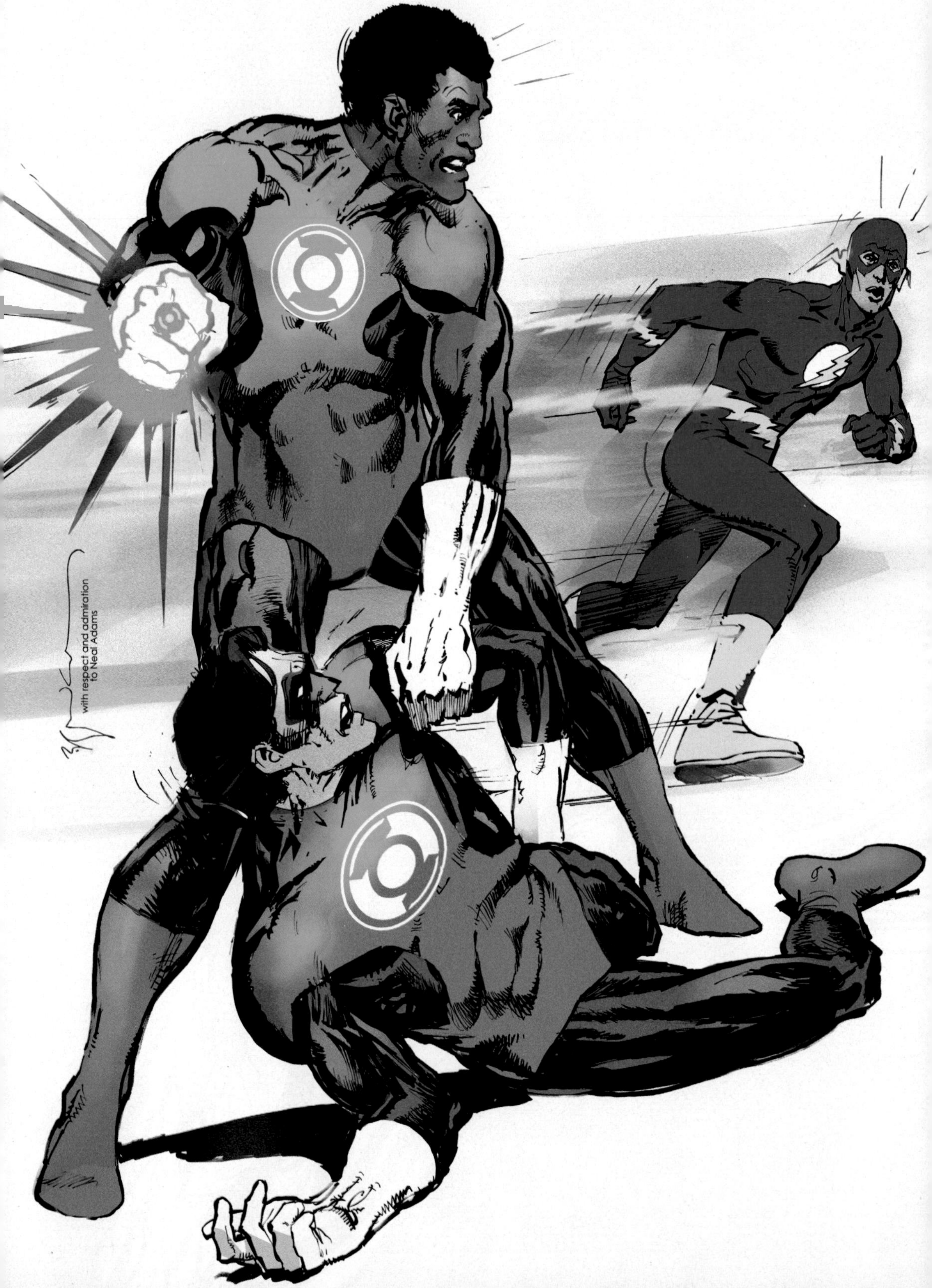
with respect and admiration
to Neal Adams

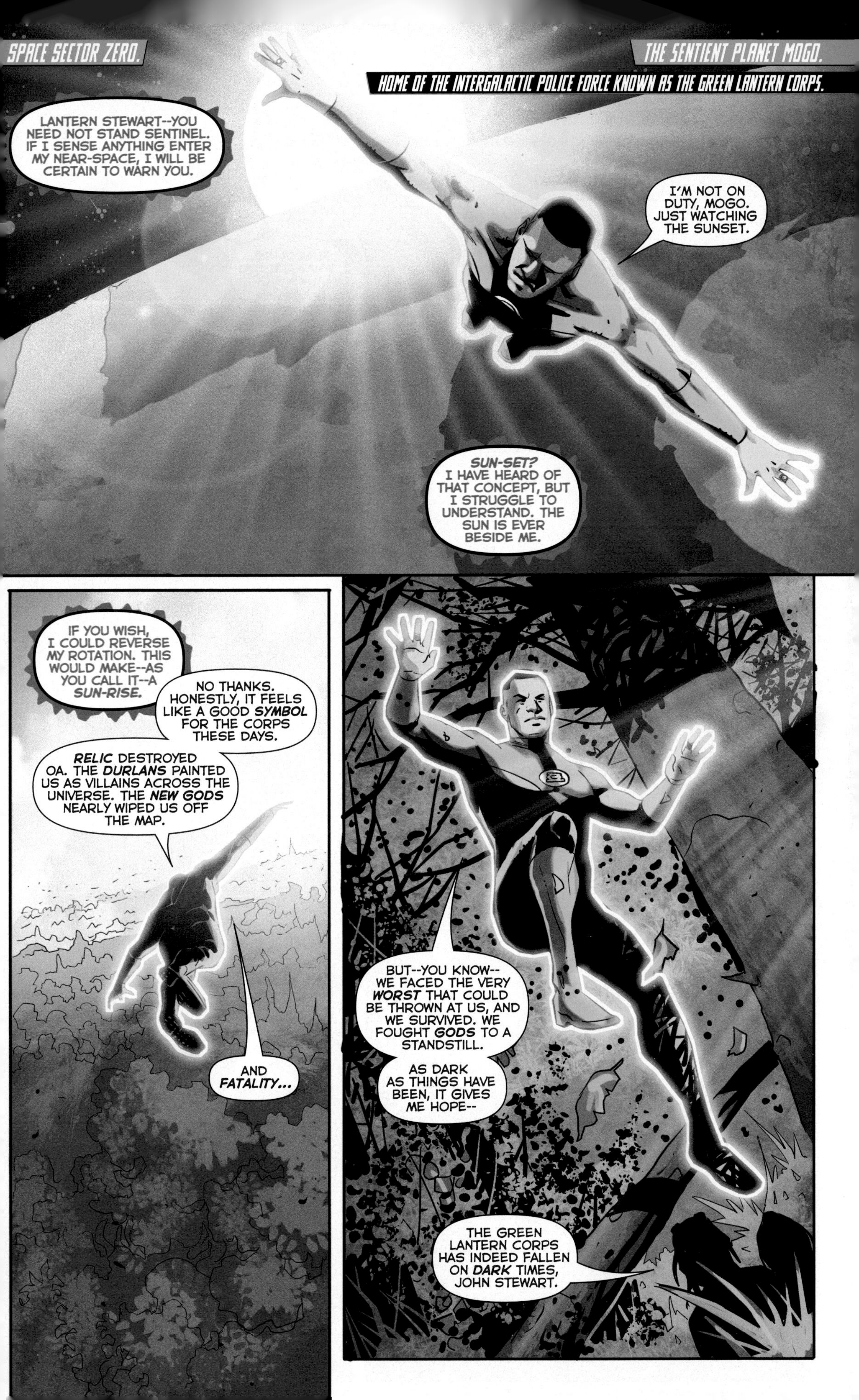
SPACE SECTOR ZERO.
THE SENTIENT PLANET MOGO.
HOME OF THE INTERGALACTIC POLICE FORCE KNOWN AS THE GREEN LANTERN CORPS.
LANTERN STEWART--YOU NEED NOT STAND SENTINEL. IF I SENSE ANYTHING ENTER MY NEAR-SPACE, I WILL BE CERTAIN TO WARN YOU.
I'M NOT ON DUTY, MOGO. JUST WATCHING THE SUNSET.
SUN-SET? I HAVE HEARD OF THAT CONCEPT, BUT I STRUGGLE TO UNDERSTAND. THE SUN IS EVER BESIDE ME.
IF YOU WISH, I COULD REVERSE MY ROTATION. THIS WOULD MAKE--AS YOU CALL IT--A SUN-RISE.
NO THANKS. HONESTLY, IT FEELS LIKE A GOOD SYMBOL FOR THE CORPS THESE DAYS.
RELIC DESTROYED OA. THE DURLANS PAINTED US AS VILLAINS ACROSS THE UNIVERSE. THE NEW GODS NEARLY WIPED US OFF THE MAP.
AND FATALITY...
BUT--YOU KNOW--WE FACED THE VERY WORST THAT COULD BE THROWN AT US, AND WE SURVIVED. WE FOUGHT GODS TO A STANDSTILL.
AS DARK AS THINGS HAVE BEEN, IT GIVES ME HOPE--
THE GREEN LANTERN CORPS HAS INDEED FALLEN ON DARK TIMES, JOHN STEWART.

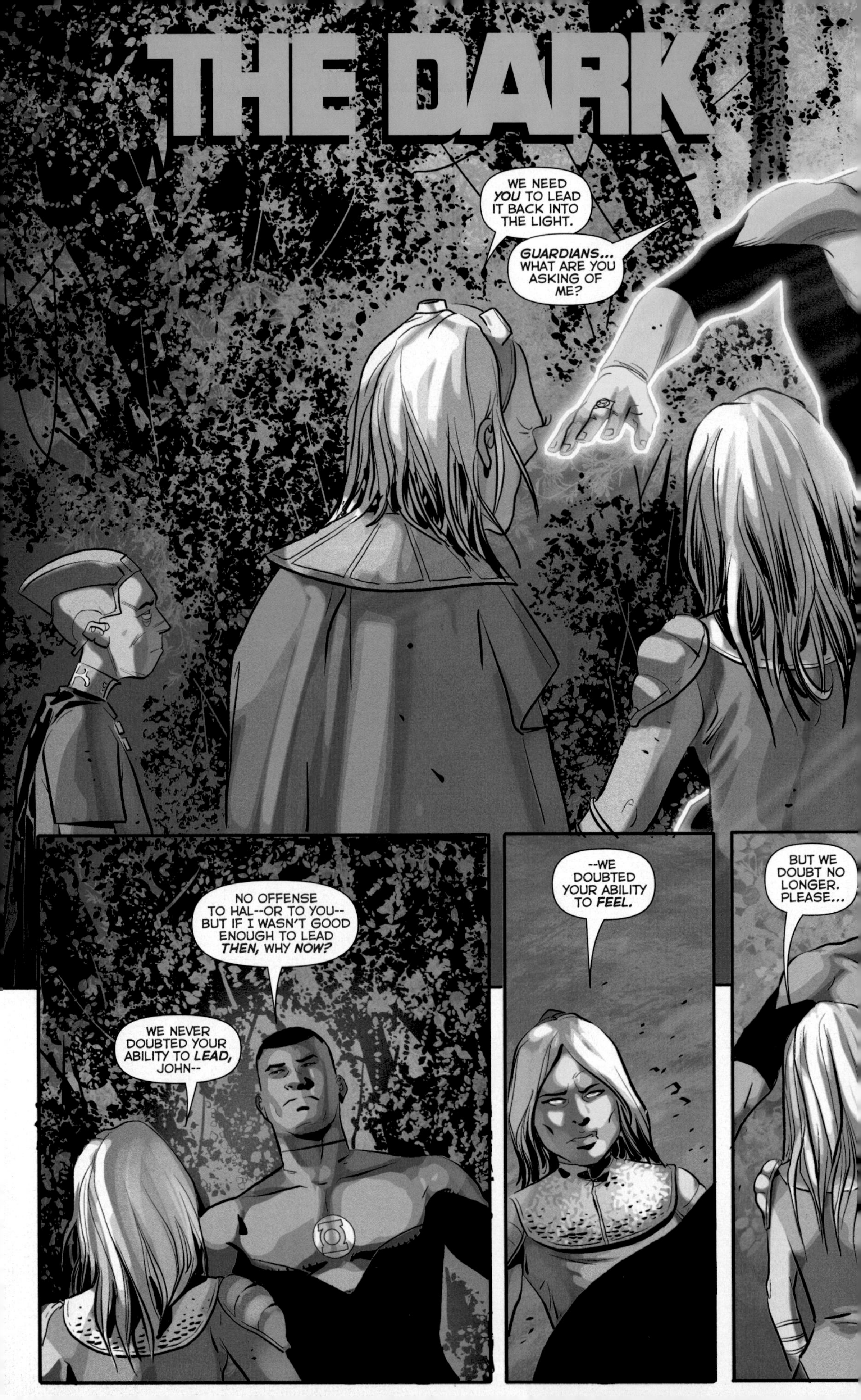
THE DARK
WE NEED YOU TO LEAD IT BACK INTO THE LIGHT.
GUARDIANS... WHAT ARE YOU ASKING OF ME?
NO OFFENSE TO HAL--OR TO YOU--BUT IF I WASN'T GOOD ENOUGH TO LEAD THEN, WHY NOW?
WE NEVER DOUBTED YOUR ABILITY TO LEAD, JOHN--
--WE DOUBTED YOUR ABILITY TO FEEL.
BUT WE DOUBT NO LONGER. PLEASE...

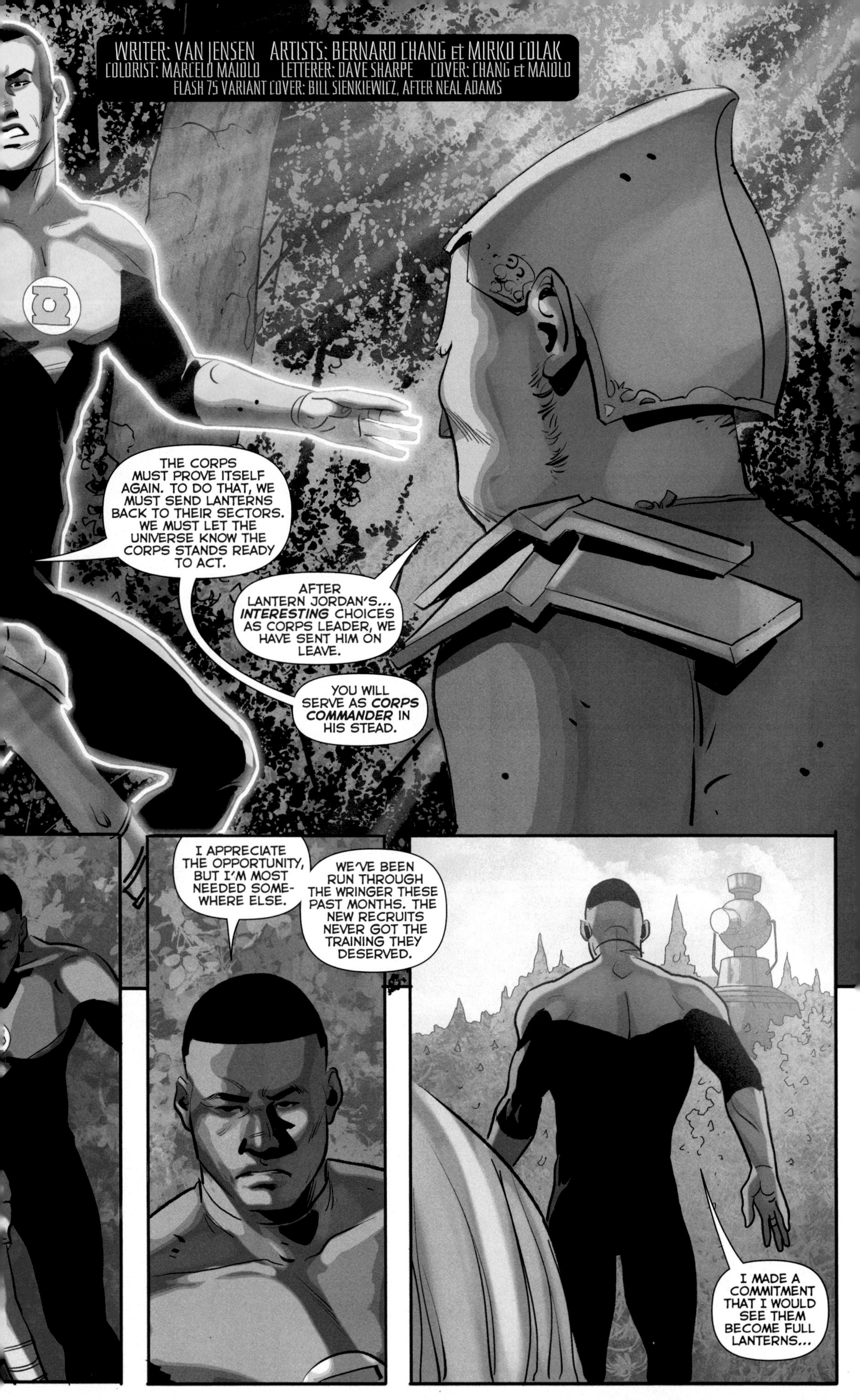
WRITER: VAN JENSEN ARTISTS: BERNARD CHANG et MIRKO COLAK
COLORIST: MARCELO MAIOLO LETTERER: DAVE SHARPE COVER: CHANG et MAIOLO
FLASH 75 VARIANT COVER: BILL SIENKIEWICZ, AFTER NEAL ADAMS
THE CORPS MUST PROVE ITSELF AGAIN. TO DO THAT, WE MUST SEND LANTERNS BACK TO THEIR SECTORS. WE MUST LET THE UNIVERSE KNOW THE CORPS STANDS READY TO ACT.
AFTER LANTERN JORDAN'S... INTERESTING CHOICES AS CORPS LEADER, WE HAVE SENT HIM ON LEAVE.
YOU WILL SERVE AS CORPS COMMANDER IN HIS STEAD.
I APPRECIATE THE OPPORTUNITY, BUT I'M MOST NEEDED SOMEWHERE ELSE.
WE'VE BEEN RUN THROUGH THE WRINGER THESE PAST MONTHS. THE NEW RECRUITS NEVER GOT THE TRAINING THEY DESERVED.
I MADE A COMMITMENT THAT I WOULD SEE THEM BECOME FULL LANTERNS...

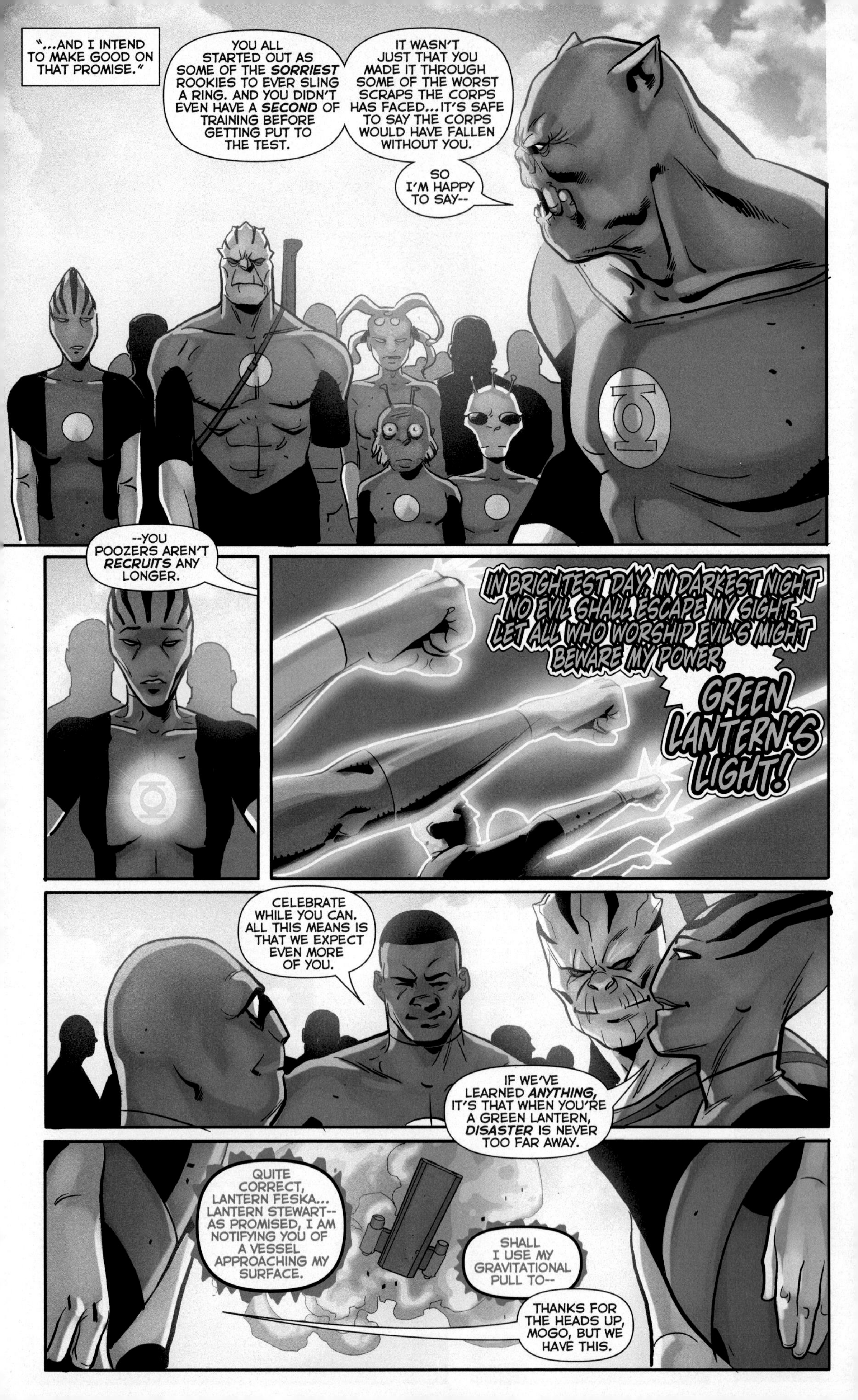
"...AND I INTEND TO MAKE GOOD ON THAT PROMISE."
YOU ALL STARTED OUT AS SOME OF THE SORRIEST ROOKIES TO EVER SLING A RING. AND YOU DIDN'T EVEN HAVE A SECOND OF TRAINING BEFORE GETTING PUT TO THE TEST.
IT WASN'T JUST THAT YOU MADE IT THROUGH SOME OF THE WORST SCRAPS THE CORPS HAS FACED...IT'S SAFE TO SAY THE CORPS WOULD HAVE FALLEN WITHOUT YOU.
SO I'M HAPPY TO SAY--
--YOU POOZERS AREN'T RECRUITS ANY LONGER.
IN BRIGHTEST DAY, IN DARKEST NIGHT NO EVIL SHALL ESCAPE MY SIGHT. LET ALL WHO WORSHIP EVIL'S MIGHT BEWARE MY POWER,
GREEN LANTERN'S LIGHT!
CELEBRATE WHILE YOU CAN. ALL THIS MEANS IS THAT WE EXPECT EVEN MORE OF YOU.
IF WE'VE LEARNED ANYTHING, IT'S THAT WHEN YOU'RE A GREEN LANTERN, DISASTER IS NEVER TOO FAR AWAY.
QUITE CORRECT, LANTERN FESKA... LANTERN STEWART-- AS PROMISED, I AM NOTIFYING YOU OF A VESSEL APPROACHING MY SURFACE.
SHALL I USE MY GRAVITATIONAL PULL TO--
THANKS FOR THE HEADS UP, MOGO, BUT WE HAVE THIS.

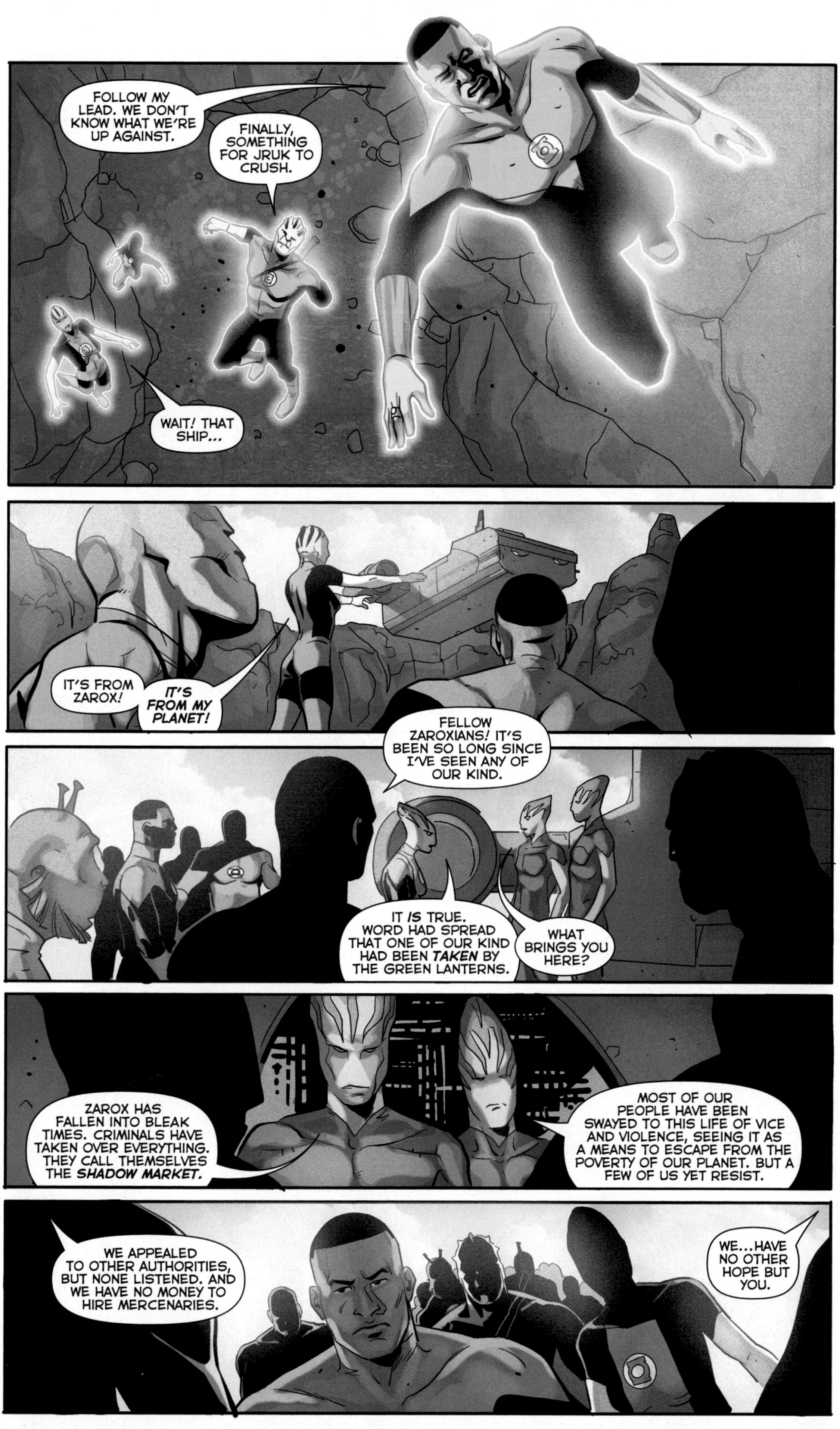
FOLLOW MY LEAD. WE DON'T KNOW WHAT WE'RE UP AGAINST.
FINALLY, SOMETHING FOR JRUK TO CRUSH.
WAIT! THAT SHIP...
IT'S FROM ZAROX!
IT'S FROM MY PLANET!
FELLOW ZAROXIANS! IT'S BEEN SO LONG SINCE I'VE SEEN ANY OF OUR KIND.
IT IS TRUE. WORD HAD SPREAD THAT ONE OF OUR KIND HAD BEEN TAKEN BY THE GREEN LANTERNS.
WHAT BRINGS YOU HERE?
ZAROX HAS FALLEN INTO BLEAK TIMES. CRIMINALS HAVE TAKEN OVER EVERYTHING. THEY CALL THEMSELVES THE SHADOW MARKET.
MOST OF OUR PEOPLE HAVE BEEN SWAYED TO THIS LIFE OF VICE AND VIOLENCE, SEEING IT AS A MEANS TO ESCAPE FROM THE POVERTY OF OUR PLANET. BUT A FEW OF US YET RESIST.
WE APPEALED TO OTHER AUTHORITIES, BUT NONE LISTENED. AND WE HAVE NO MONEY TO HIRE MERCENARIES.
WE...HAVE NO OTHER HOPE BUT YOU.

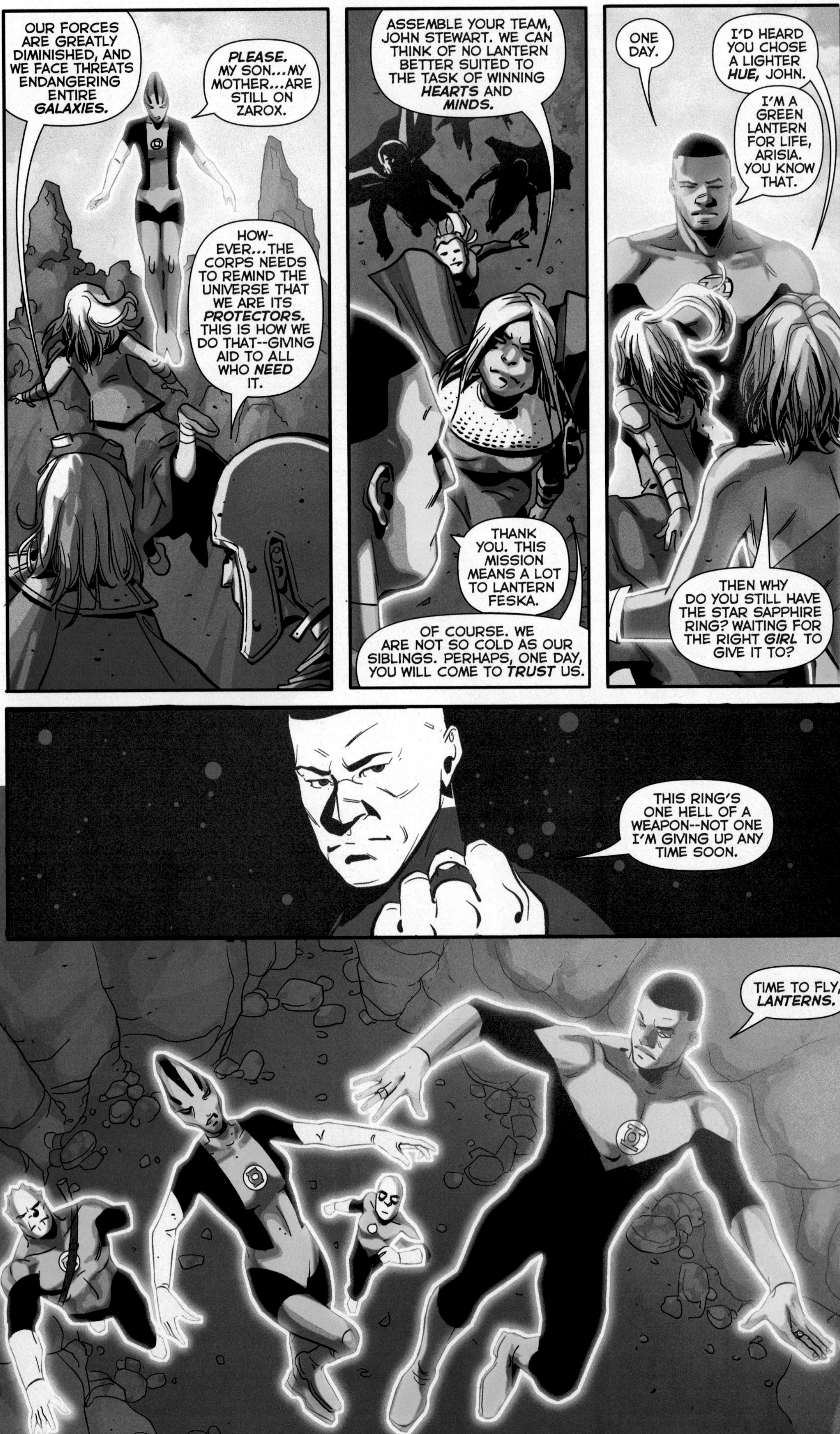
OUR FORCES ARE GREATLY DIMINISHED, AND WE FACE THREATS ENDANGERING ENTIRE GALAXIES.
PLEASE. MY SON...MY MOTHER...ARE STILL ON ZAROX.
HOW-EVER...THE CORPS NEEDS TO REMIND THE UNIVERSE THAT WE ARE ITS PROTECTORS. THIS IS HOW WE DO THAT--GIVING AID TO ALL WHO NEED IT.
ASSEMBLE YOUR TEAM, JOHN STEWART. WE CAN THINK OF NO LANTERN BETTER SUITED TO THE TASK OF WINNING HEARTS AND MINDS.
THANK YOU. THIS MISSION MEANS A LOT TO LANTERN FESKA.
OF COURSE. WE ARE NOT SO COLD AS OUR SIBLINGS. PERHAPS, ONE DAY, YOU WILL COME TO TRUST US.
ONE DAY.
I'D HEARD YOU CHOSE A LIGHTER HUE, JOHN.
I'M A GREEN LANTERN FOR LIFE, ARISIA. YOU KNOW THAT.
THEN WHY DO YOU STILL HAVE THE STAR SAPPHIRE RING? WAITING FOR THE RIGHT GIRL TO GIVE IT TO?
THIS RING'S ONE HELL OF A WEAPON--NOT ONE I'M GIVING UP ANY TIME SOON.
TIME TO FLY, LANTERNS.

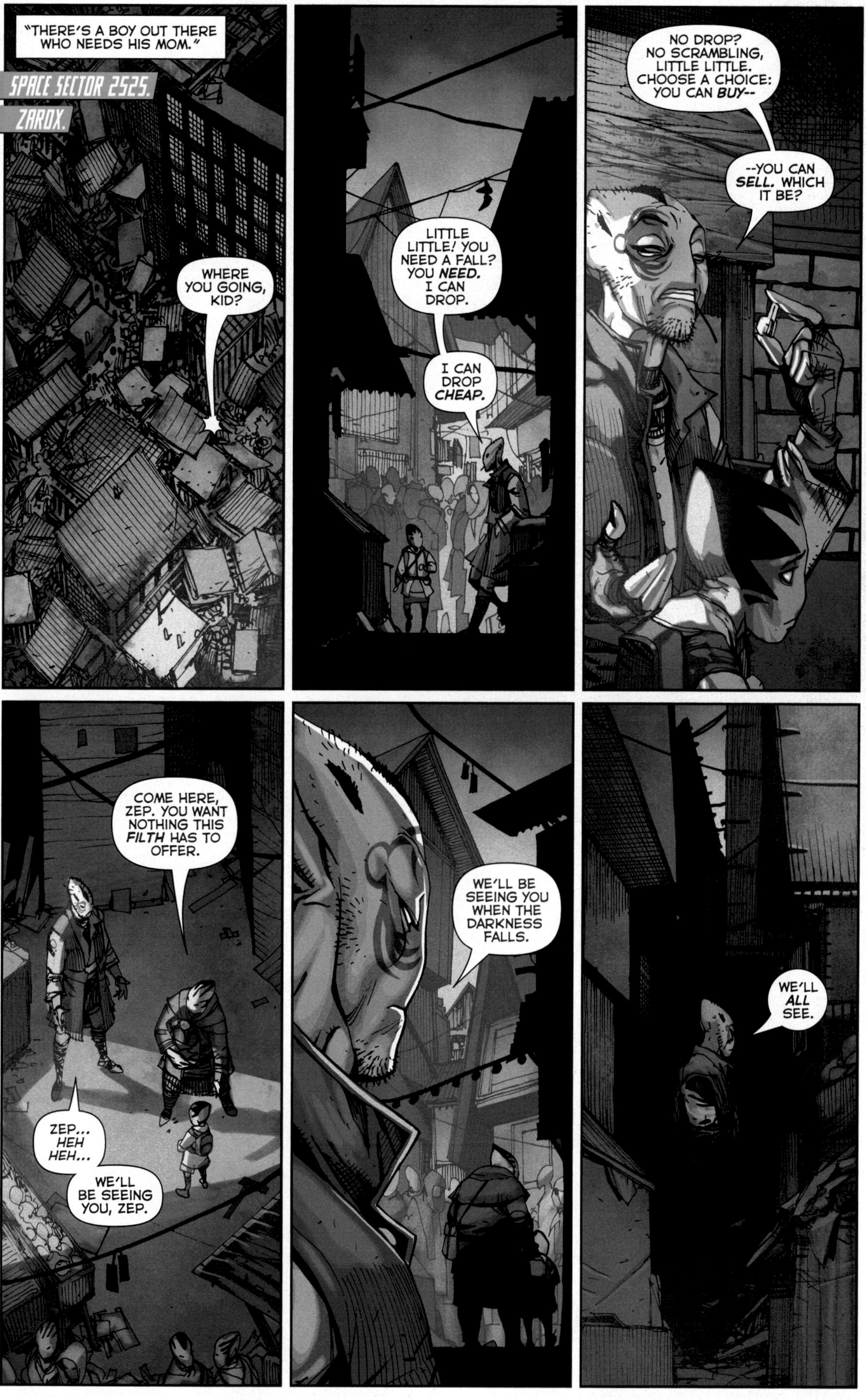
"THERE'S A BOY OUT THERE WHO NEEDS HIS MOM."
SPACE SECTOR 2525.
ZAROX.
WHERE YOU GOING, KID?
LITTLE LITTLE! YOU NEED A FALL? YOU NEED. I CAN DROP.
I CAN DROP CHEAP.
NO DROP? NO SCRAMBLING, LITTLE LITTLE. CHOOSE A CHOICE: YOU CAN BUY--
--YOU CAN SELL. WHICH IT BE?
COME HERE, ZEP. YOU WANT NOTHING THIS FILTH HAS TO OFFER.
ZEP... HEH HEH...
WE'LL BE SEEING YOU, ZEP.
WE'LL BE SEEING YOU WHEN THE DARKNESS FALLS.
WE'LL ALL SEE.

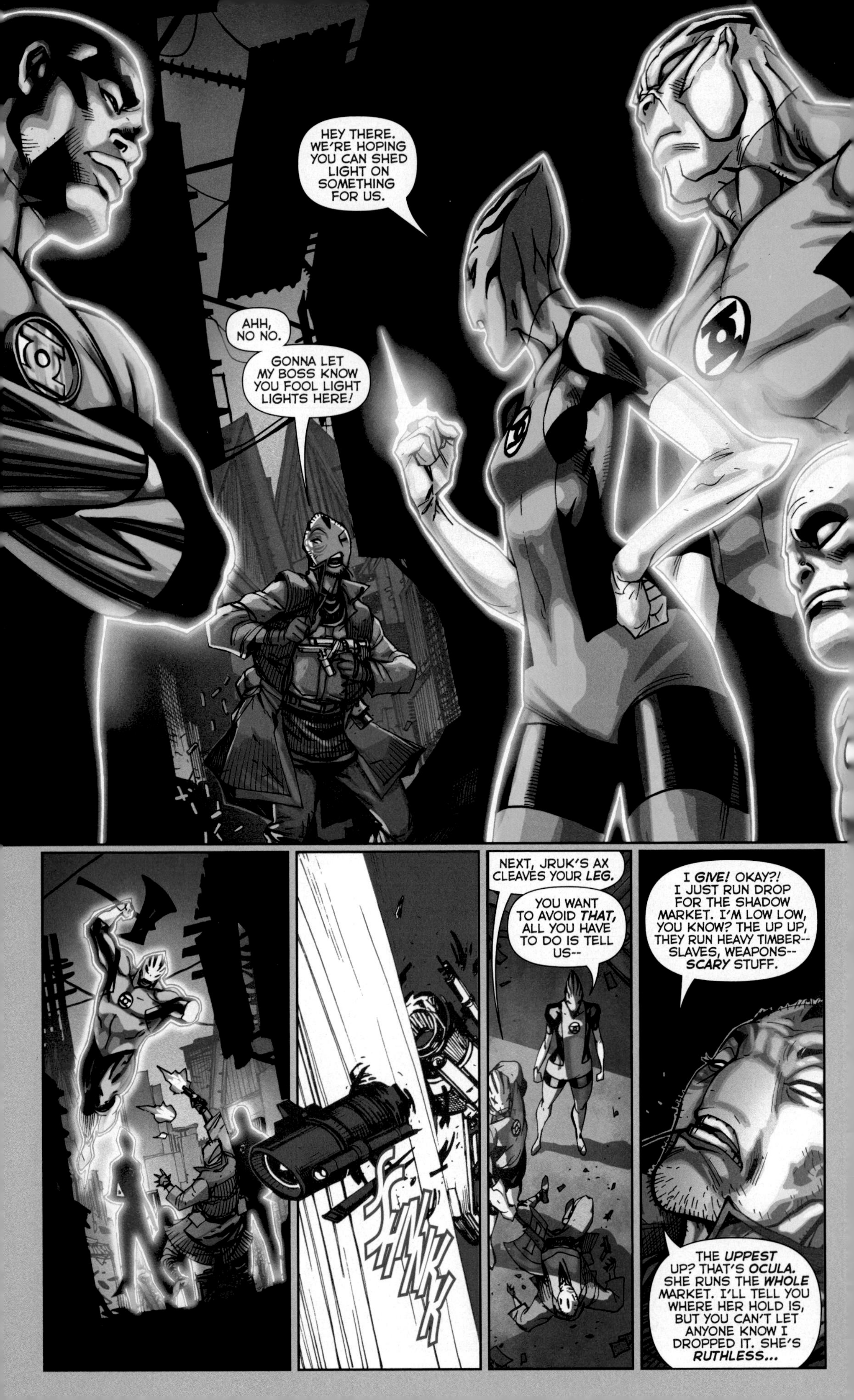
HEY THERE. WE'RE HOPING YOU CAN SHED LIGHT ON SOMETHING FOR US.
AHH, NO NO.
GONNA LET MY BOSS KNOW YOU FOOL LIGHT LIGHTS HERE!
SHNNK
NEXT, JRUK'S AX CLEAVES YOUR LEG.
YOU WANT TO AVOID THAT, ALL YOU HAVE TO DO IS TELL US--
I GIVE! OKAY?! I JUST RUN DROP FOR THE SHADOW MARKET. I'M LOW LOW, YOU KNOW? THE UP UP, THEY RUN HEAVY TIMBER-- SLAVES, WEAPONS-- SCARY STUFF.
THE UPPEST UP? THAT'S OCULA. SHE RUNS THE WHOLE MARKET. I'LL TELL YOU WHERE HER HOLD IS, BUT YOU CAN'T LET ANYONE KNOW I DROPPED IT. SHE'S RUTHLESS...

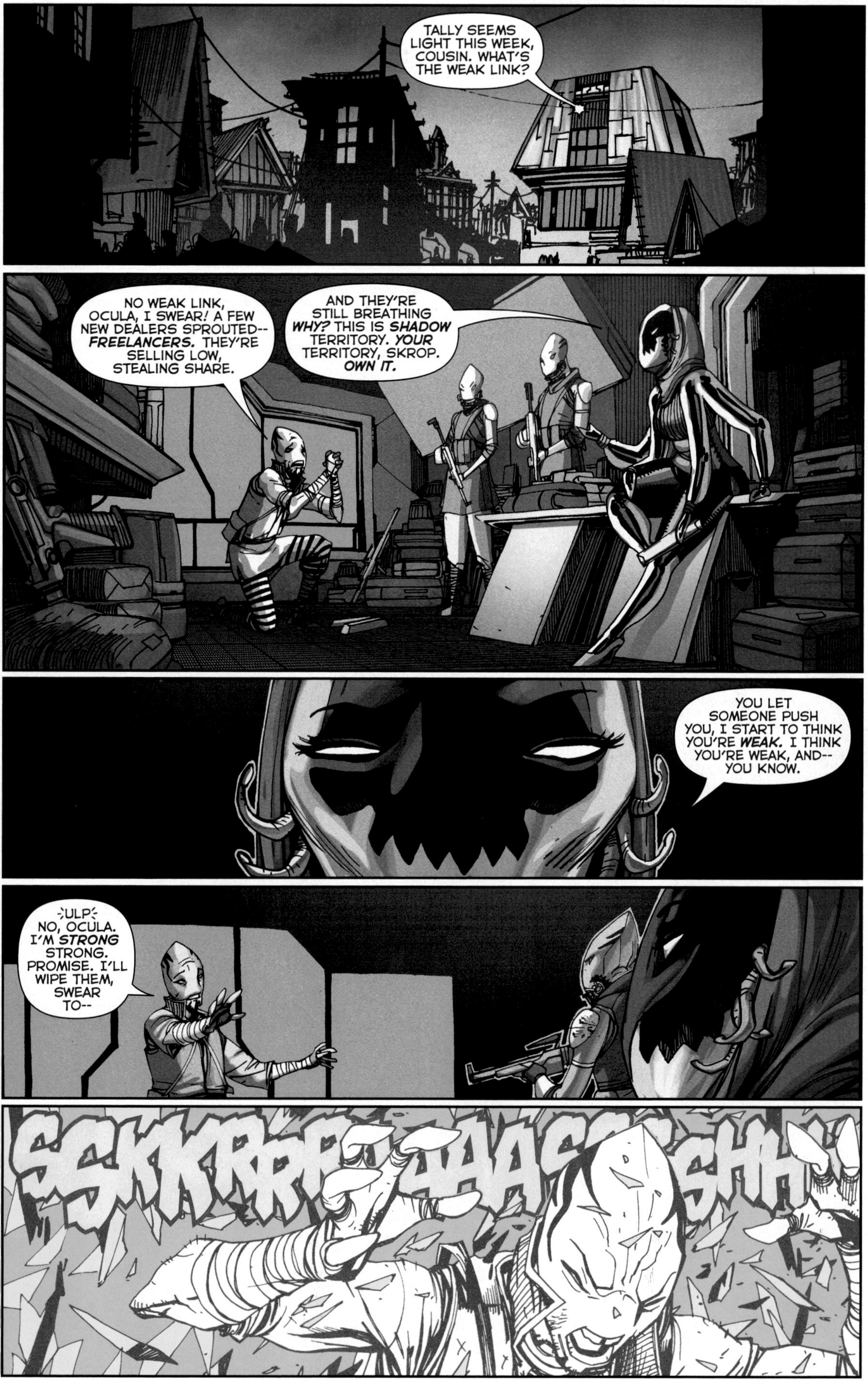
TALLY SEEMS LIGHT THIS WEEK, COUSIN. WHAT'S THE WEAK LINK?
NO WEAK LINK, OCULA, I SWEAR! A FEW NEW DEALERS SPROUTED-- FREELANCERS. THEY'RE SELLING LOW, STEALING SHARE.
AND THEY'RE STILL BREATHING WHY? THIS IS SHADOW TERRITORY. YOUR TERRITORY, SKROP. OWN IT.
YOU LET SOMEONE PUSH YOU, I START TO THINK YOU'RE WEAK. I THINK YOU'RE WEAK, AND-- YOU KNOW.
ULP NO, OCULA. I'M STRONG STRONG. PROMISE. I'LL WIPE THEM, SWEAR TO--

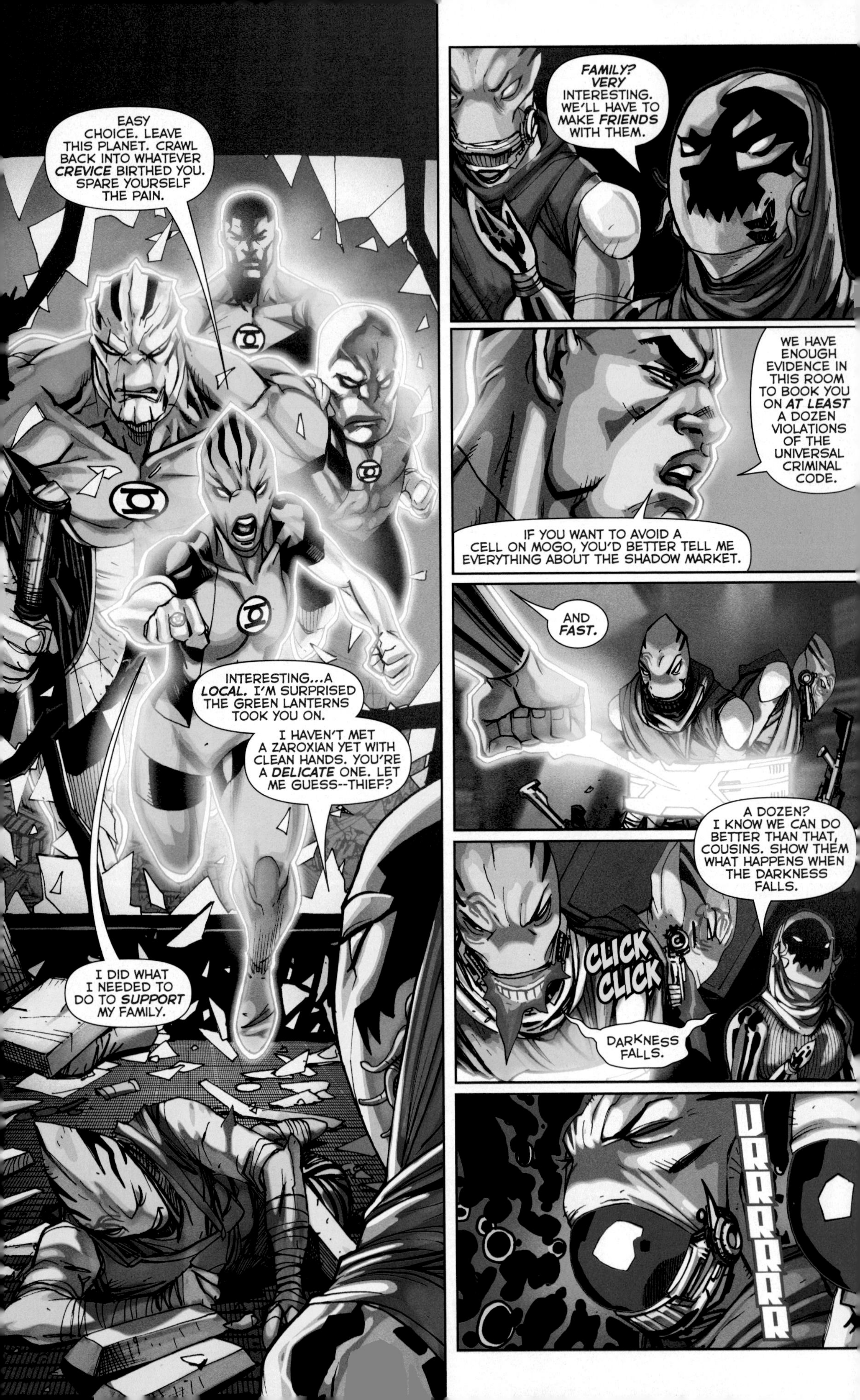
EASY CHOICE. LEAVE THIS PLANET. CRAWL BACK INTO WHATEVER CREVICE BIRTHED YOU. SPARE YOURSELF THE PAIN.
INTERESTING...A LOCAL. I'M SURPRISED THE GREEN LANTERNS TOOK YOU ON.
I HAVEN'T MET A ZAROXIAN YET WITH CLEAN HANDS. YOU'RE A DELICATE ONE. LET ME GUESS--THIEF?
I DID WHAT I NEEDED TO DO TO SUPPORT MY FAMILY.
FAMILY? VERY INTERESTING. WE'LL HAVE TO MAKE FRIENDS WITH THEM.
WE HAVE ENOUGH EVIDENCE IN THIS ROOM TO BOOK YOU ON AT LEAST A DOZEN VIOLATIONS OF THE UNIVERSAL CRIMINAL CODE.
IF YOU WANT TO AVOID A CELL ON MOGO, YOU'D BETTER TELL ME EVERYTHING ABOUT THE SHADOW MARKET.
AND FAST.
A DOZEN? I KNOW WE CAN DO BETTER THAN THAT, COUSINS. SHOW THEM WHAT HAPPENS WHEN THE DARKNESS FALLS.
CLICK CLICK
DARKNESS FALLS.
URRRRRR

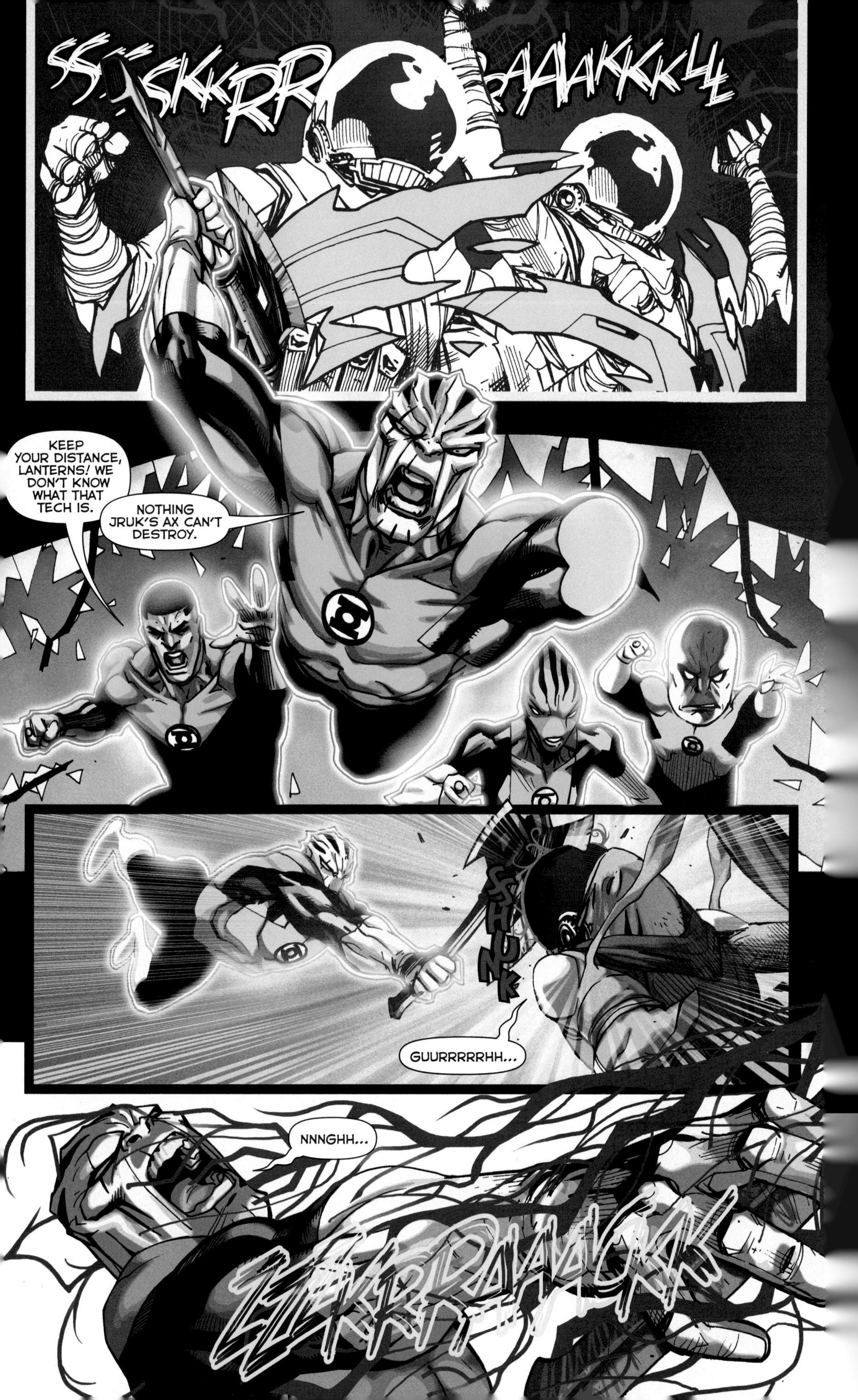
SSSKKRRAAAKKK
KEEP YOUR DISTANCE, LANTERNS! WE DON'T KNOW WHAT THAT TECH IS.
NOTHING JRUK'S AX CAN'T DESTROY.
SSHUNK
GUURRRRRHH...
NNNGHH...
ZZKKRRAAKKK

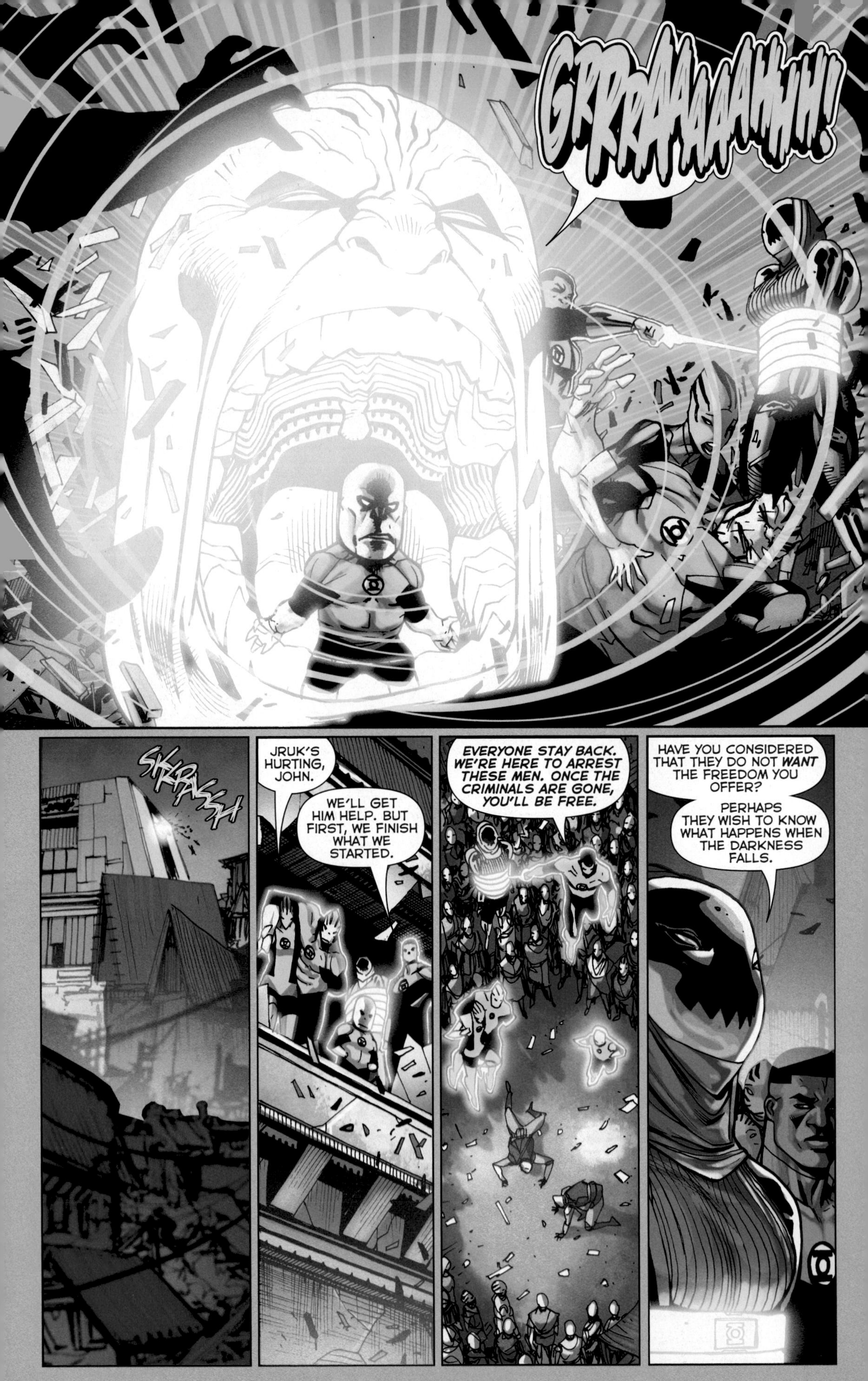
GRRRAAAAAHHH!
SKRASSH
JRUK'S HURTING, JOHN.
WE'LL GET HIM HELP. BUT FIRST, WE FINISH WHAT WE STARTED.
EVERYONE STAY BACK. WE'RE HERE TO ARREST THESE MEN. ONCE THE CRIMINALS ARE GONE, YOU'LL BE FREE.
HAVE YOU CONSIDERED THAT THEY DO NOT WANT THE FREEDOM YOU OFFER?
PERHAPS THEY WISH TO KNOW WHAT HAPPENS WHEN THE DARKNESS FALLS.

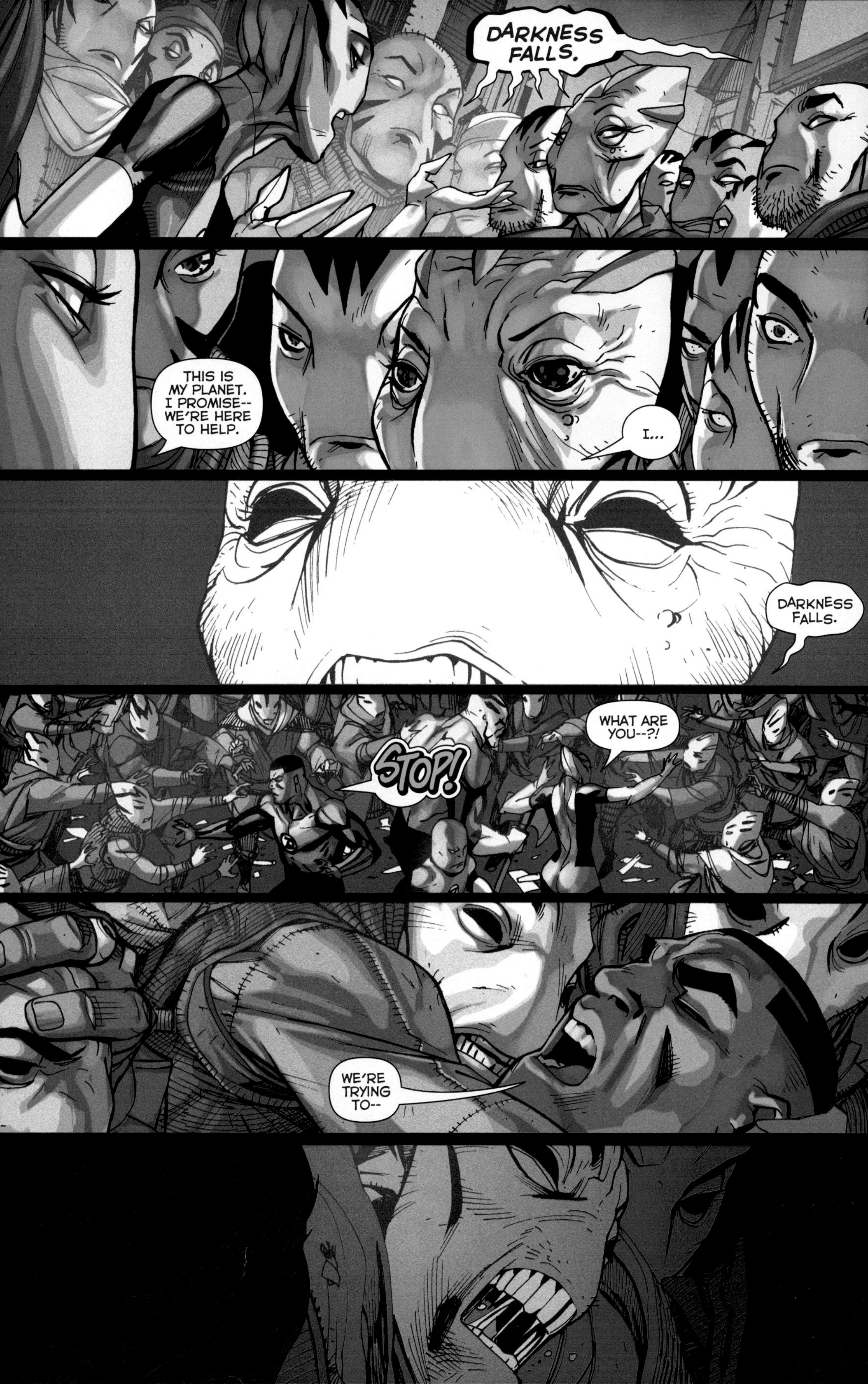
DARKNESS FALLS.
THIS IS MY PLANET. I PROMISE-- WE'RE HERE TO HELP.
I...
DARKNESS FALLS.
STOP!
WHAT ARE YOU--?!
WE'RE TRYING TO--

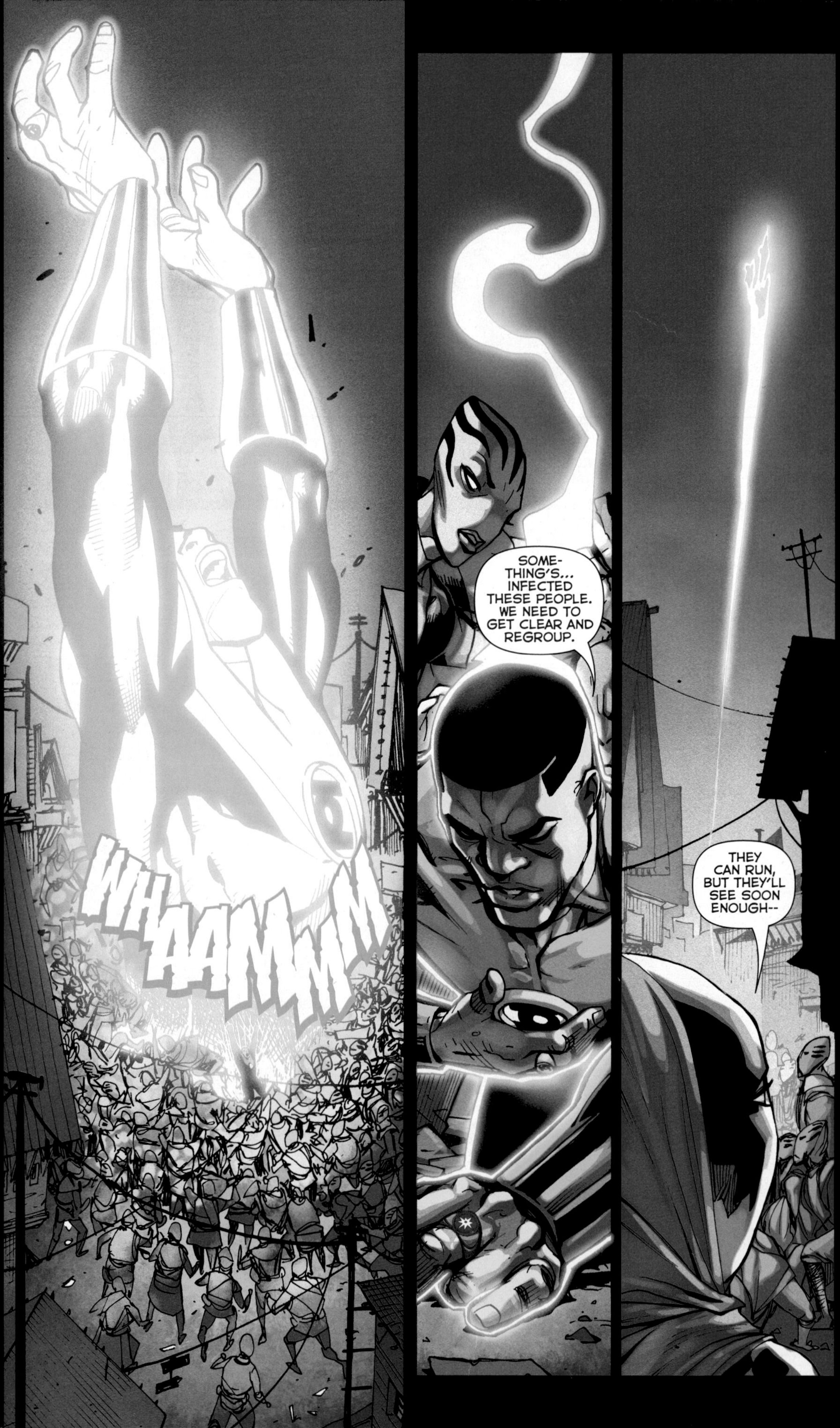
WHAAMMM
SOME-THING'S... INFECTED THESE PEOPLE. WE NEED TO GET CLEAR AND REGROUP.
THEY CAN RUN, BUT THEY'LL SEE SOON ENOUGH--

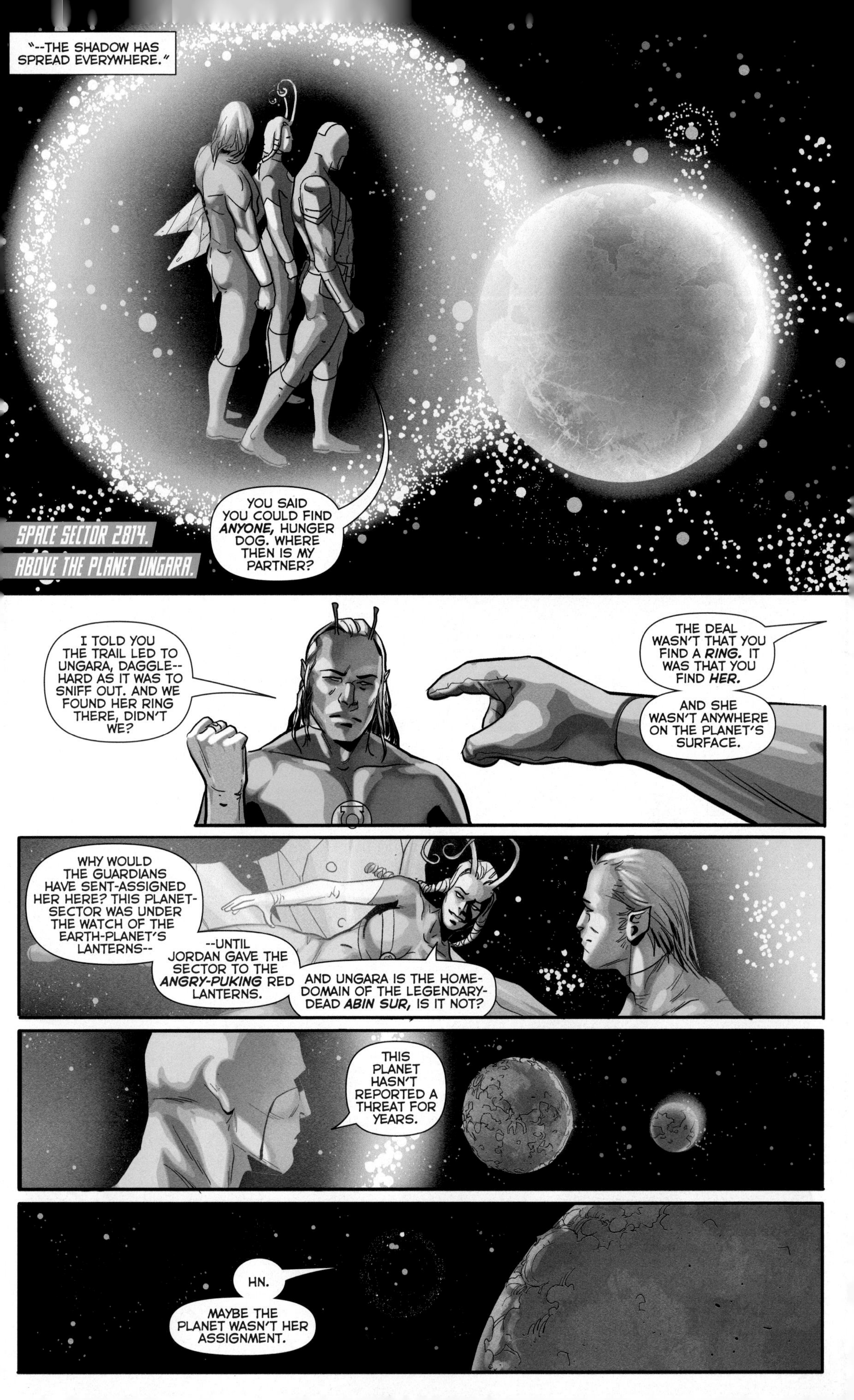
"--THE SHADOW HAS SPREAD EVERYWHERE."
SPACE SECTOR 2814.
ABOVE THE PLANET UNGARA.
YOU SAID YOU COULD FIND ANYONE, HUNGER DOG. WHERE THEN IS MY PARTNER?
I TOLD YOU THE TRAIL LED TO UNGARA, DAGGLE-- HARD AS IT WAS TO SNIFF OUT. AND WE FOUND HER RING THERE, DIDN'T WE?
THE DEAL WASN'T THAT YOU FIND A RING. IT WAS THAT YOU FIND HER.
AND SHE WASN'T ANYWHERE ON THE PLANET'S SURFACE.
WHY WOULD THE GUARDIANS HAVE SENT-ASSIGNED HER HERE? THIS PLANET-SECTOR WAS UNDER THE WATCH OF THE EARTH-PLANET'S LANTERNS--
--UNTIL JORDAN GAVE THE SECTOR TO THE ANGRY-PUKING RED LANTERNS.
AND UNGARA IS THE HOME-DOMAIN OF THE LEGENDARY-DEAD ABIN SUR, IS IT NOT?
THIS PLANET HASN'T REPORTED A THREAT FOR YEARS.
HN.
MAYBE THE PLANET WASN'T HER ASSIGNMENT.

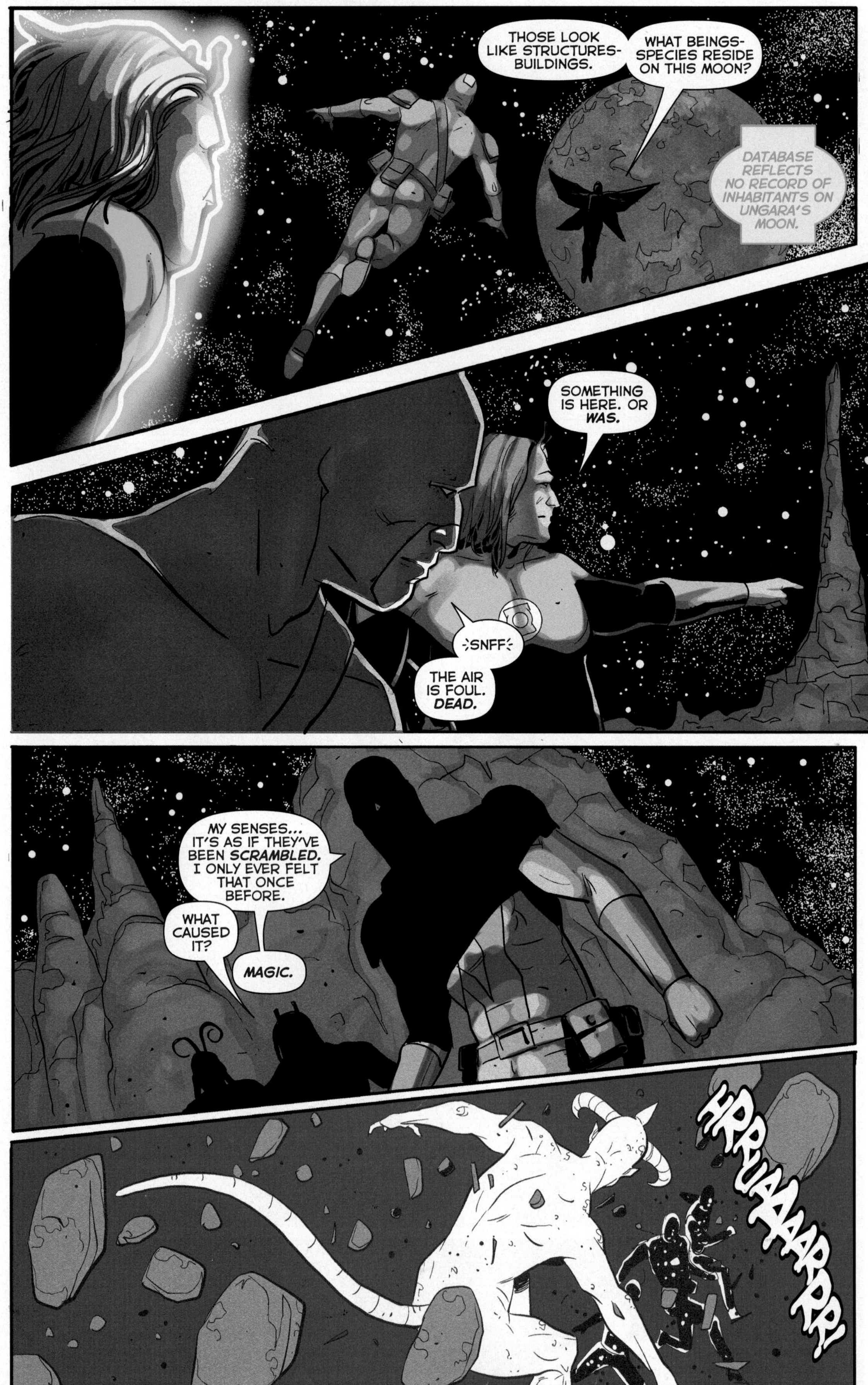

THOSE LOOK LIKE STRUCTURES- BUILDINGS.
WHAT BEINGS- SPECIES RESIDE ON THIS MOON?
DATABASE REFLECTS NO RECORD OF INHABITANTS ON UNGARA'S MOON.
SOMETHING IS HERE. OR *WAS.*
-SNFF-
THE AIR IS FOUL. *DEAD.*
MY SENSES... IT'S AS IF THEY'VE BEEN *SCRAMBLED.* I ONLY EVER FELT THAT ONCE BEFORE.
WHAT CAUSED IT?
MAGIC.
HRRUAAAARRR!

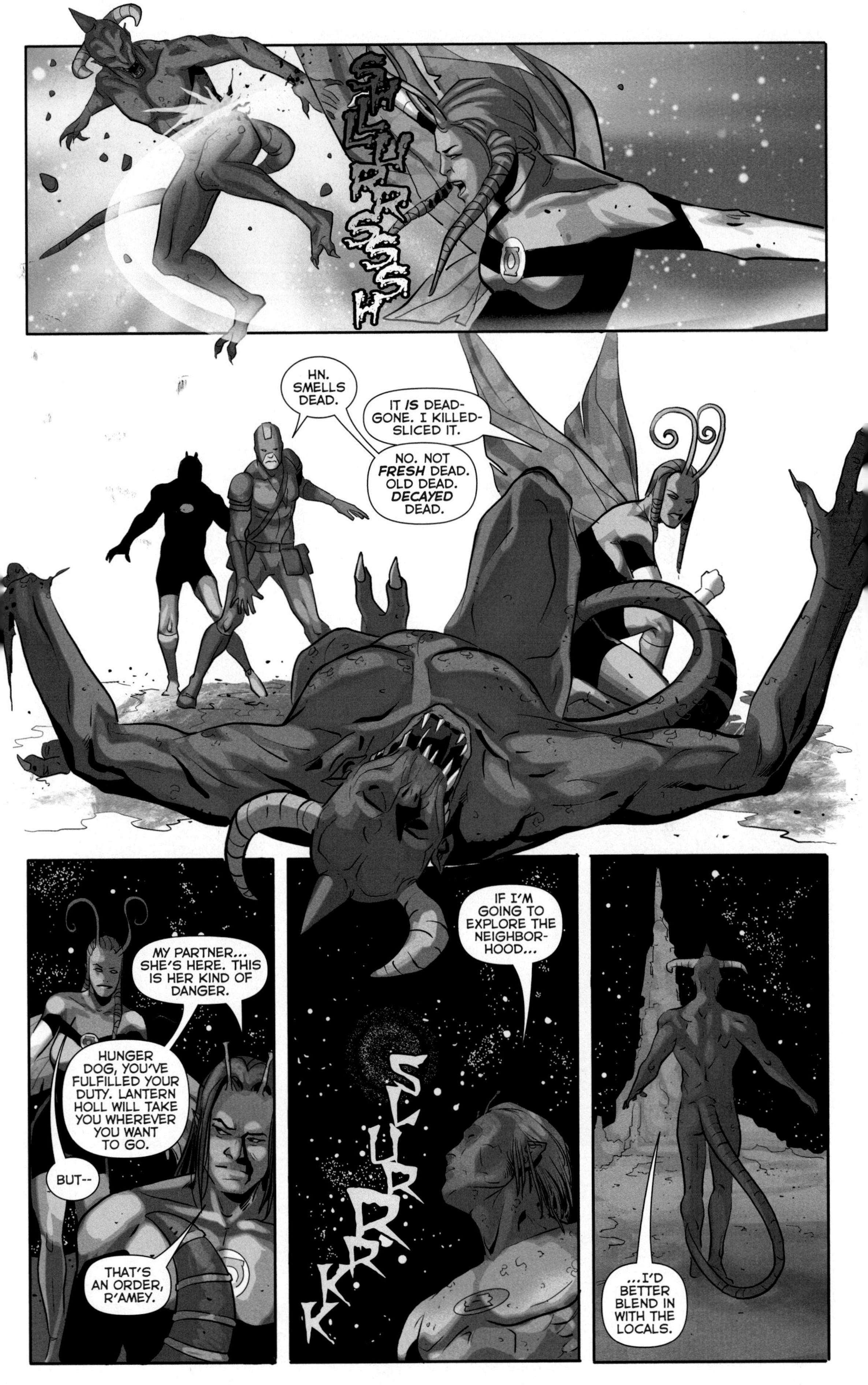
SHLURRSSSH
HN. SMELLS DEAD.
IT IS DEAD-GONE. I KILLED-SLICED IT.
NO. NOT FRESH DEAD. OLD DEAD. DECAYED DEAD.
MY PARTNER... SHE'S HERE. THIS IS HER KIND OF DANGER.
HUNGER DOG, YOU'VE FULFILLED YOUR DUTY. LANTERN HOLL WILL TAKE YOU WHEREVER YOU WANT TO GO.
BUT--
THAT'S AN ORDER, R'AMEY.
IF I'M GOING TO EXPLORE THE NEIGHBOR-HOOD...
SLURRRKK
...I'D BETTER BLEND IN WITH THE LOCALS.

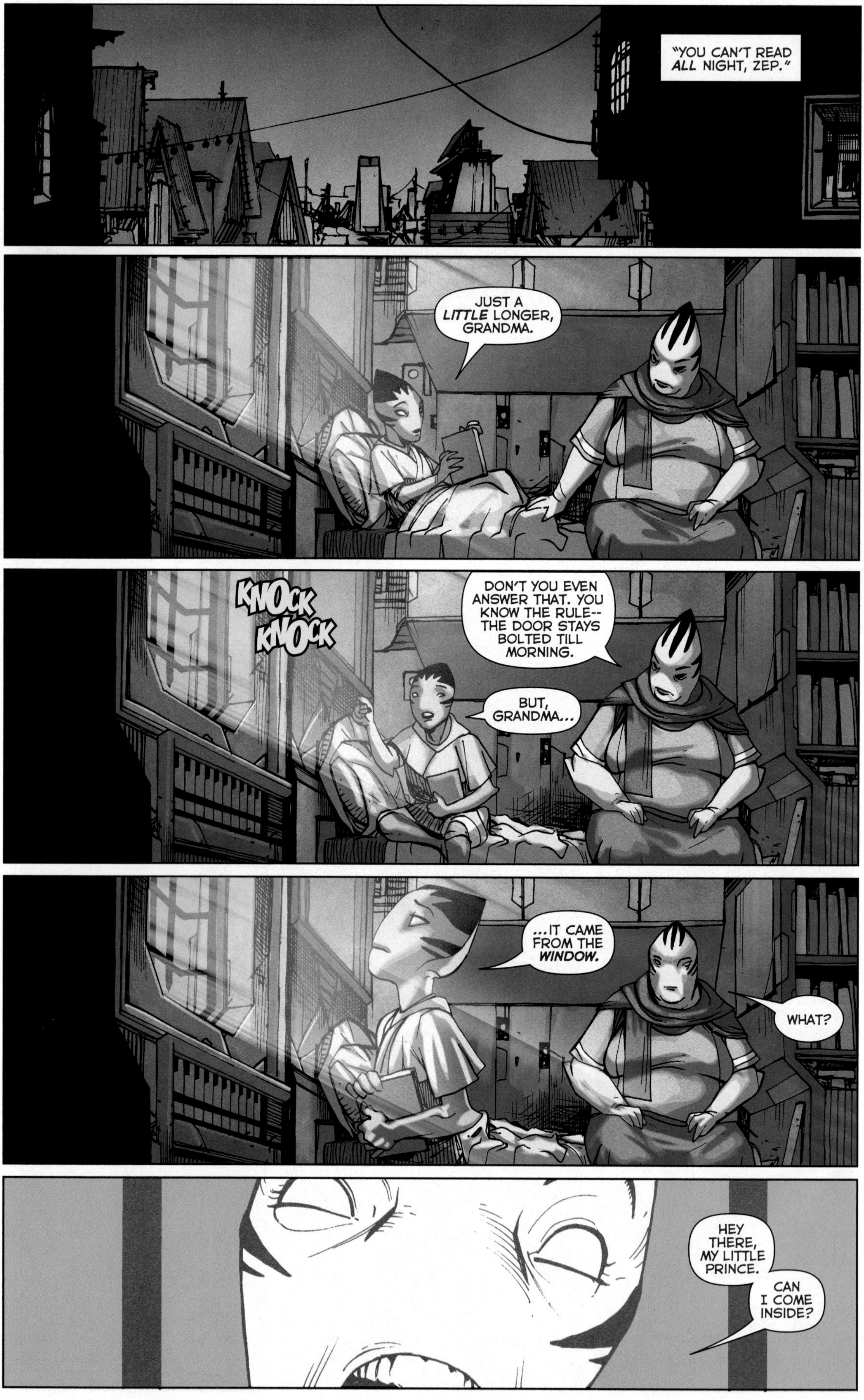
"YOU CAN'T READ ALL NIGHT, ZEP."
JUST A LITTLE LONGER, GRANDMA.
KNOCK KNOCK
DON'T YOU EVEN ANSWER THAT. YOU KNOW THE RULE-- THE DOOR STAYS BOLTED TILL MORNING.
BUT, GRANDMA...
...IT CAME FROM THE WINDOW.
WHAT?
HEY THERE, MY LITTLE PRINCE.
CAN I COME INSIDE?

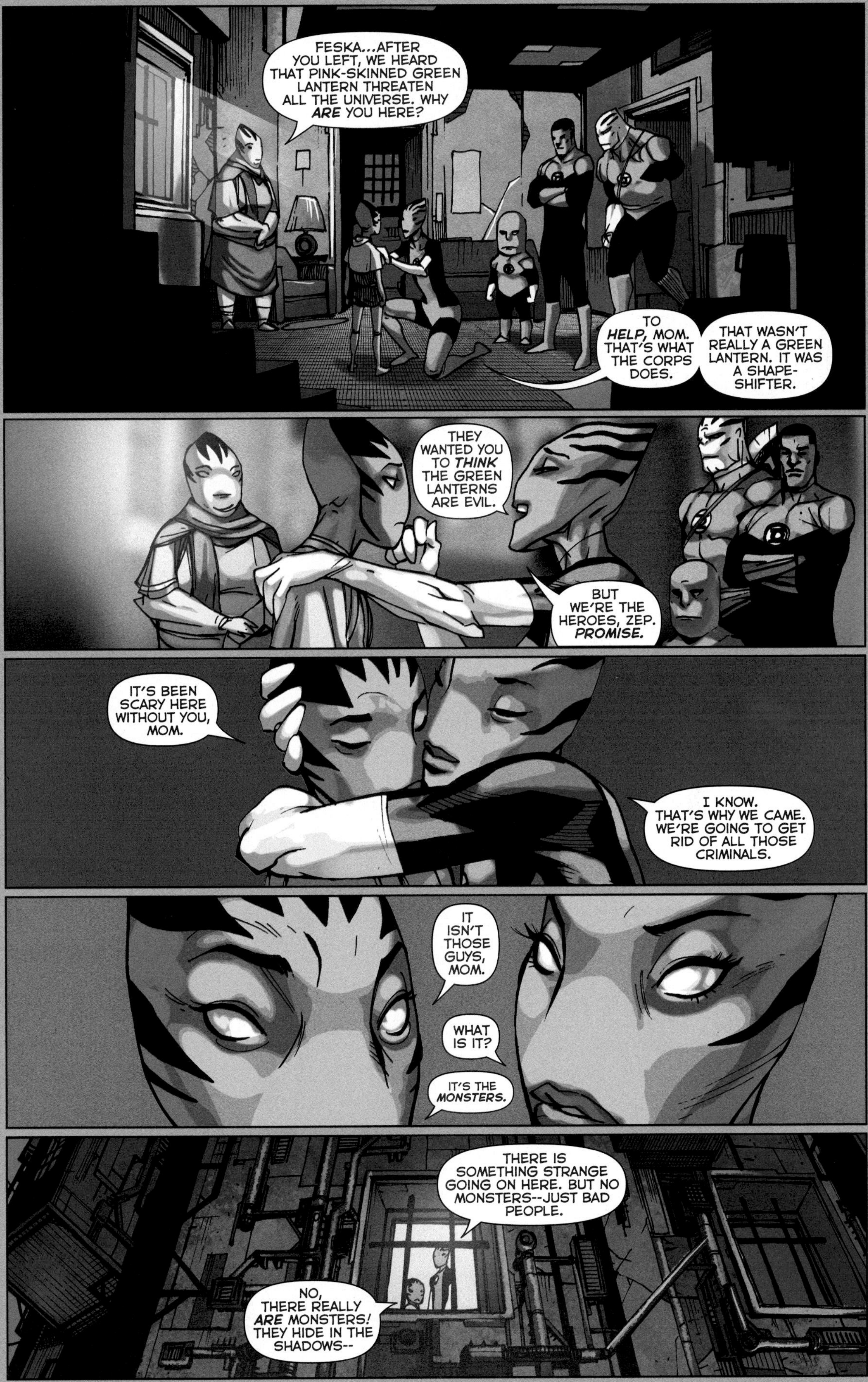
FESKA...AFTER YOU LEFT, WE HEARD THAT PINK-SKINNED GREEN LANTERN THREATEN ALL THE UNIVERSE. WHY ARE YOU HERE?
TO HELP, MOM. THAT'S WHAT THE CORPS DOES.
THAT WASN'T REALLY A GREEN LANTERN. IT WAS A SHAPE-SHIFTER.
THEY WANTED YOU TO THINK THE GREEN LANTERNS ARE EVIL.
BUT WE'RE THE HEROES, ZEP. PROMISE.
IT'S BEEN SCARY HERE WITHOUT YOU, MOM.
I KNOW. THAT'S WHY WE CAME. WE'RE GOING TO GET RID OF ALL THOSE CRIMINALS.
IT ISN'T THOSE GUYS, MOM.
WHAT IS IT?
IT'S THE MONSTERS.
THERE IS SOMETHING STRANGE GOING ON HERE. BUT NO MONSTERS--JUST BAD PEOPLE.
NO, THERE REALLY ARE MONSTERS! THEY HIDE IN THE SHADOWS--

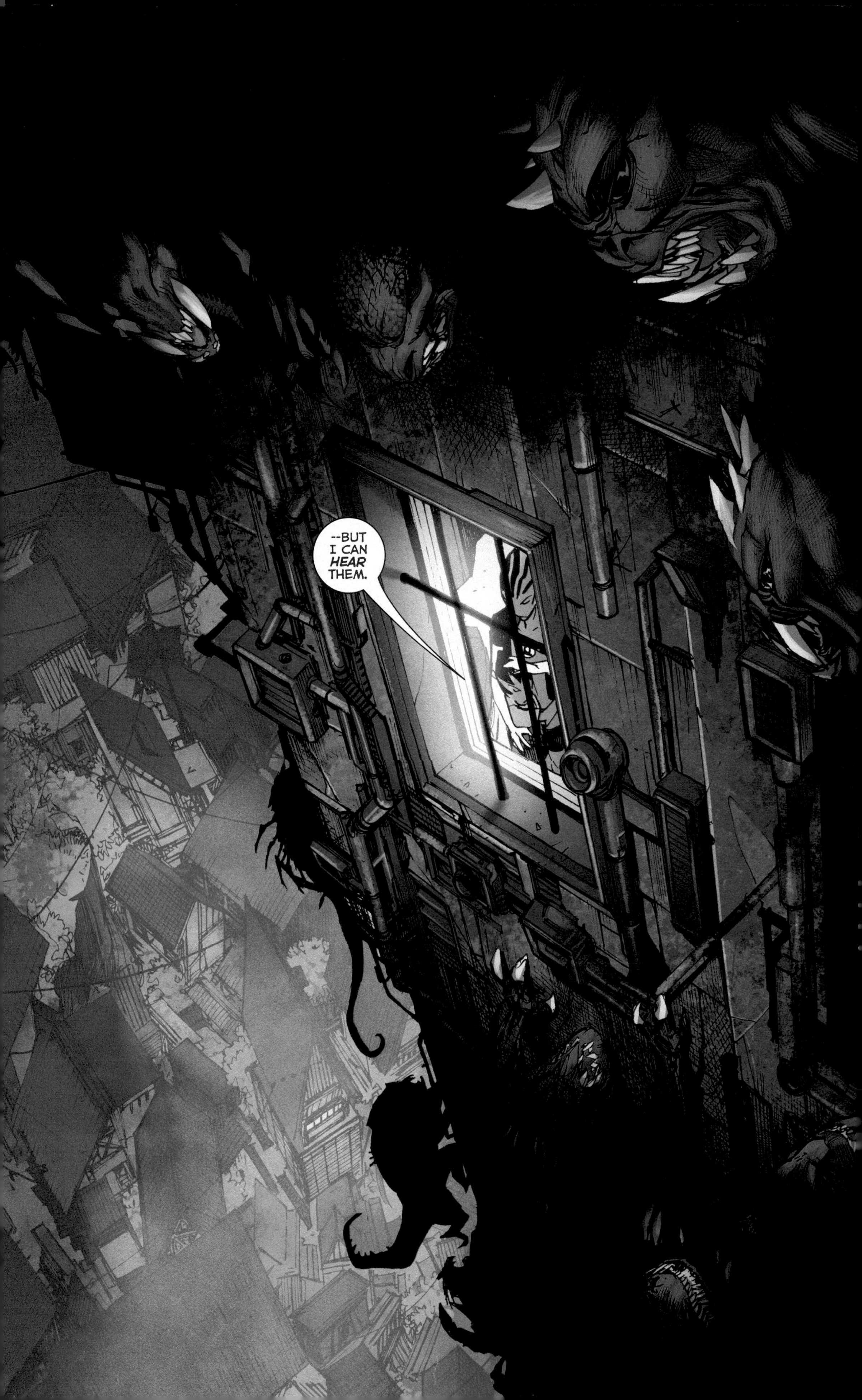
--BUT I CAN *HEAR* THEM.

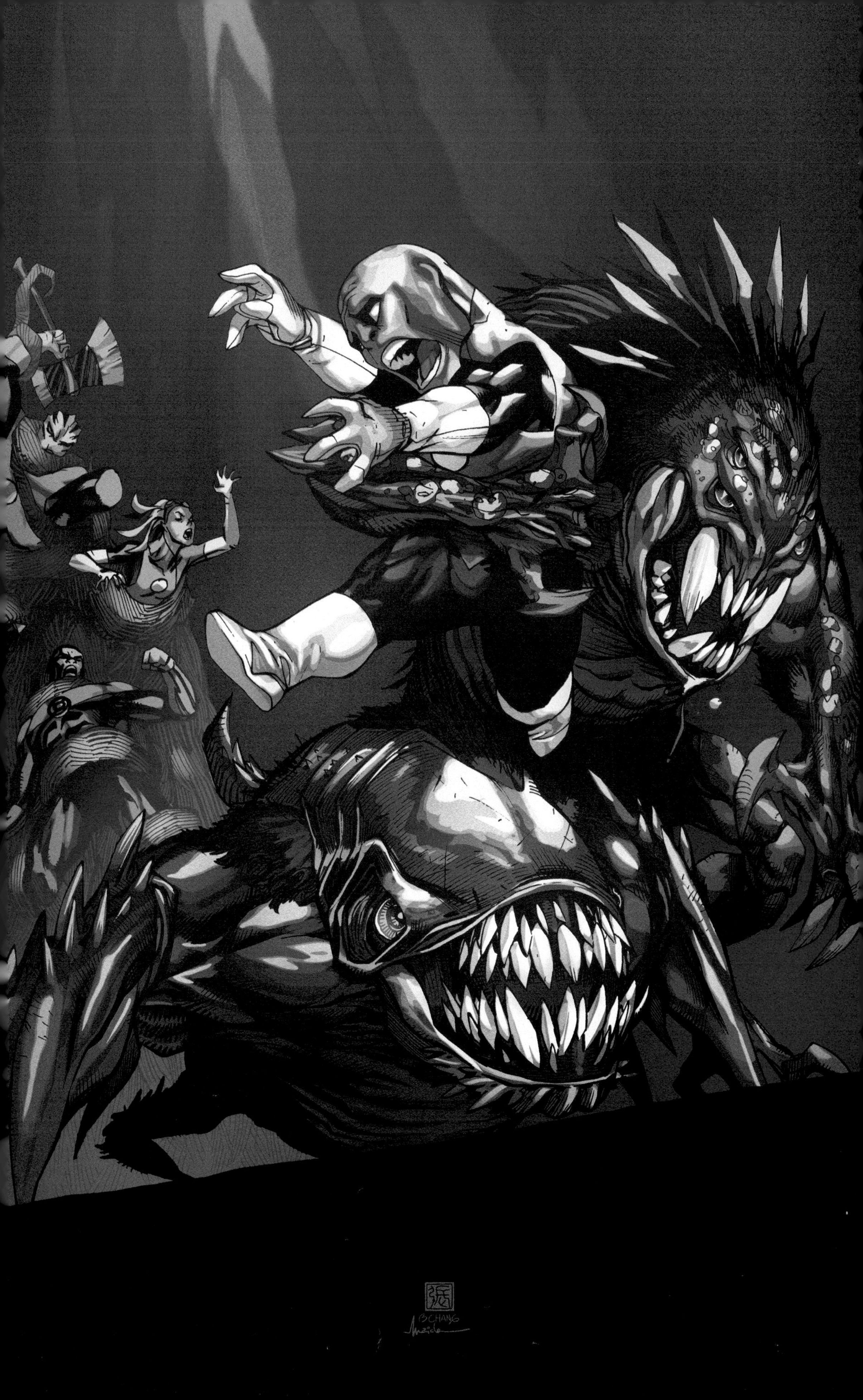
B CHANG

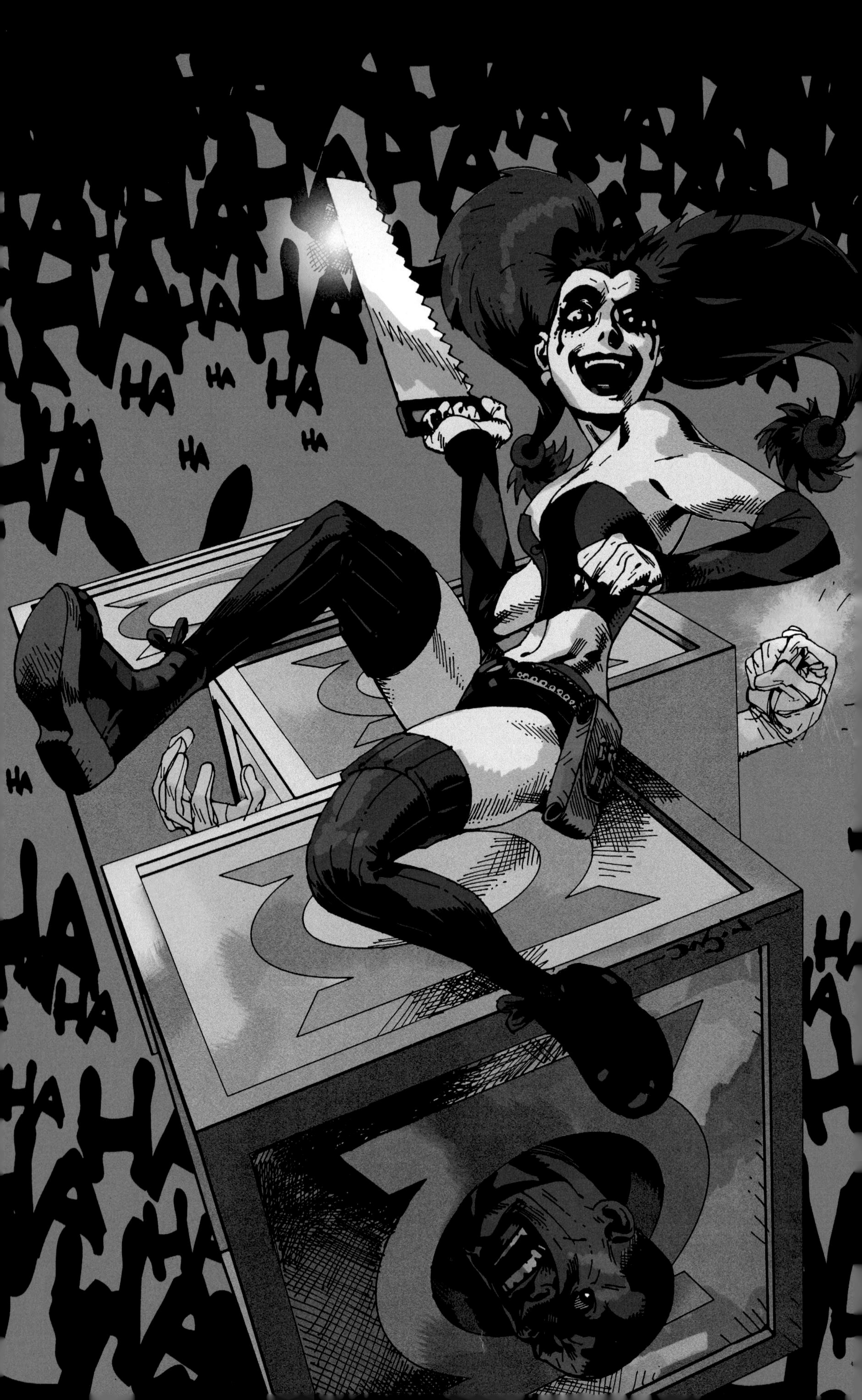
HA HA HA
HA HA
HA

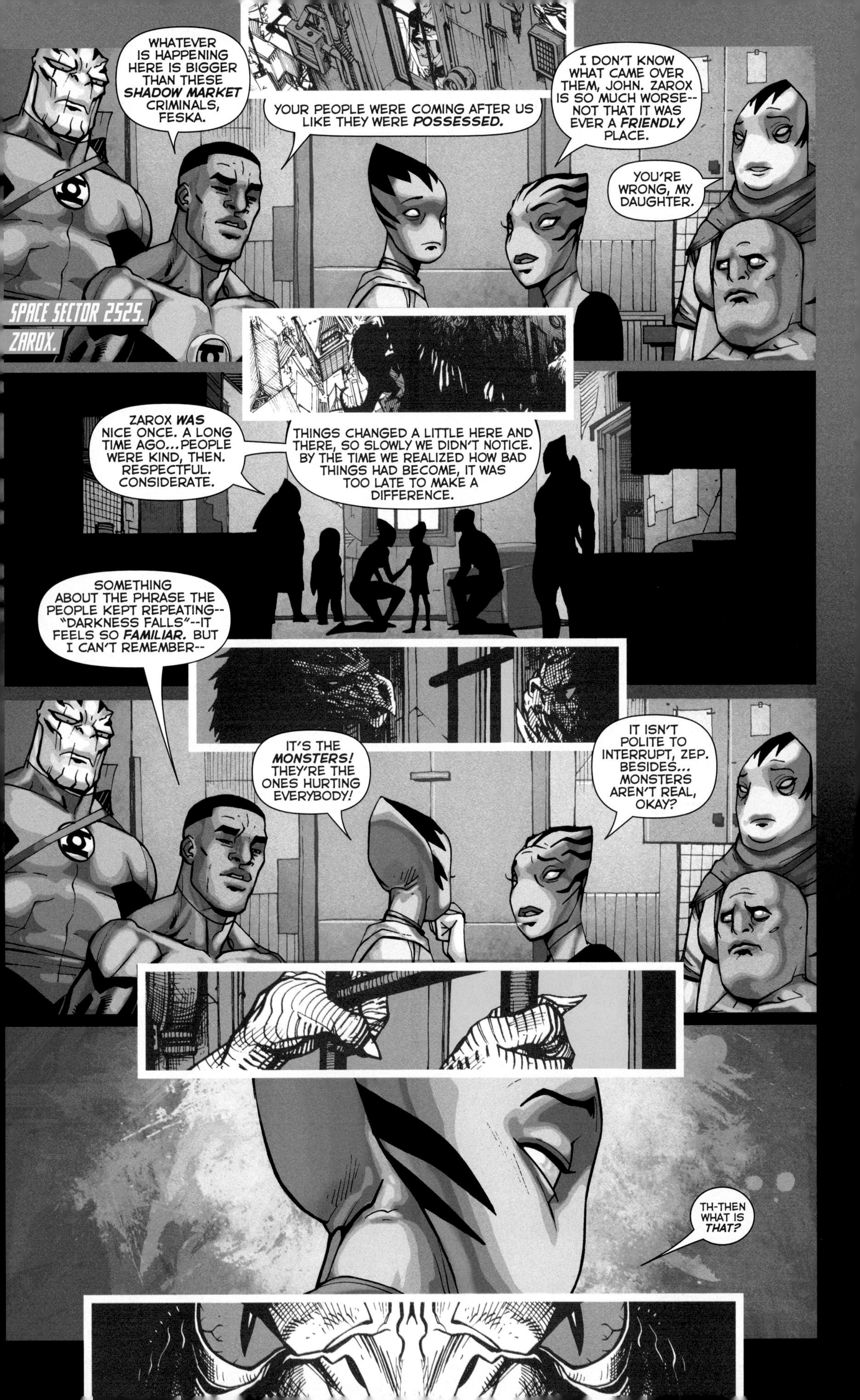
SPACE SECTOR 2525.
ZAROX.
WHATEVER IS HAPPENING HERE IS BIGGER THAN THESE SHADOW MARKET CRIMINALS, FESKA.
YOUR PEOPLE WERE COMING AFTER US LIKE THEY WERE POSSESSED.
I DON'T KNOW WHAT CAME OVER THEM, JOHN. ZAROX IS SO MUCH WORSE--NOT THAT IT WAS EVER A FRIENDLY PLACE.
YOU'RE WRONG, MY DAUGHTER.
ZAROX WAS NICE ONCE. A LONG TIME AGO...PEOPLE WERE KIND, THEN. RESPECTFUL. CONSIDERATE.
THINGS CHANGED A LITTLE HERE AND THERE, SO SLOWLY WE DIDN'T NOTICE. BY THE TIME WE REALIZED HOW BAD THINGS HAD BECOME, IT WAS TOO LATE TO MAKE A DIFFERENCE.
SOMETHING ABOUT THE PHRASE THE PEOPLE KEPT REPEATING--"DARKNESS FALLS"--IT FEELS SO FAMILIAR. BUT I CAN'T REMEMBER--
IT'S THE MONSTERS! THEY'RE THE ONES HURTING EVERYBODY!
IT ISN'T POLITE TO INTERRUPT, ZEP. BESIDES... MONSTERS AREN'T REAL, OKAY?
TH-THEN WHAT IS THAT?

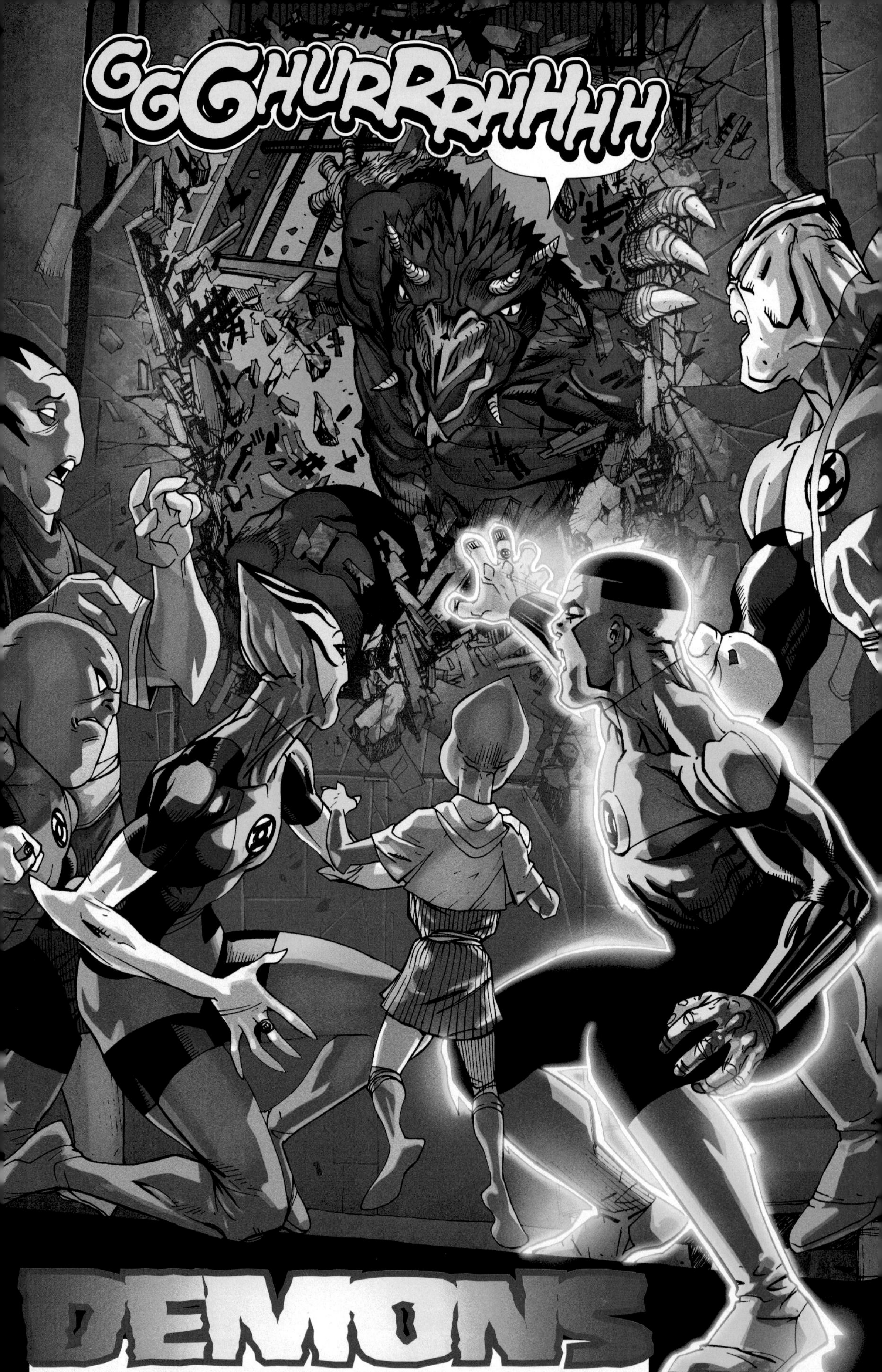
GGGHURRRHHHH
DEMONS

WRITER: VAN JENSEN ARTIST: BERNARD CHANG COLORIST: MARCELO MAIOLO
LETTERER: DAVE SHARPE COVER: CHANG & MAIOLO HARLEY QUINN VARIANT: JASON PEARSON

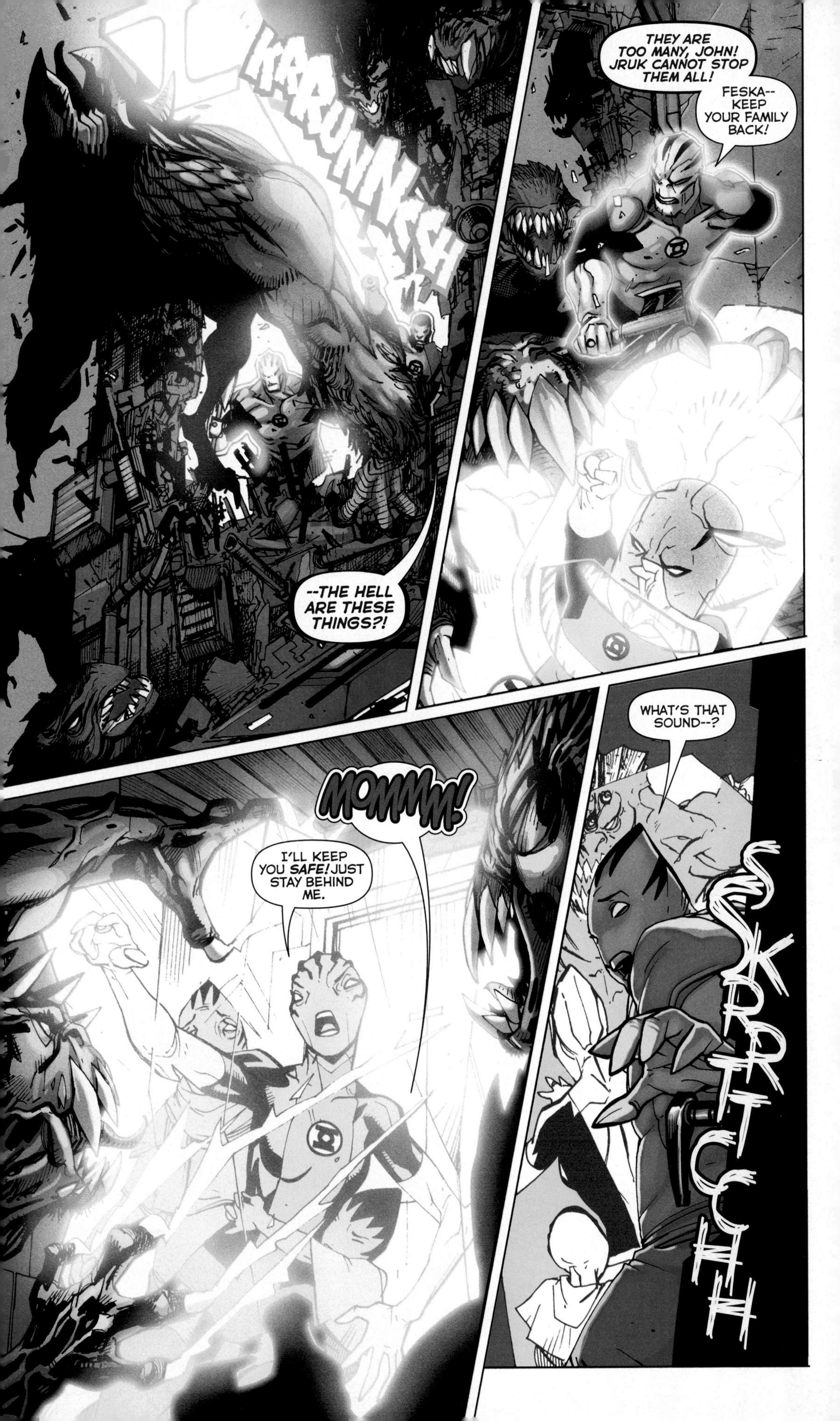
KRUNNCH
--THE HELL ARE THESE THINGS?!
THEY ARE TOO MANY, JOHN! JRUK CANNOT STOP THEM ALL!
FESKA-- KEEP YOUR FAMILY BACK!
MOMMM!
I'LL KEEP YOU SAFE! JUST STAY BEHIND ME.
WHAT'S THAT SOUND--?
SKRRITCHH

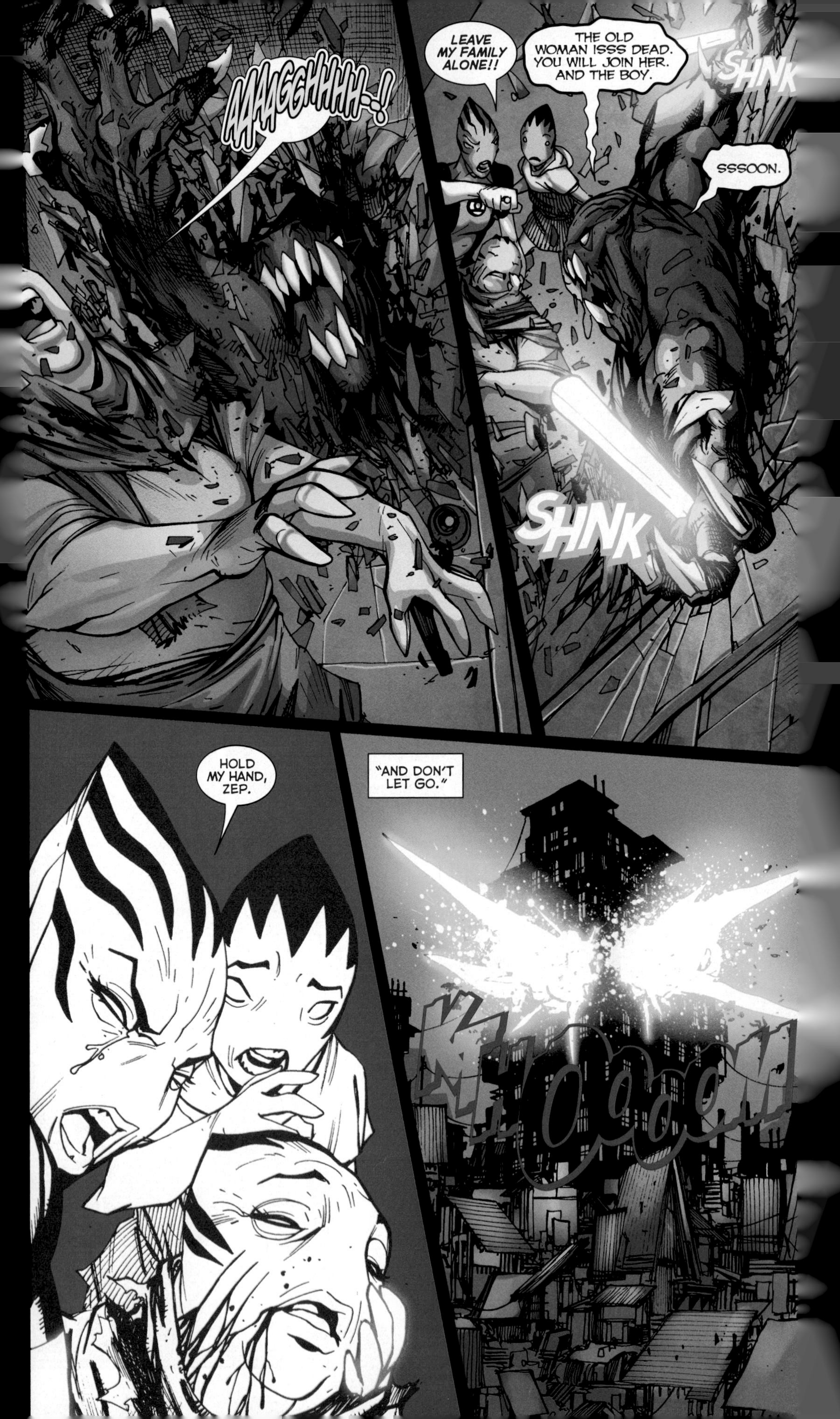
AAAAGGHHHH--!
LEAVE MY FAMILY ALONE!!
THE OLD WOMAN ISSS DEAD. YOU WILL JOIN HER. AND THE BOY.
SHNK
SSSOON.
SHNK
HOLD MY HAND, ZEP.
"AND DON'T LET GO."

NO! MARO!

I'M NOT LOSING ONE OF MY TEAM!

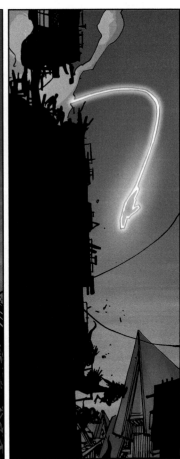

THERE'S NO SHADOW DARK ENOUGH TO HIDE YOU FROM ME.

WHERE--?

JOHN...I TRIED TO GRAB EVERYONE. I TRIED...

WE HAVE TO KEEP HUNTING. THEY HAVE TO BE NEAR HERE.

WE NEED TO REGROUP, KEEP THE BOY SAFE. WHATEVER WE'RE UP AGAINST...

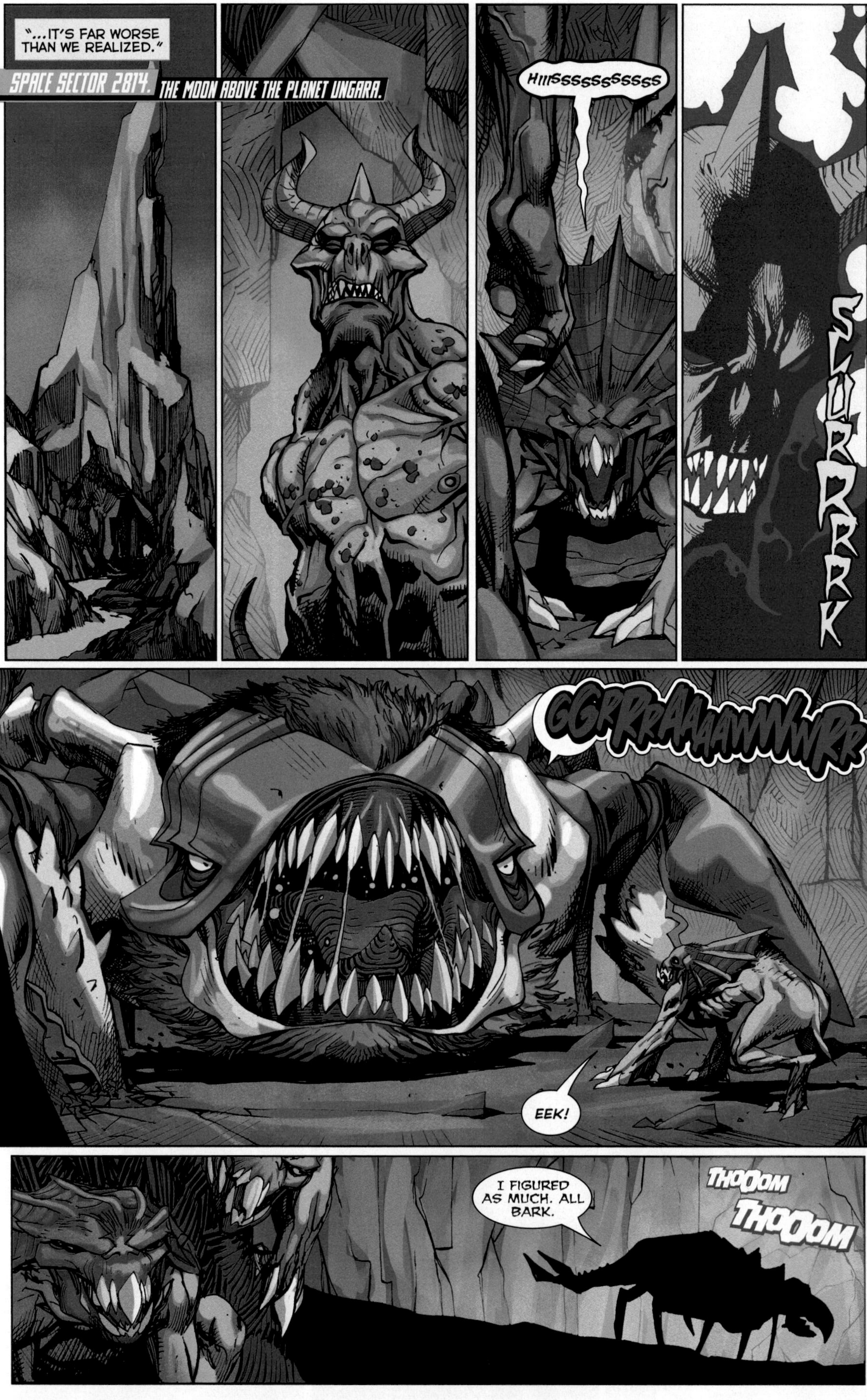
"...IT'S FAR WORSE THAN WE REALIZED."
SPACE SECTOR 2814.
THE MOON ABOVE THE PLANET UNGARA.
HIIISSSSSSSSSSS
SLURRRRK
GGRRRAAAAWWRR
EEK!
I FIGURED AS MUCH. ALL BARK.
THOOOM
THOOOM

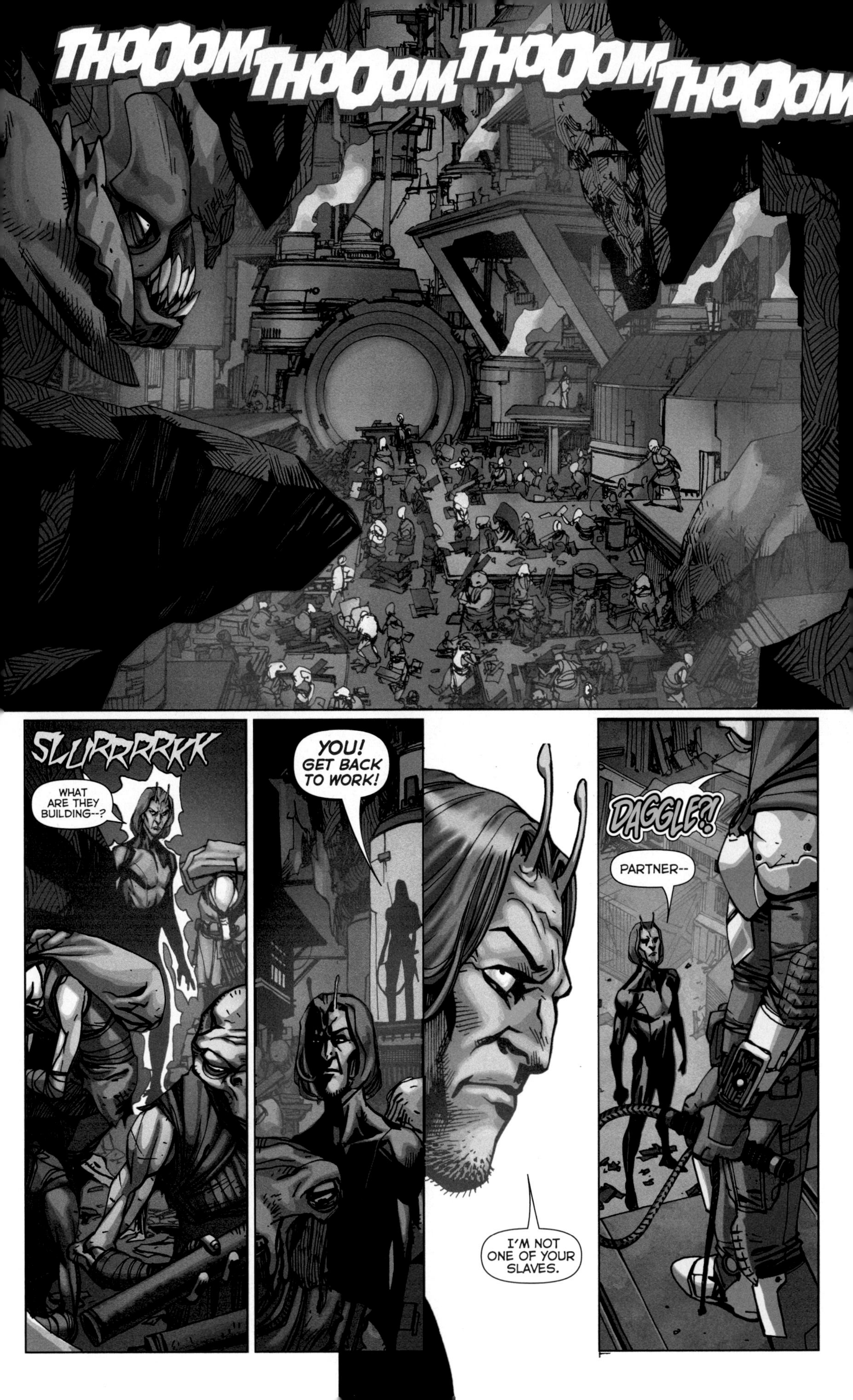
THOOOM THOOOM THOOOM THOOOM
SLURRRRKK
WHAT ARE THEY BUILDING--?
YOU! GET BACK TO WORK!
I'M NOT ONE OF YOUR SLAVES.
DAGGLE?!
PARTNER--

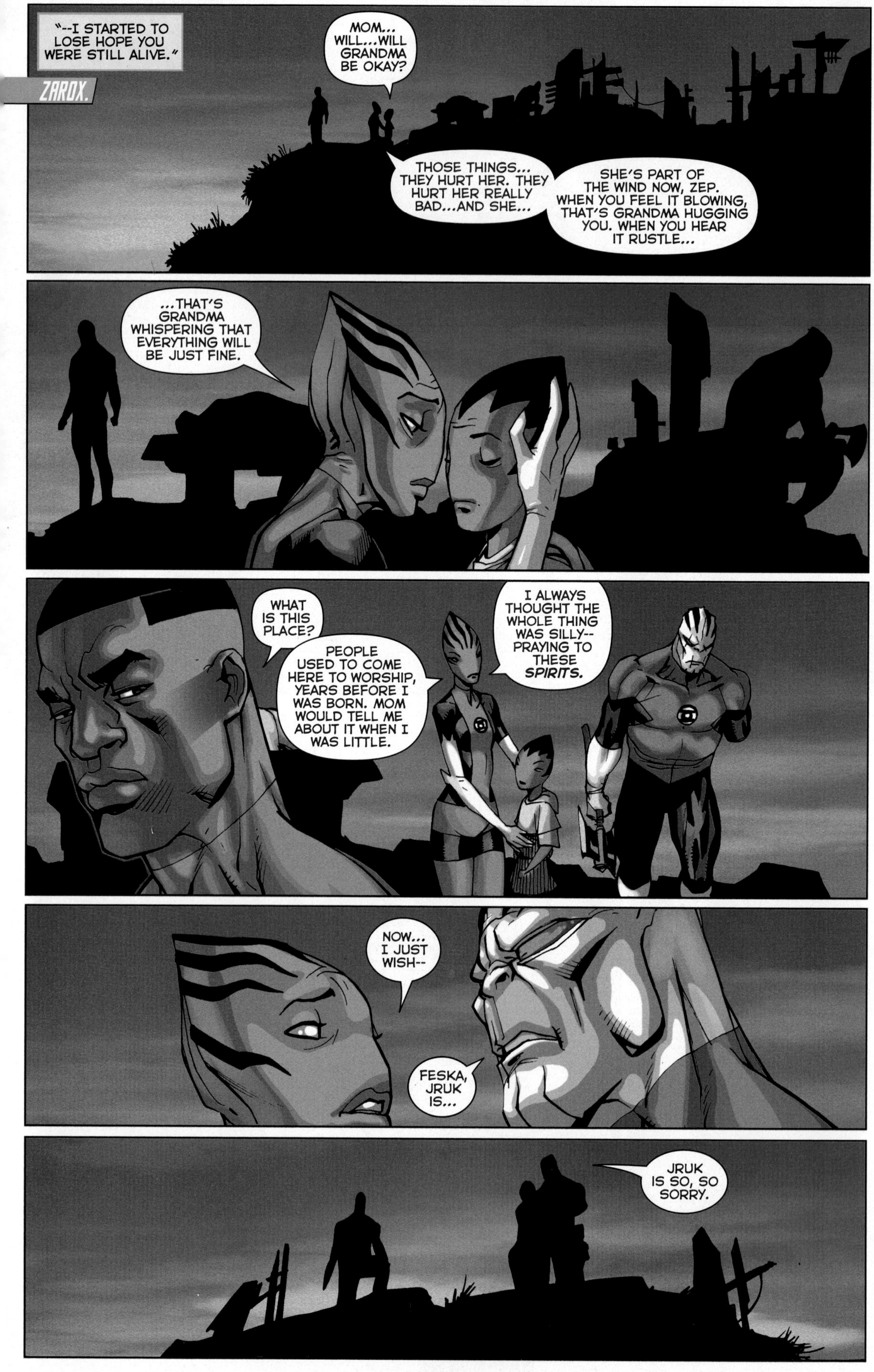
"--I STARTED TO LOSE HOPE YOU WERE STILL ALIVE."
ZAROX.
MOM... WILL...WILL GRANDMA BE OKAY?
THOSE THINGS... THEY HURT HER. THEY HURT HER REALLY BAD...AND SHE...
SHE'S PART OF THE WIND NOW, ZEP. WHEN YOU FEEL IT BLOWING, THAT'S GRANDMA HUGGING YOU. WHEN YOU HEAR IT RUSTLE...
...THAT'S GRANDMA WHISPERING THAT EVERYTHING WILL BE JUST FINE.
WHAT IS THIS PLACE?
PEOPLE USED TO COME HERE TO WORSHIP, YEARS BEFORE I WAS BORN. MOM WOULD TELL ME ABOUT IT WHEN I WAS LITTLE.
I ALWAYS THOUGHT THE WHOLE THING WAS SILLY-- PRAYING TO THESE *SPIRITS.*
NOW... I JUST WISH--
FESKA, JRUK IS...
JRUK IS SO, SO SORRY.

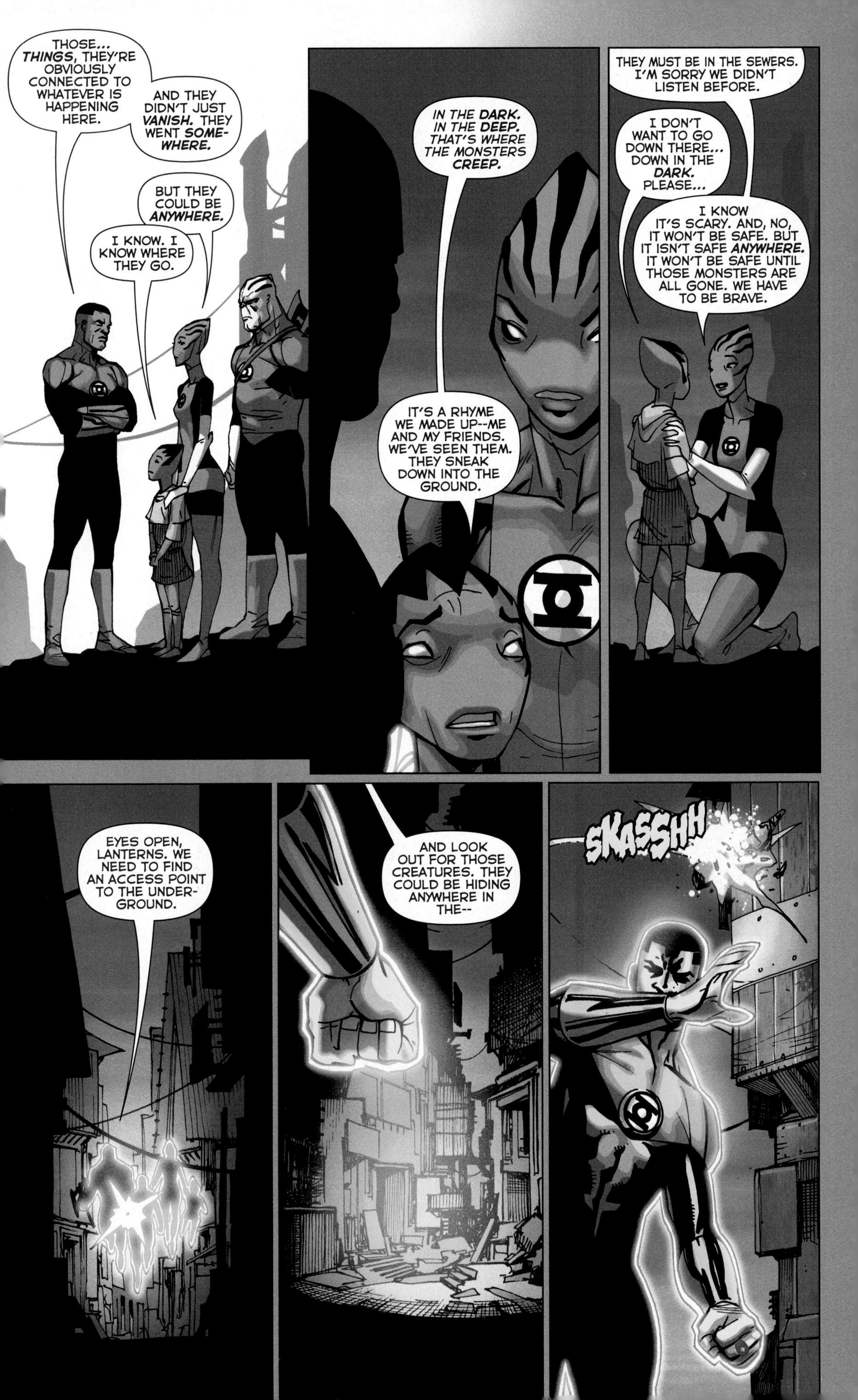
THOSE... THINGS, THEY'RE OBVIOUSLY CONNECTED TO WHATEVER IS HAPPENING HERE.
AND THEY DIDN'T JUST VANISH. THEY WENT SOME-WHERE.
BUT THEY COULD BE ANYWHERE.
I KNOW. I KNOW WHERE THEY GO.
IN THE DARK. IN THE DEEP. THAT'S WHERE THE MONSTERS CREEP.
IT'S A RHYME WE MADE UP--ME AND MY FRIENDS. WE'VE SEEN THEM. THEY SNEAK DOWN INTO THE GROUND.
THEY MUST BE IN THE SEWERS. I'M SORRY WE DIDN'T LISTEN BEFORE.
I DON'T WANT TO GO DOWN THERE... DOWN IN THE DARK. PLEASE...
I KNOW IT'S SCARY. AND, NO, IT WON'T BE SAFE. BUT IT ISN'T SAFE ANYWHERE. IT WON'T BE SAFE UNTIL THOSE MONSTERS ARE ALL GONE. WE HAVE TO BE BRAVE.
EYES OPEN, LANTERNS. WE NEED TO FIND AN ACCESS POINT TO THE UNDER-GROUND.
AND LOOK OUT FOR THOSE CREATURES. THEY COULD BE HIDING ANYWHERE IN THE--
SKASSHH

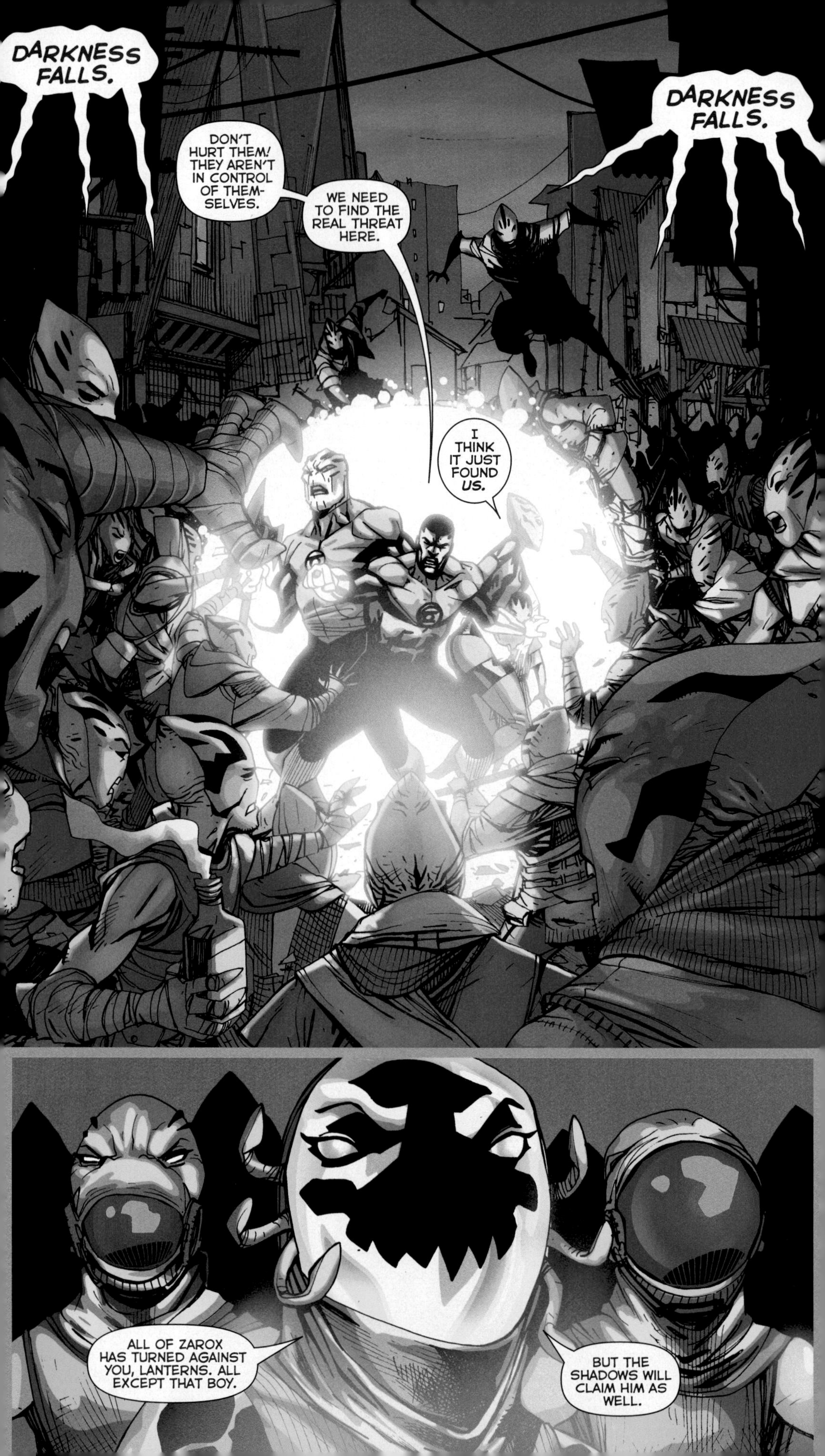
DARKNESS FALLS.
DON'T HURT THEM! THEY AREN'T IN CONTROL OF THEM-SELVES.
WE NEED TO FIND THE REAL THREAT HERE.
DARKNESS FALLS.
I THINK IT JUST FOUND US.
ALL OF ZAROX HAS TURNED AGAINST YOU, LANTERNS. ALL EXCEPT THAT BOY.
BUT THE SHADOWS WILL CLAIM HIM AS WELL.

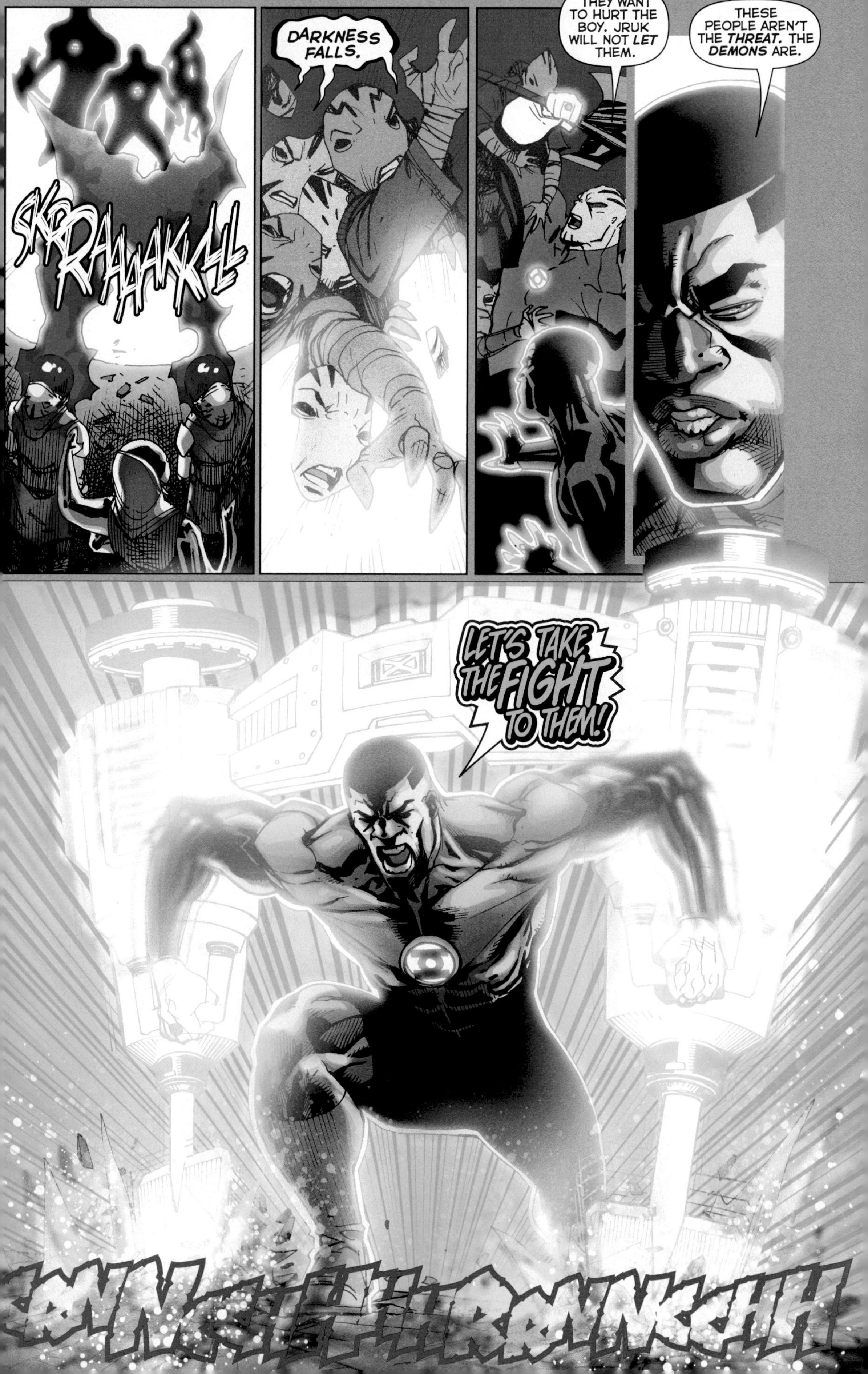
SKRRAAAKKLL
DARKNESS FALLS.
THEY WANT TO HURT THE BOY. JRUK WILL NOT LET THEM.
THESE PEOPLE AREN'T THE THREAT. THE DEMONS ARE.
LET'S TAKE THE FIGHT TO THEM!

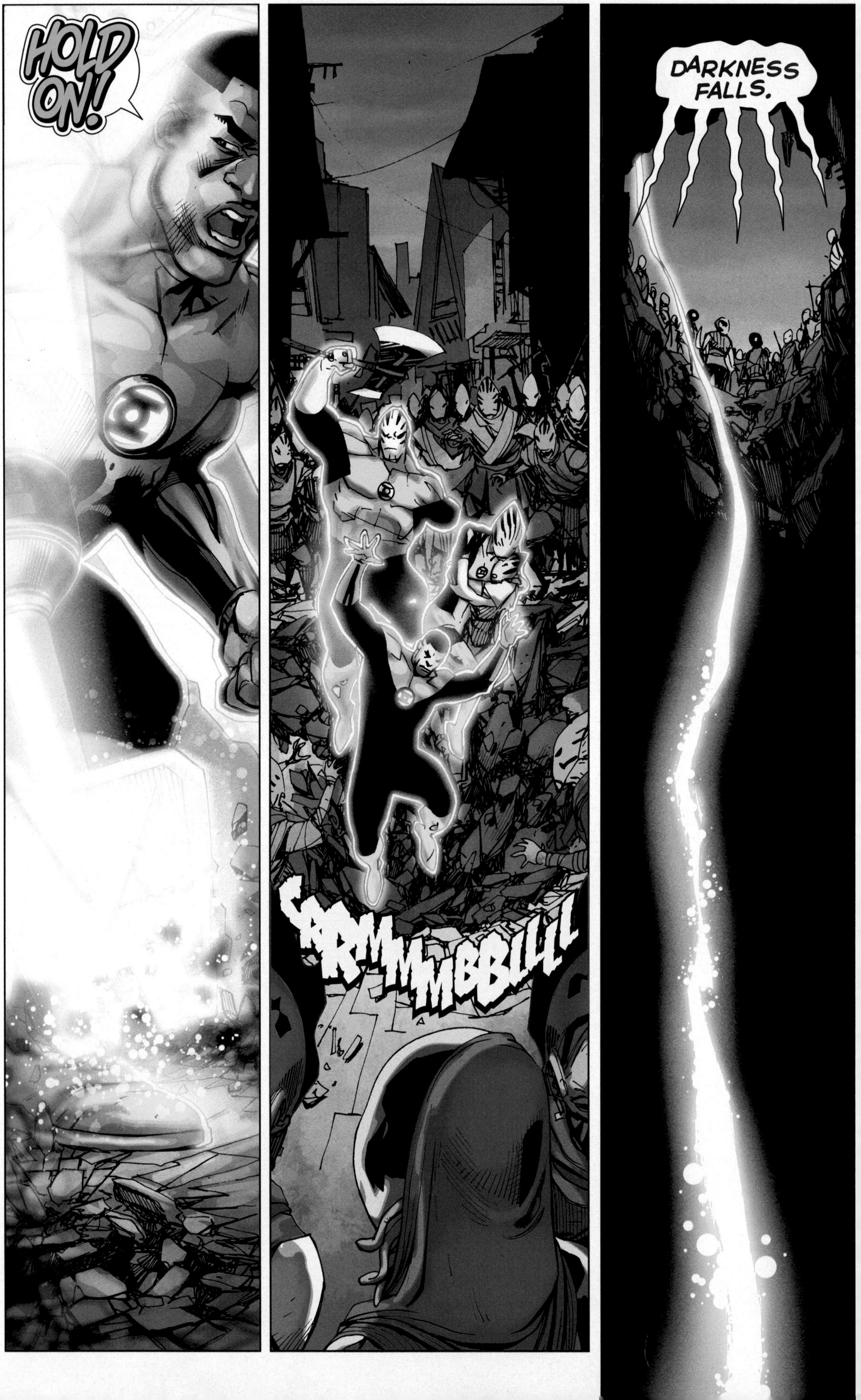
HOLD ON!
CRMMMBBLLL
DARKNESS FALLS.

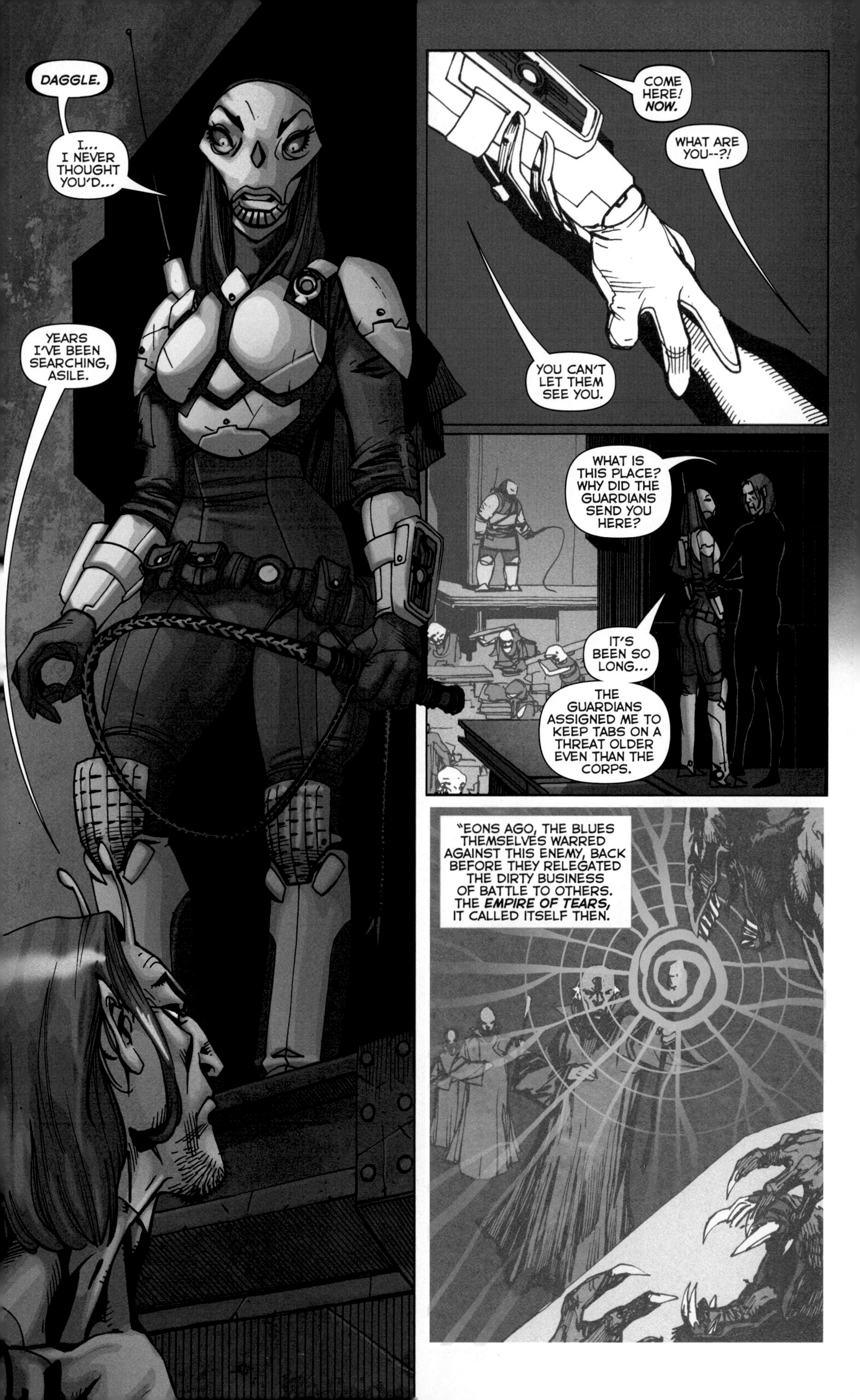
DAGGLE.
I... I NEVER THOUGHT YOU'D...
YEARS I'VE BEEN SEARCHING, ASILE.
COME HERE! NOW.
WHAT ARE YOU--?!
YOU CAN'T LET THEM SEE YOU.
WHAT IS THIS PLACE? WHY DID THE GUARDIANS SEND YOU HERE?
IT'S BEEN SO LONG...
THE GUARDIANS ASSIGNED ME TO KEEP TABS ON A THREAT OLDER EVEN THAN THE CORPS.
"EONS AGO, THE BLUES THEMSELVES WARRED AGAINST THIS ENEMY, BACK BEFORE THEY RELEGATED THE DIRTY BUSINESS OF BATTLE TO OTHERS. THE EMPIRE OF TEARS, IT CALLED ITSELF THEN.

"THE GUARDIANS *DEFEATED* THE EMPIRE, BELIEVING ITS SERVANTS FOREVER *IMPRISONED* ON YSMAULT.

"BUT THE PRISON WOULDN'T REMAIN ISOLATED. ONE DAY, THE PILOT OF A DAMAGED SHIP SAW YSMAULT AS HIS ONLY HOPE.

"HE WOULD'VE BEEN BETTER OFF DYING IN SPACE.

"BUT A CHILD, HIS *DAUGHTER,* SURVIVED THE CRASH. SHE DIDN'T SPEND LONG ON THE PLANET-- SEVERAL HOURS--BUT IT WAS *ENOUGH.* AFTER ALL...

"THESE DEMONS ONLY NEEDED *MINUTES* TO POISON THE MIND OF *ABIN SUR* WITH VISIONS OF THE *BLACKEST NIGHT.*

"ABIN SUR RESCUED THE CHILD, TAKING HER TO HIS HOME PLANET OF UNGARA. HE THOUGHT HE HAD SAVED A LIFE. BUT IT WASN'T JUST THE GREEN LANTERN THAT HAD BEEN *INFECTED.*

"THE GIRL BORE A *DISEASE* DEEP INSIDE HER, ONE THAT *FESTERED,* GREW...READYING TO SPREAD."

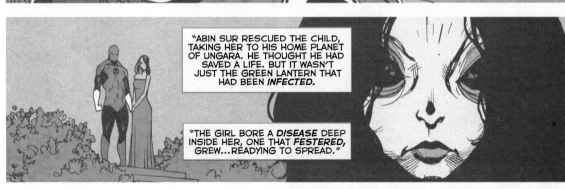

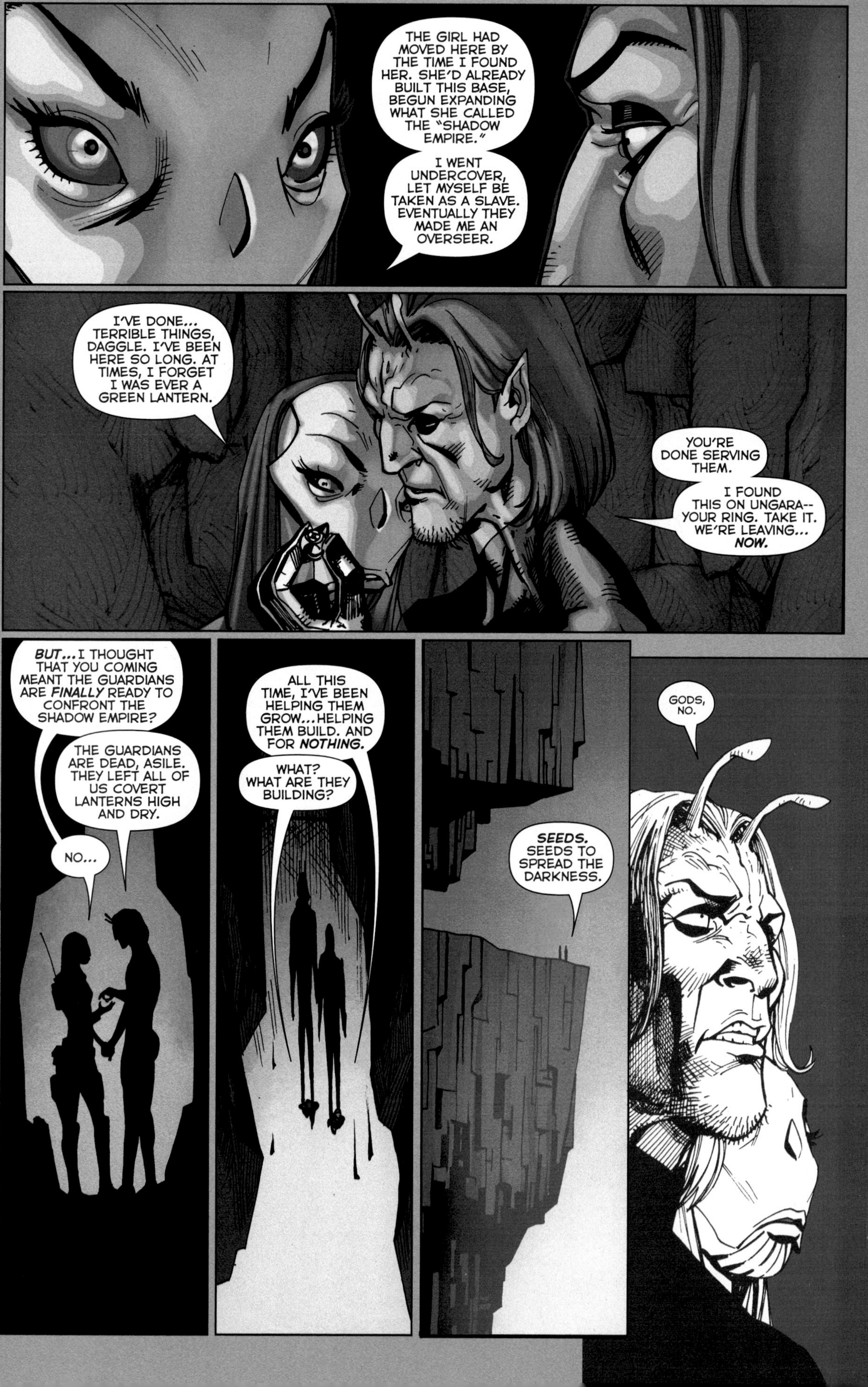
THE GIRL HAD MOVED HERE BY THE TIME I FOUND HER. SHE'D ALREADY BUILT THIS BASE, BEGUN EXPANDING WHAT SHE CALLED THE "SHADOW EMPIRE."
I WENT UNDERCOVER, LET MYSELF BE TAKEN AS A SLAVE. EVENTUALLY THEY MADE ME AN OVERSEER.
I'VE DONE... TERRIBLE THINGS, DAGGLE. I'VE BEEN HERE SO LONG. AT TIMES, I FORGET I WAS EVER A GREEN LANTERN.
YOU'RE DONE SERVING THEM.
I FOUND THIS ON UNGARA-- YOUR RING. TAKE IT. WE'RE LEAVING... NOW.
BUT... I THOUGHT THAT YOU COMING MEANT THE GUARDIANS ARE FINALLY READY TO CONFRONT THE SHADOW EMPIRE?
THE GUARDIANS ARE DEAD, ASILE. THEY LEFT ALL OF US COVERT LANTERNS HIGH AND DRY.
NO...
ALL THIS TIME, I'VE BEEN HELPING THEM GROW... HELPING THEM BUILD. AND FOR NOTHING.
WHAT? WHAT ARE THEY BUILDING?
SEEDS. SEEDS TO SPREAD THE DARKNESS.
GODS, NO.

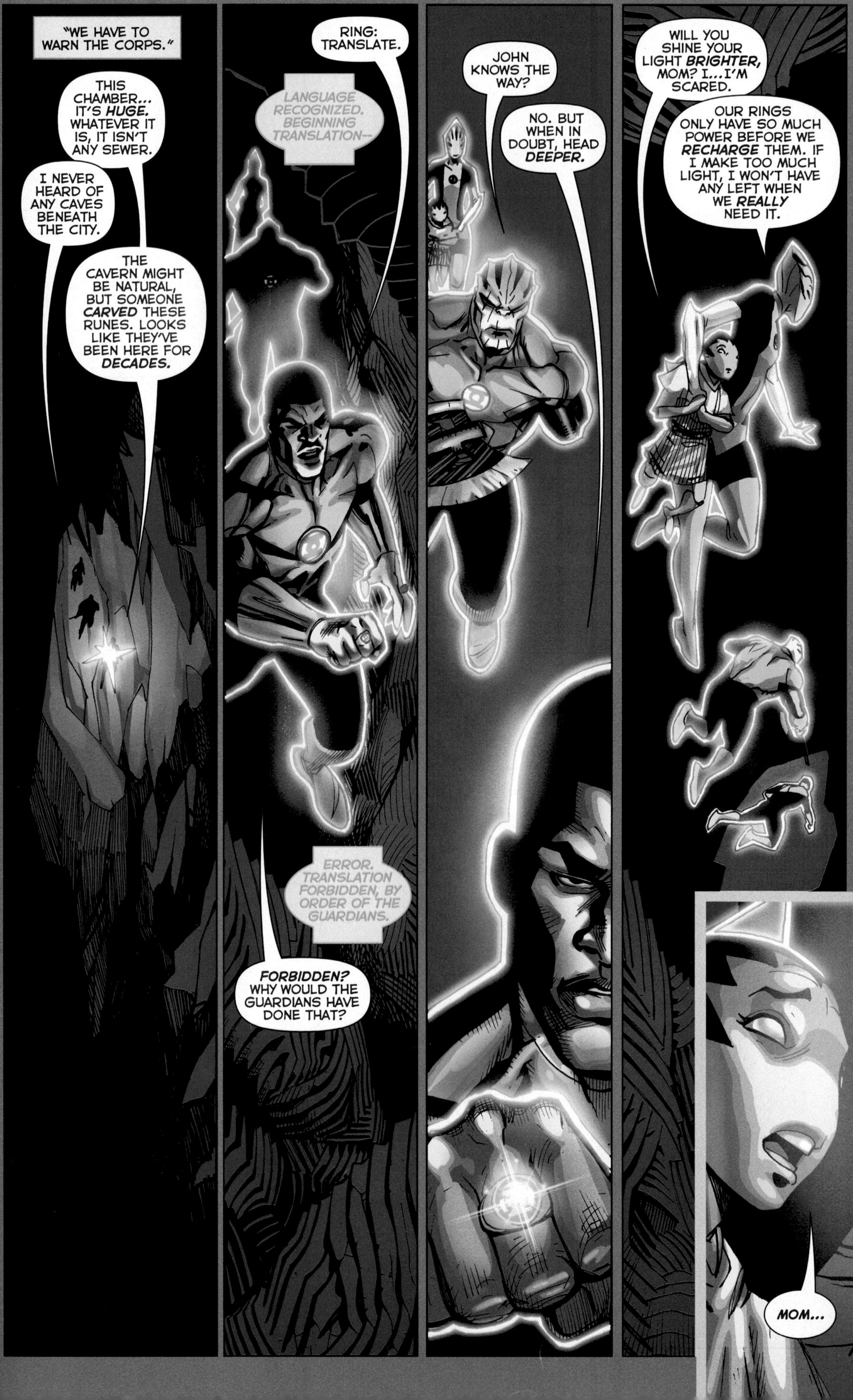
"WE HAVE TO WARN THE CORPS."
THIS CHAMBER... IT'S *HUGE.* WHATEVER IT IS, IT ISN'T ANY SEWER.
I NEVER HEARD OF ANY CAVES BENEATH THE CITY.
THE CAVERN MIGHT BE NATURAL, BUT SOMEONE *CARVED* THESE RUNES. LOOKS LIKE THEY'VE BEEN HERE FOR *DECADES.*
RING: TRANSLATE.
LANGUAGE RECOGNIZED. BEGINNING TRANSLATION--
ERROR. TRANSLATION FORBIDDEN, BY ORDER OF THE GUARDIANS.
FORBIDDEN? WHY WOULD THE GUARDIANS HAVE DONE THAT?
JOHN KNOWS THE WAY?
NO. BUT WHEN IN DOUBT, HEAD *DEEPER.*
WILL YOU SHINE YOUR LIGHT *BRIGHTER,* MOM? I...I'M SCARED.
OUR RINGS ONLY HAVE SO MUCH POWER BEFORE WE *RECHARGE* THEM. IF I MAKE TOO MUCH LIGHT, I WON'T HAVE ANY LEFT WHEN WE *REALLY* NEED IT.
MOM...

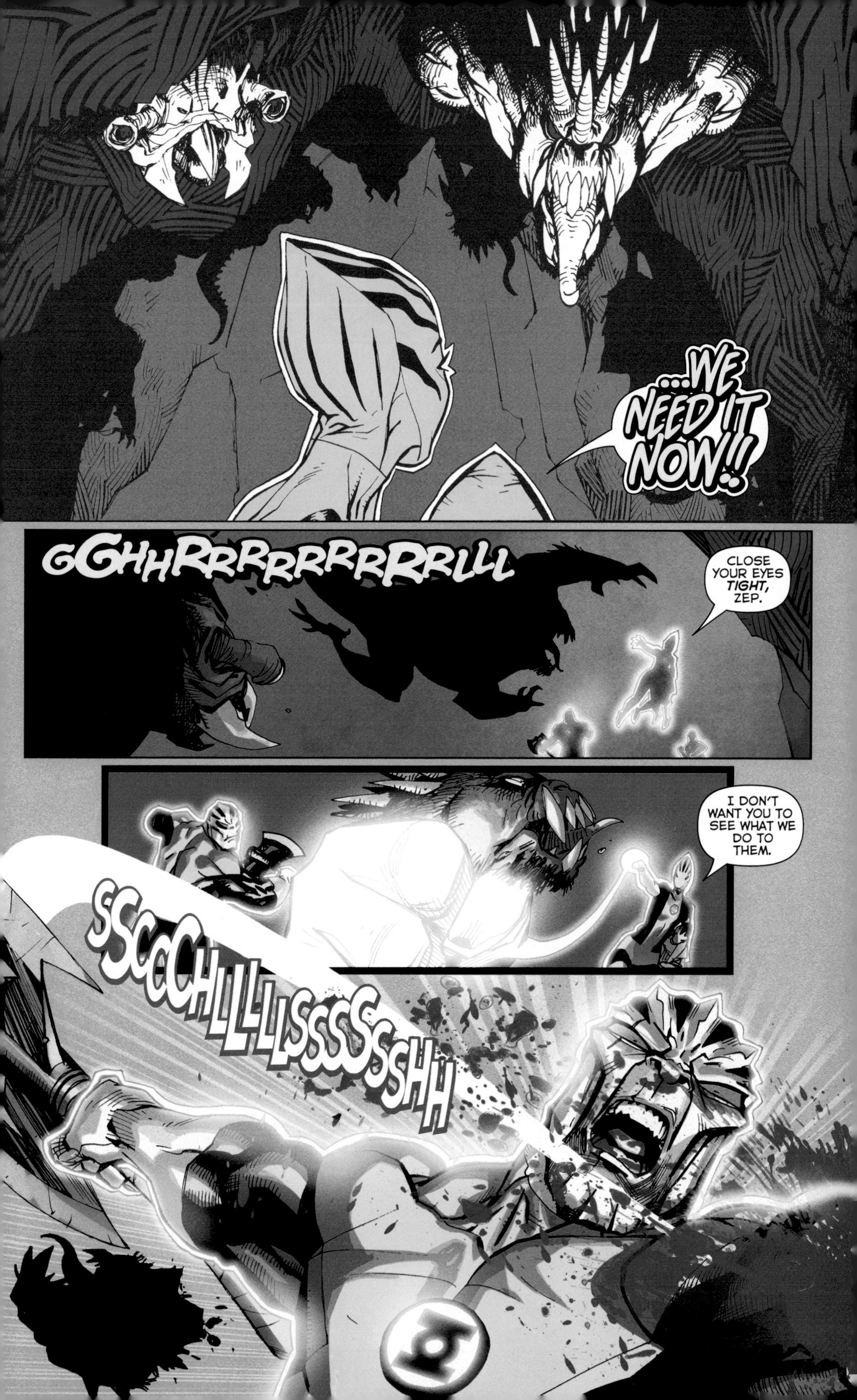
...WE NEED IT NOW!!
GGHHRRRRRRRRRLLL
CLOSE YOUR EYES TIGHT, ZEP.
I DON'T WANT YOU TO SEE WHAT WE DO TO THEM.
SSCCCHLLLLLSSSSSSHH

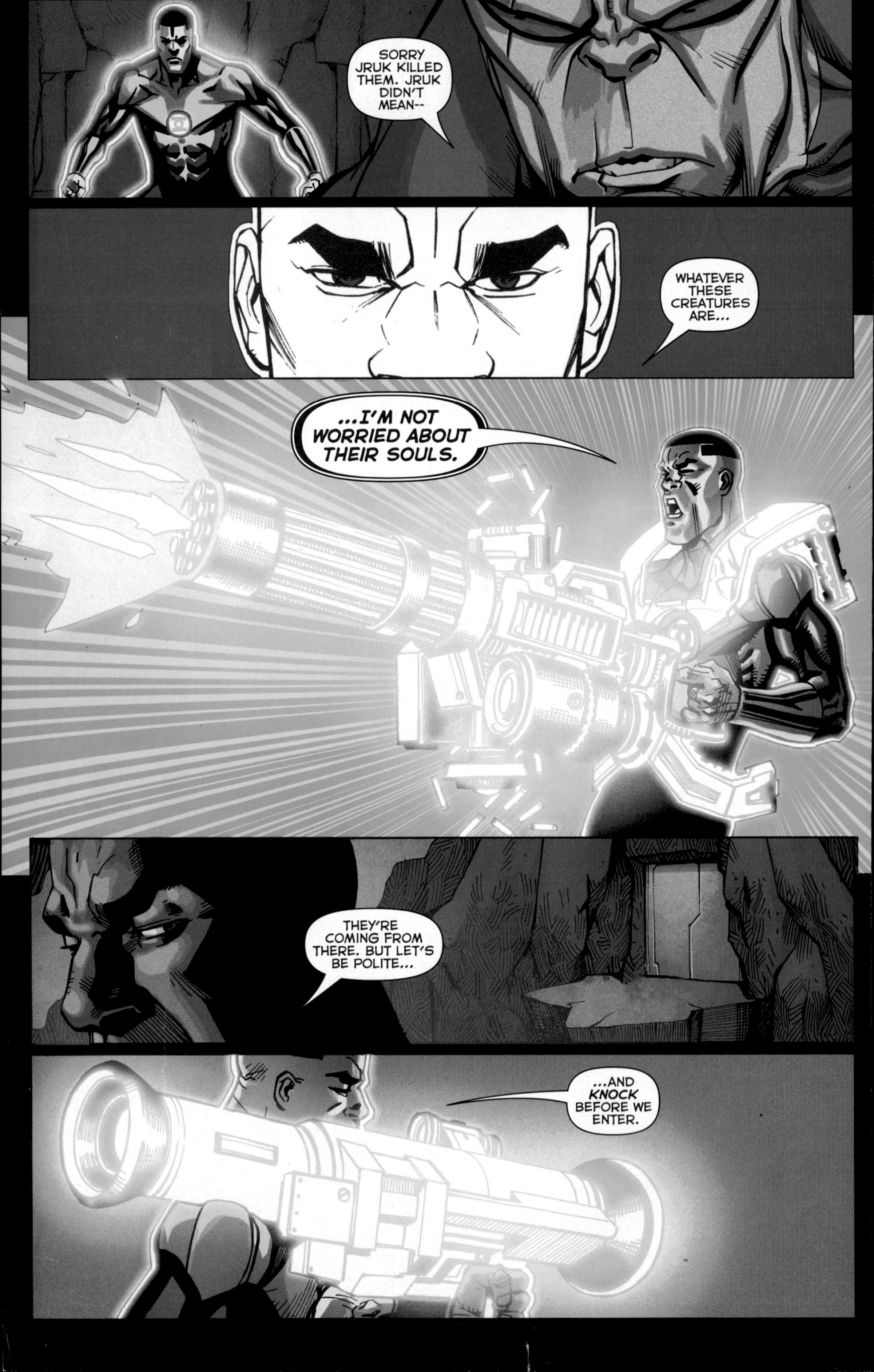

SORRY JRUK KILLED THEM. JRUK DIDN'T MEAN--
WHATEVER THESE CREATURES ARE...
...I'M NOT WORRIED ABOUT THEIR SOULS.
THEY'RE COMING FROM THERE. BUT LET'S BE POLITE...
...AND *KNOCK* BEFORE WE ENTER.

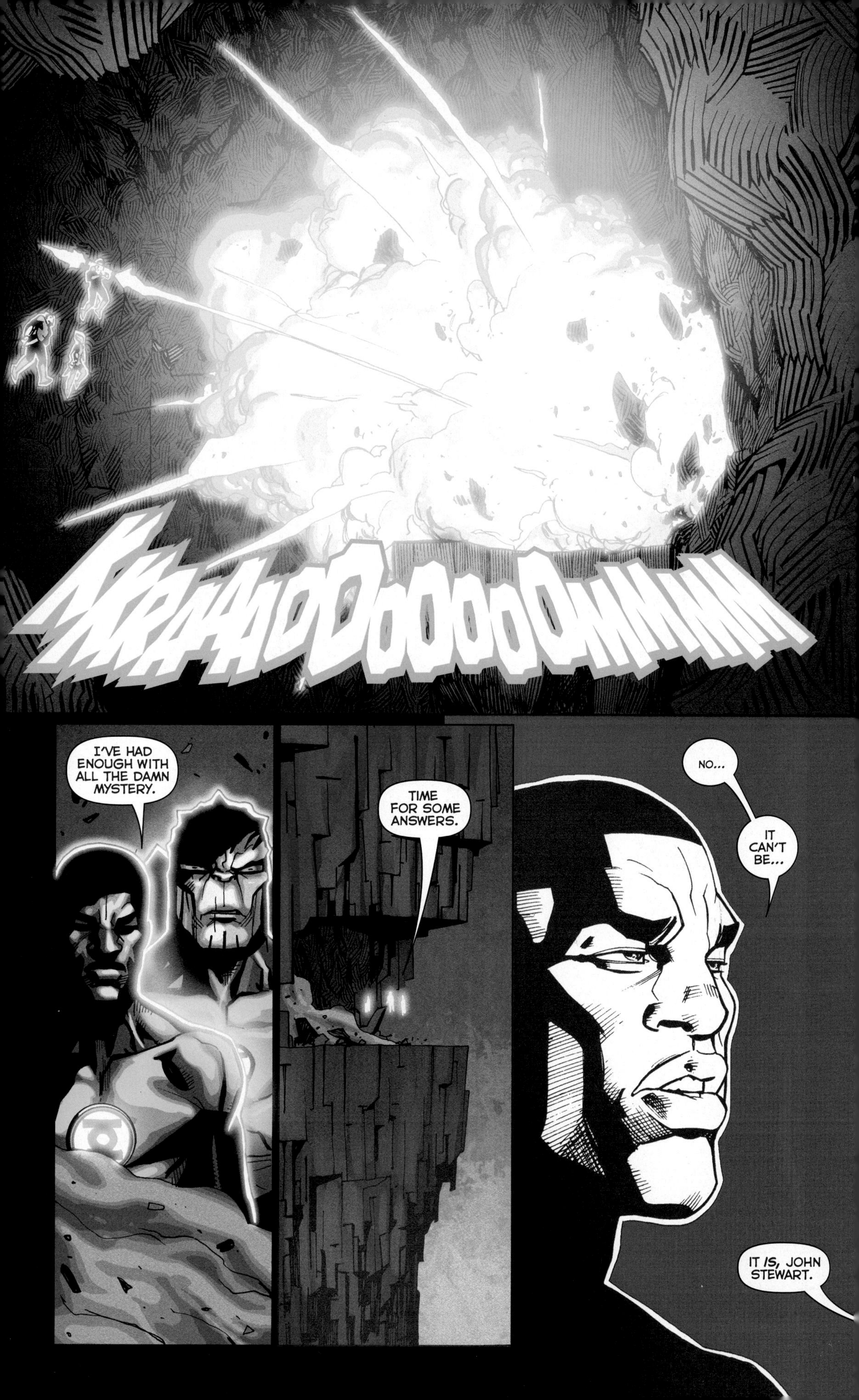
I'VE HAD ENOUGH WITH ALL THE DAMN MYSTERY.
TIME FOR SOME ANSWERS.
NO...
IT CAN'T BE...
IT *IS*, JOHN STEWART.

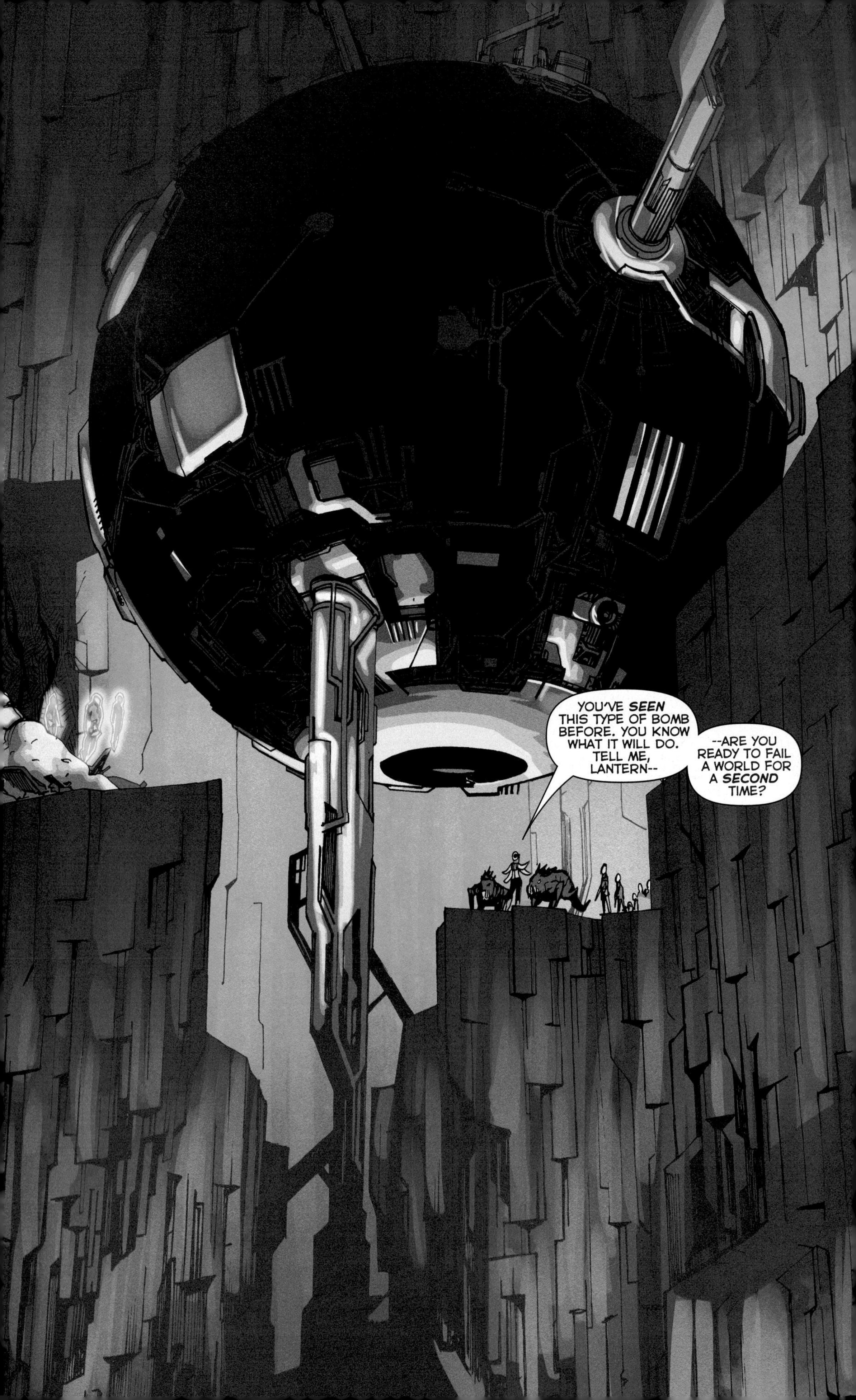
YOU'VE SEEN THIS TYPE OF BOMB BEFORE. YOU KNOW WHAT IT WILL DO. TELL ME, LANTERN--
--ARE YOU READY TO FAIL A WORLD FOR A SECOND TIME?

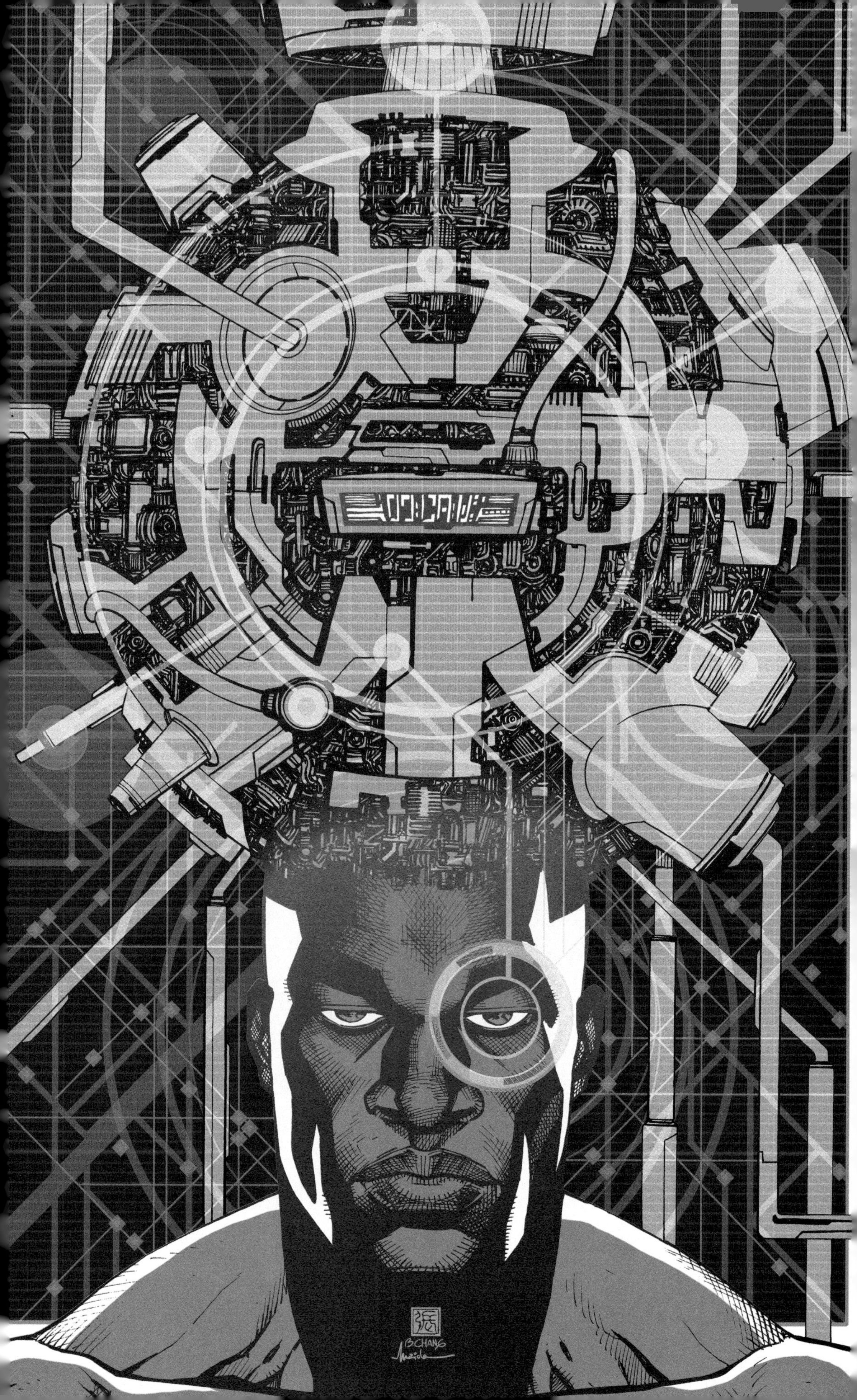
B.CHANG

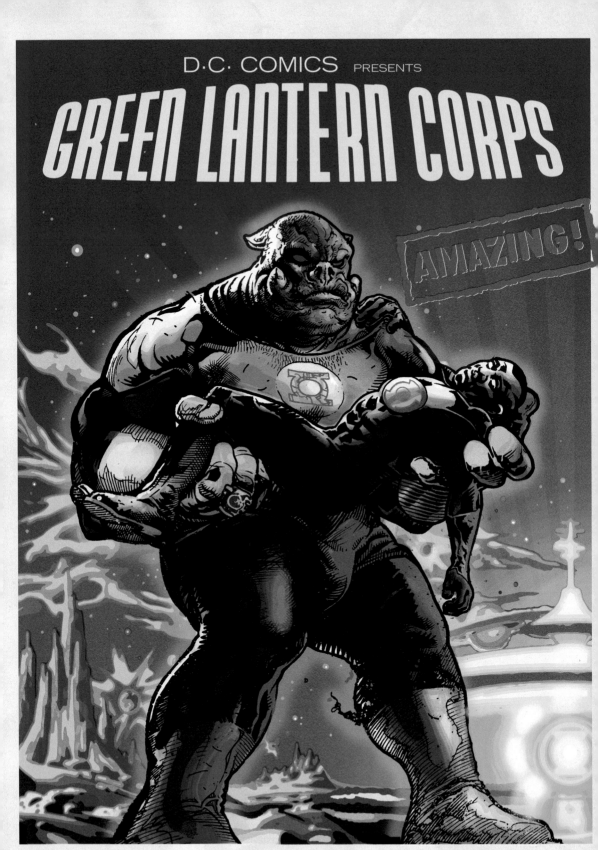

D·C· COMICS PRESENTS

GREEN LANTERN CORPS

AMAZING!

GREEN LANTERN CORPS ISSUE FORTY   VAN JENSEN WRITER   BERNARD CHANG ARTIST   MARCELO MAIOLO COLORIST

DAVE SHARPE LETTERER   JASON PEARSON MOVIE POSTER VARIANT COVER   DARREN SHAN ASSOCIATE EDITOR   MATT IDELSON GROUP EDITOR   BOB HARRAS SENIOR VP — EDITOR-IN-CHIEF, DC COMICS

RATED T TEEN   DAN DIDIO AND JIM LEE CO-PUBLISHERS   GEOFF JOHNS CHIEF CREATIVE OFFICER   DIANE NELSON PRESIDENT   DC COMICS™

MAY 2015

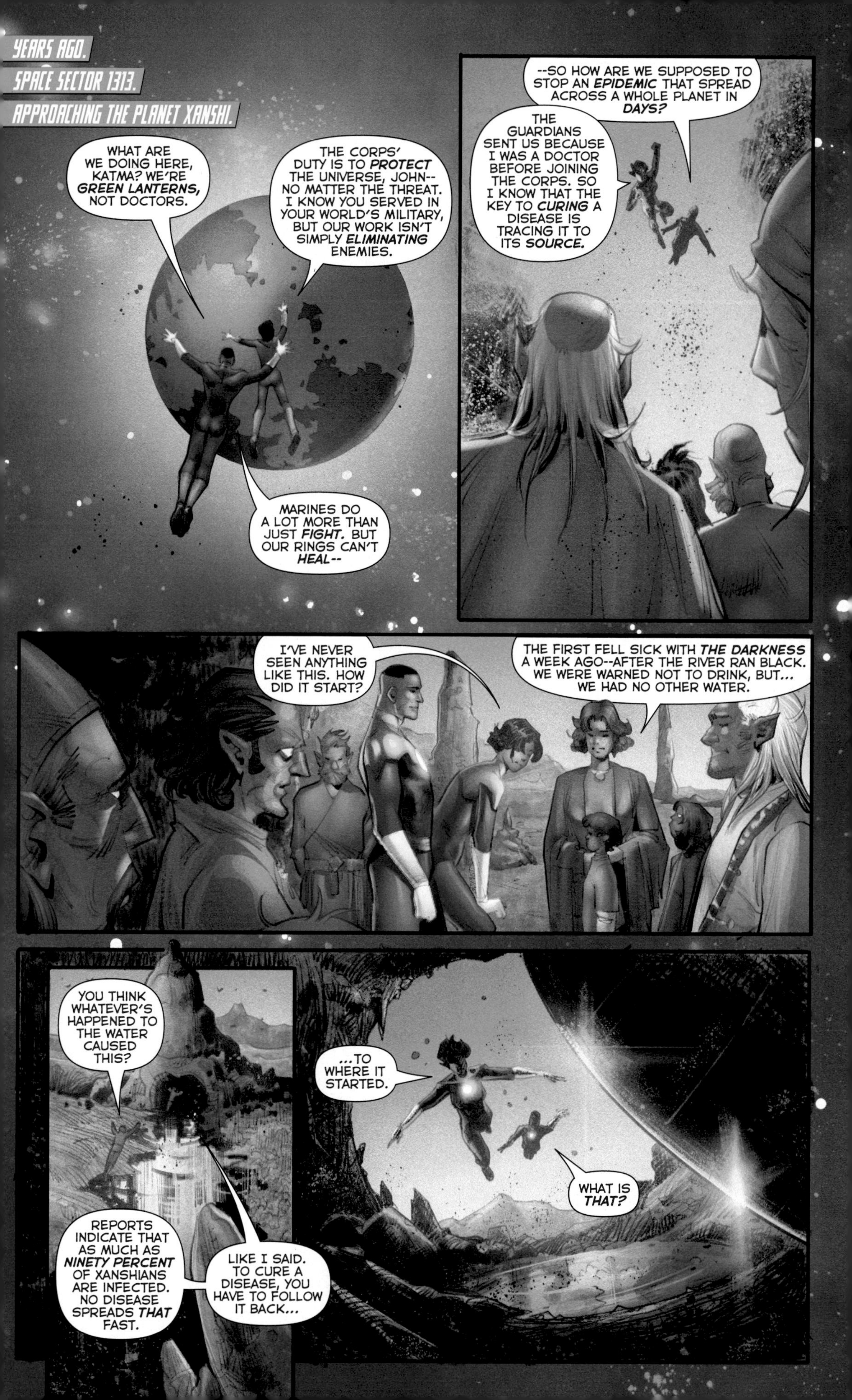
YEARS AGO.
SPACE SECTOR 1313.
APPROACHING THE PLANET XANSHI.
WHAT ARE WE DOING HERE, KATMA? WE'RE GREEN LANTERNS, NOT DOCTORS.
THE CORPS' DUTY IS TO PROTECT THE UNIVERSE, JOHN--NO MATTER THE THREAT. I KNOW YOU SERVED IN YOUR WORLD'S MILITARY, BUT OUR WORK ISN'T SIMPLY ELIMINATING ENEMIES.
MARINES DO A LOT MORE THAN JUST FIGHT. BUT OUR RINGS CAN'T HEAL--
--SO HOW ARE WE SUPPOSED TO STOP AN EPIDEMIC THAT SPREAD ACROSS A WHOLE PLANET IN DAYS?
THE GUARDIANS SENT US BECAUSE I WAS A DOCTOR BEFORE JOINING THE CORPS. SO I KNOW THAT THE KEY TO CURING A DISEASE IS TRACING IT TO ITS SOURCE.
I'VE NEVER SEEN ANYTHING LIKE THIS. HOW DID IT START?
THE FIRST FELL SICK WITH THE DARKNESS A WEEK AGO--AFTER THE RIVER RAN BLACK. WE WERE WARNED NOT TO DRINK, BUT... WE HAD NO OTHER WATER.
YOU THINK WHATEVER'S HAPPENED TO THE WATER CAUSED THIS?
REPORTS INDICATE THAT AS MUCH AS NINETY PERCENT OF XANSHIANS ARE INFECTED. NO DISEASE SPREADS THAT FAST.
LIKE I SAID. TO CURE A DISEASE, YOU HAVE TO FOLLOW IT BACK...
...TO WHERE IT STARTED.
WHAT IS THAT?

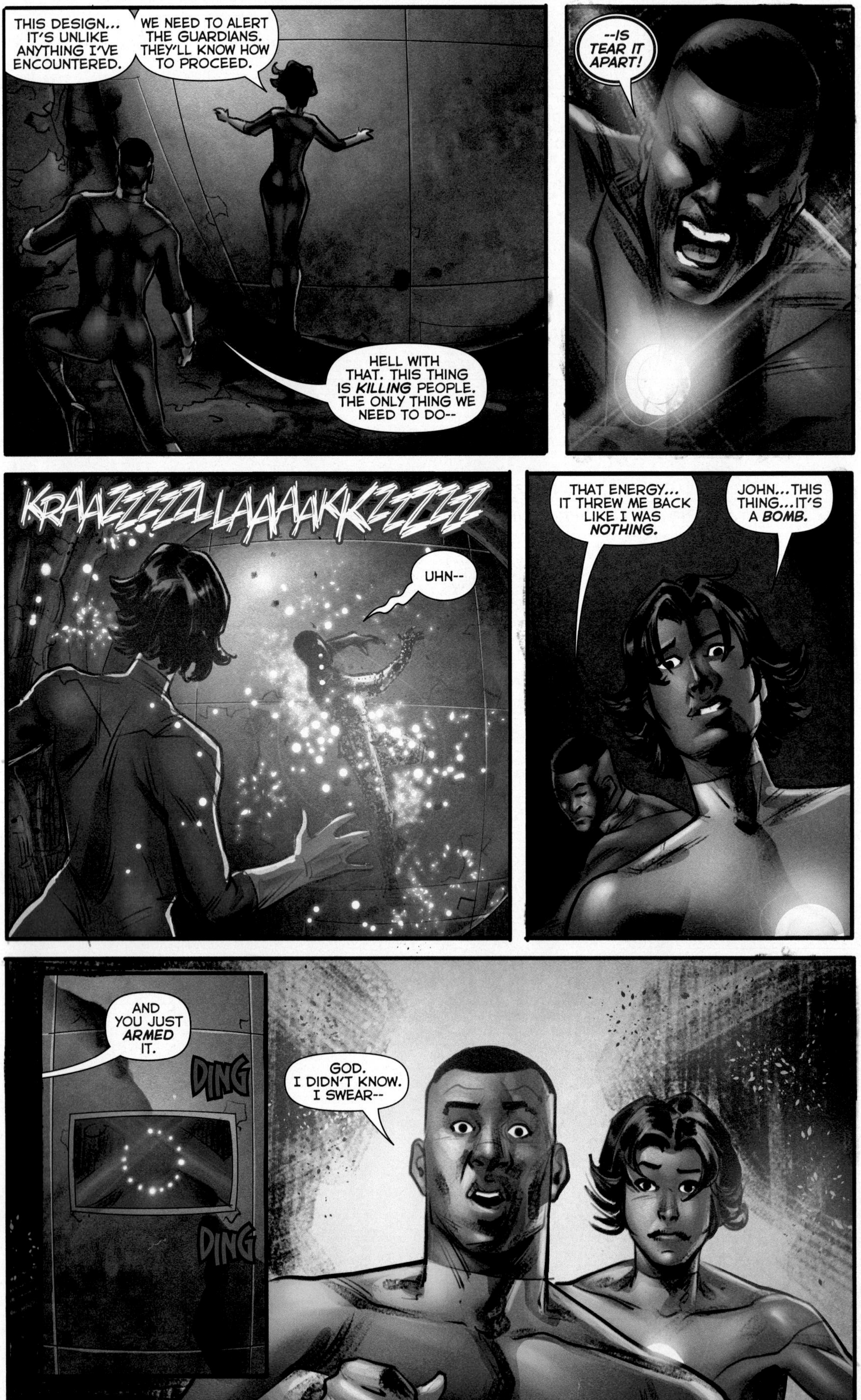

THIS DESIGN... IT'S UNLIKE ANYTHING I'VE ENCOUNTERED.
WE NEED TO ALERT THE GUARDIANS. THEY'LL KNOW HOW TO PROCEED.
HELL WITH THAT. THIS THING IS *KILLING* PEOPLE. THE ONLY THING WE NEED TO DO--
--IS *TEAR IT APART!*
KRAAZZZZZLAAAAKKZZZZZZ
UHN--
THAT ENERGY... IT THREW ME BACK LIKE I WAS *NOTHING.*
JOHN...THIS THING...IT'S A *BOMB.*
AND YOU JUST *ARMED* IT.
DING
DING
GOD. I DIDN'T KNOW. I SWEAR--

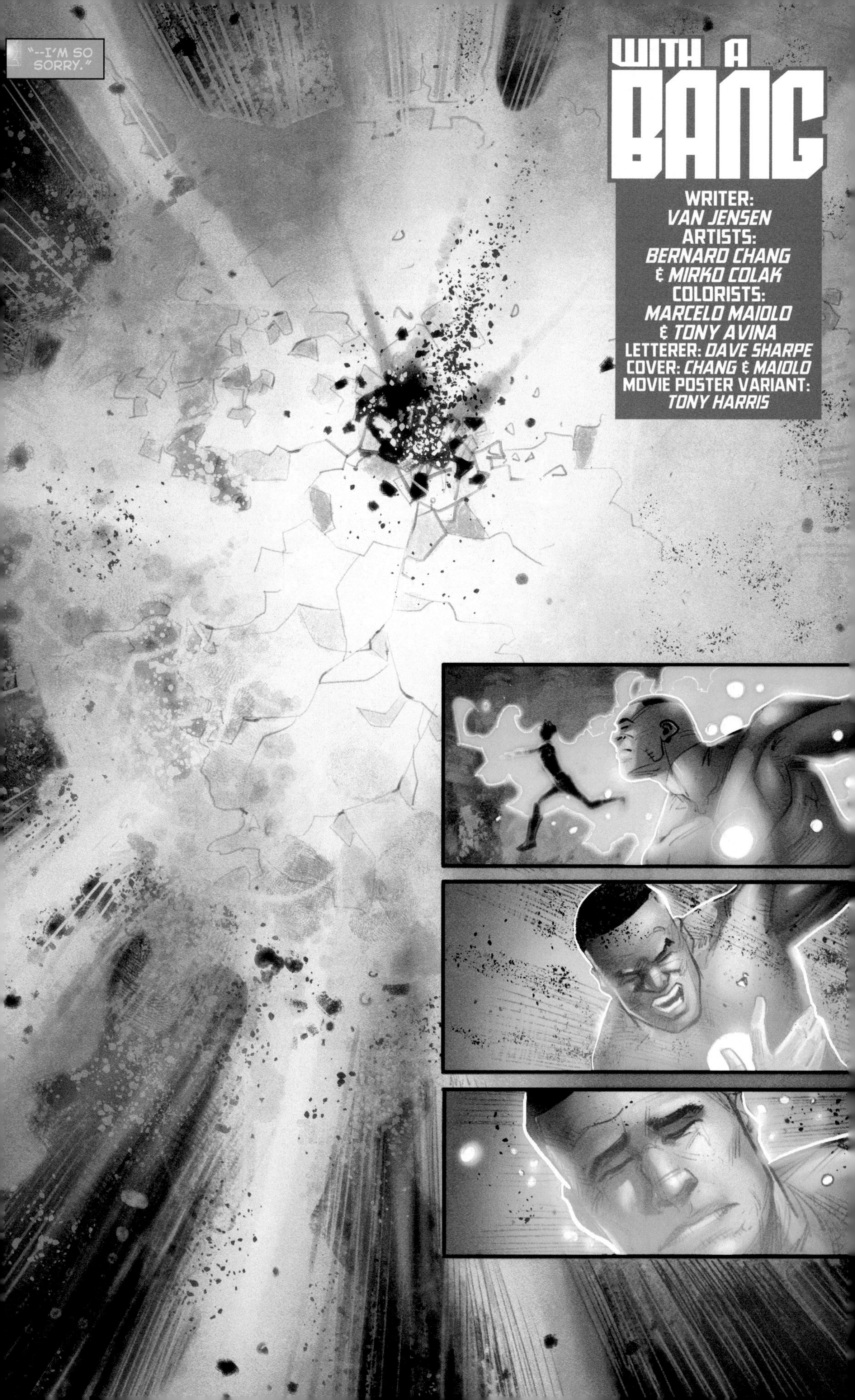
"--I'M SO SORRY."
WITH A BANG
WRITER: VAN JENSEN
ARTISTS: BERNARD CHANG & MIRKO COLAK
COLORISTS: MARCELO MAIOLO & TONY AVINA
LETTERER: DAVE SHARPE
COVER: CHANG & MAIOLO
MOVIE POSTER VARIANT: TONY HARRIS

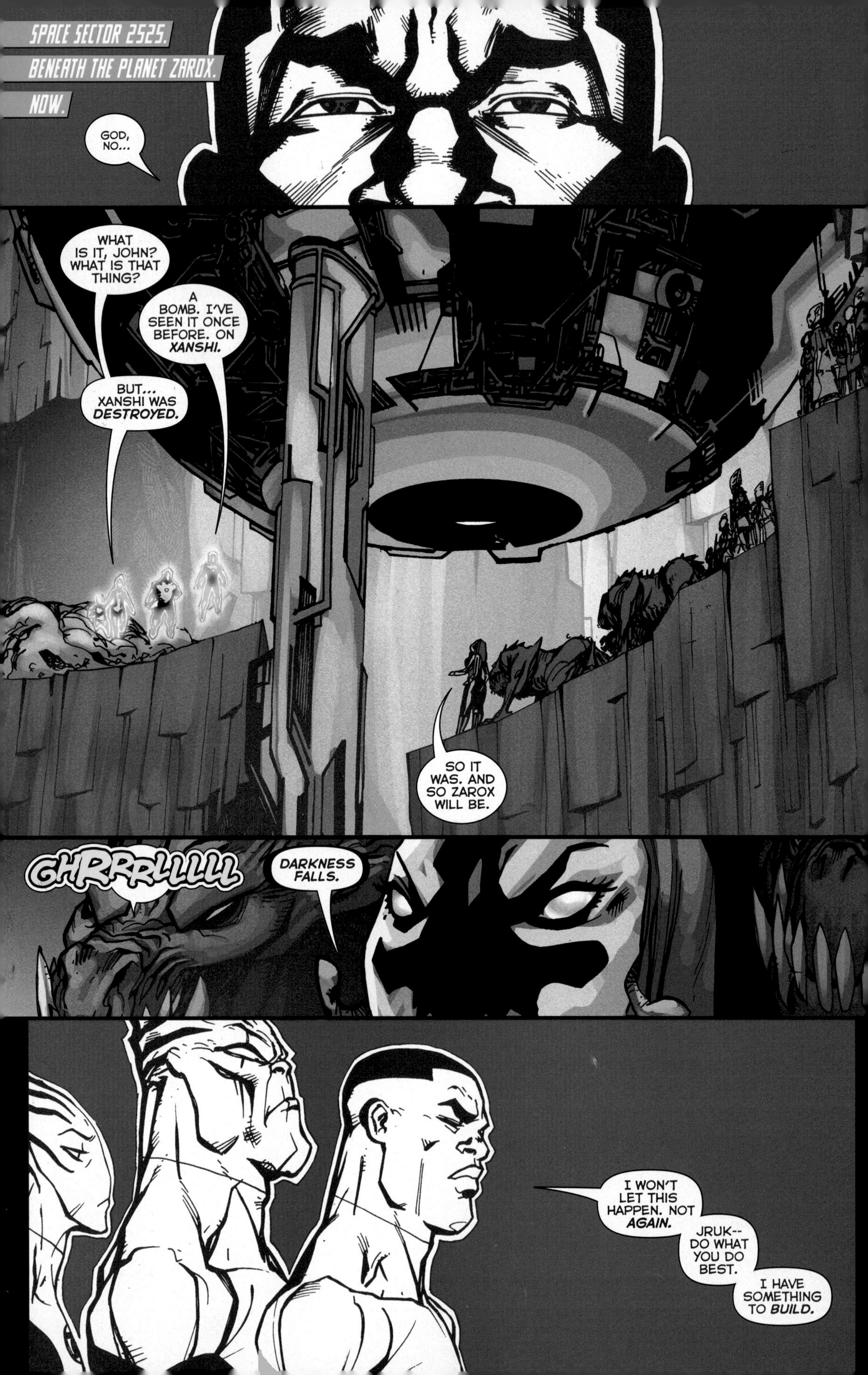
SPACE SECTOR 2525.
BENEATH THE PLANET ZAROX.
NOW.
GOD, NO...
WHAT IS IT, JOHN? WHAT IS THAT THING?
A BOMB. I'VE SEEN IT ONCE BEFORE. ON XANSHI.
BUT... XANSHI WAS DESTROYED.
SO IT WAS. AND SO ZAROX WILL BE.
GHRRRLLLLL
DARKNESS FALLS.
I WON'T LET THIS HAPPEN. NOT AGAIN.
JRUK-- DO WHAT YOU DO BEST.
I HAVE SOMETHING TO BUILD.

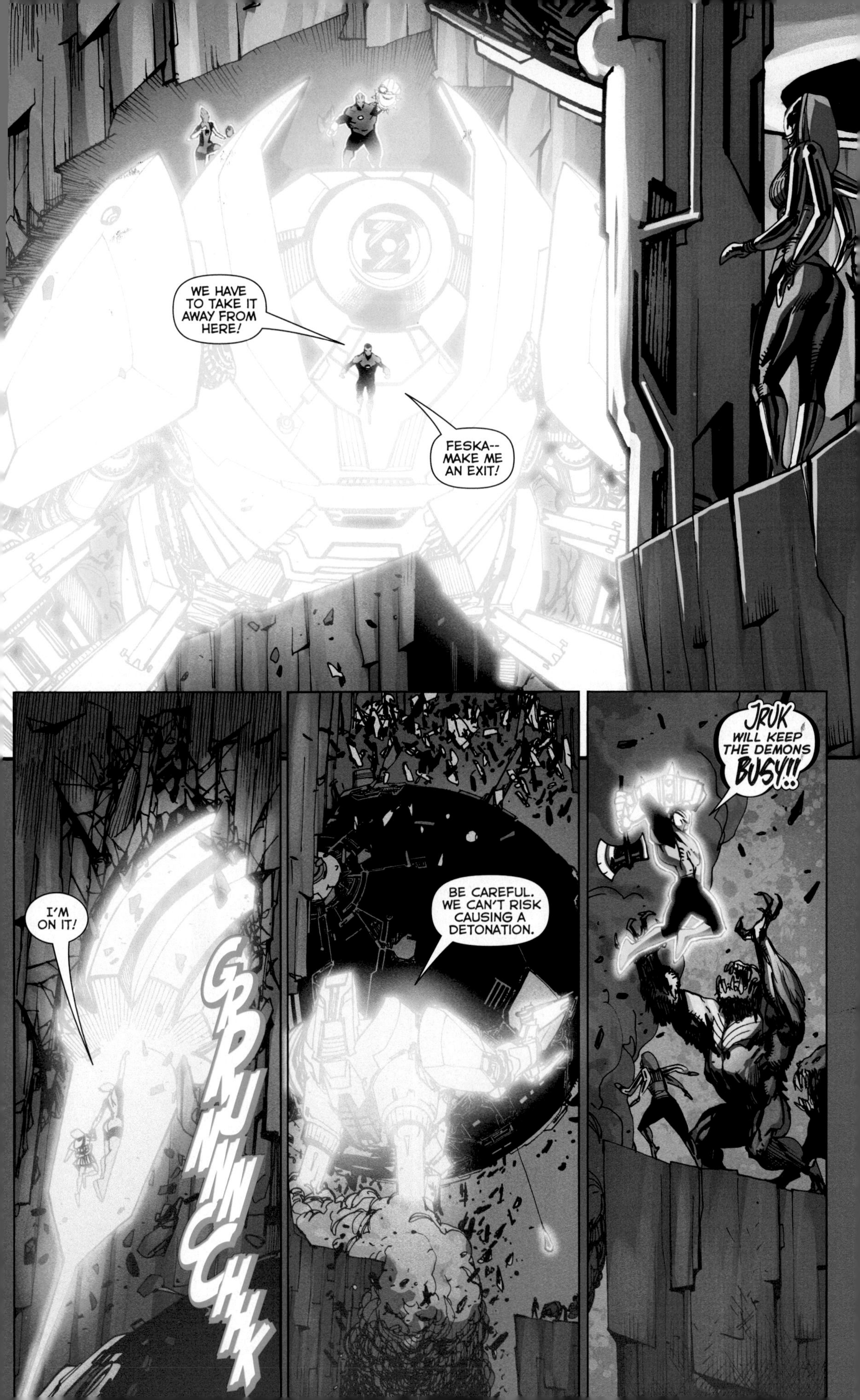
WE HAVE TO TAKE IT AWAY FROM HERE!
FESKA-- MAKE ME AN EXIT!
I'M ON IT!
GRUNNNCHHK
BE CAREFUL. WE CAN'T RISK CAUSING A DETONATION.
JRUK WILL KEEP THE DEMONS BUSY!!

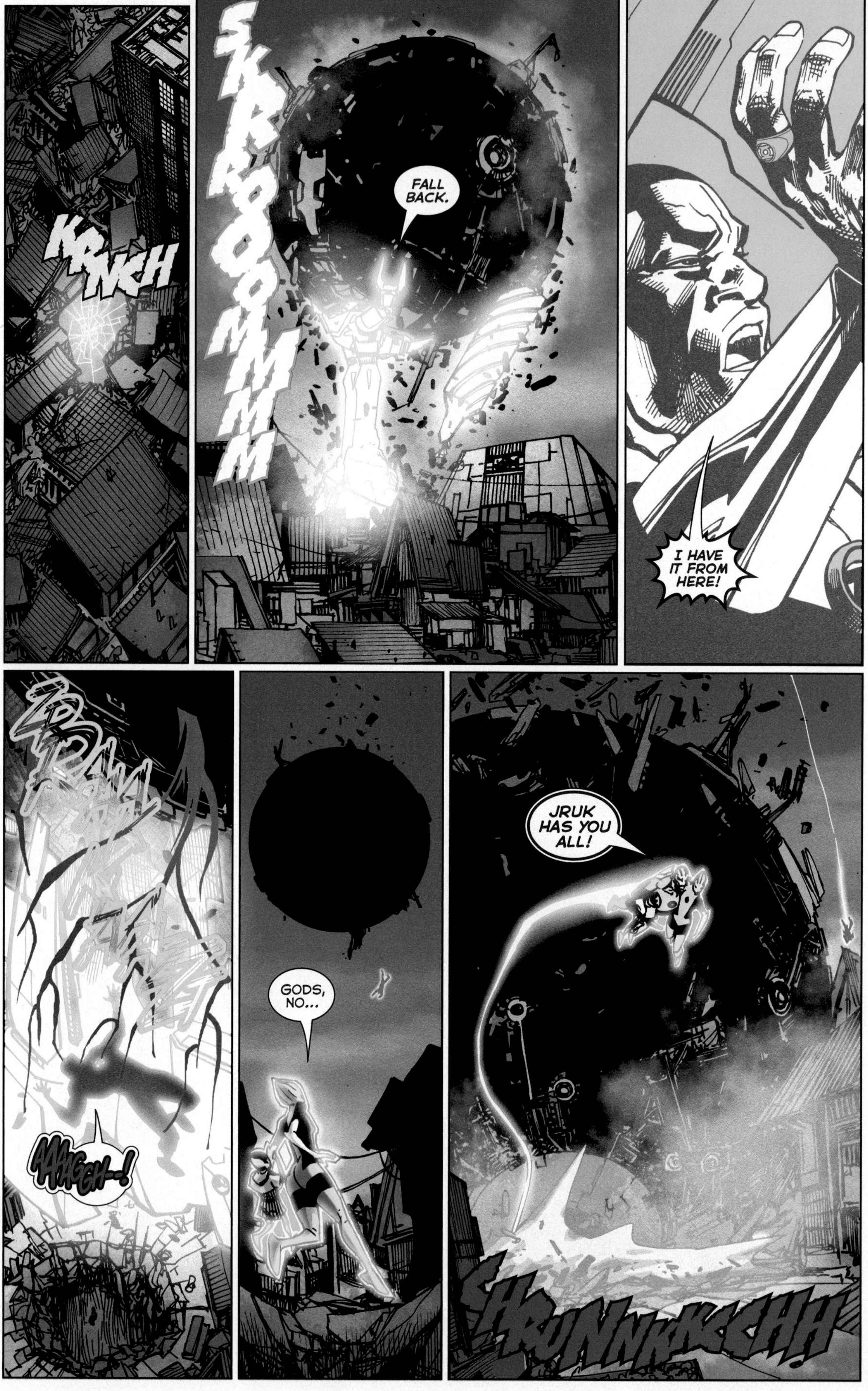
KRNCH
SKROOMMM
FALL BACK.
I HAVE IT FROM HERE!
AAAAGGH--!
GODS, NO...
JRUK HAS YOU ALL!
SHRUNNKKCHH

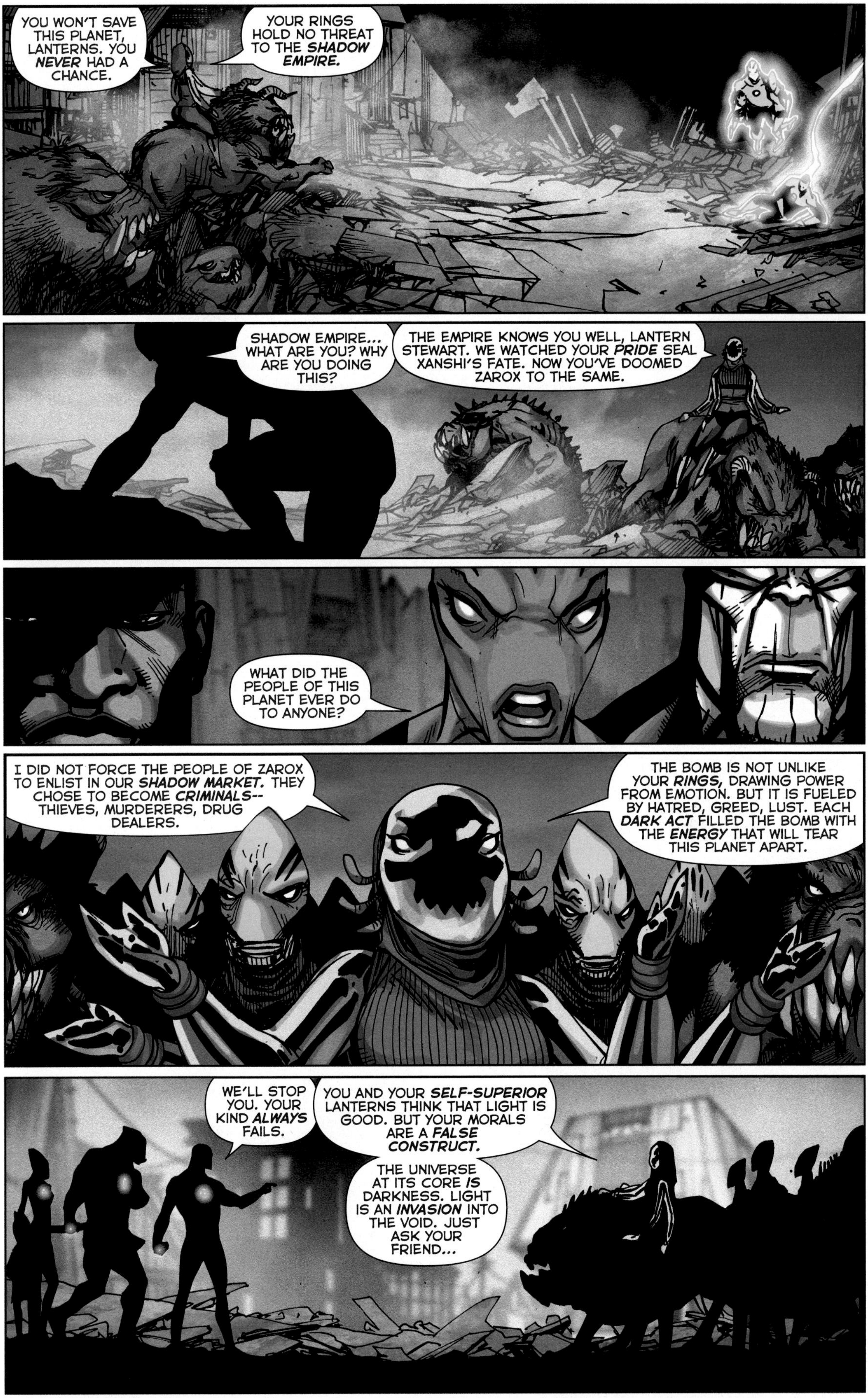
YOU WON'T SAVE THIS PLANET, LANTERNS. YOU NEVER HAD A CHANCE.
YOUR RINGS HOLD NO THREAT TO THE SHADOW EMPIRE.
SHADOW EMPIRE... WHAT ARE YOU? WHY ARE YOU DOING THIS?
THE EMPIRE KNOWS YOU WELL, LANTERN STEWART. WE WATCHED YOUR PRIDE SEAL XANSHI'S FATE. NOW YOU'VE DOOMED ZAROX TO THE SAME.
WHAT DID THE PEOPLE OF THIS PLANET EVER DO TO ANYONE?
I DID NOT FORCE THE PEOPLE OF ZAROX TO ENLIST IN OUR SHADOW MARKET. THEY CHOSE TO BECOME CRIMINALS-- THIEVES, MURDERERS, DRUG DEALERS.
THE BOMB IS NOT UNLIKE YOUR RINGS, DRAWING POWER FROM EMOTION. BUT IT IS FUELED BY HATRED, GREED, LUST. EACH DARK ACT FILLED THE BOMB WITH THE ENERGY THAT WILL TEAR THIS PLANET APART.
WE'LL STOP YOU. YOUR KIND ALWAYS FAILS.
YOU AND YOUR SELF-SUPERIOR LANTERNS THINK THAT LIGHT IS GOOD. BUT YOUR MORALS ARE A FALSE CONSTRUCT.
THE UNIVERSE AT ITS CORE IS DARKNESS. LIGHT IS AN INVASION INTO THE VOID. JUST ASK YOUR FRIEND...

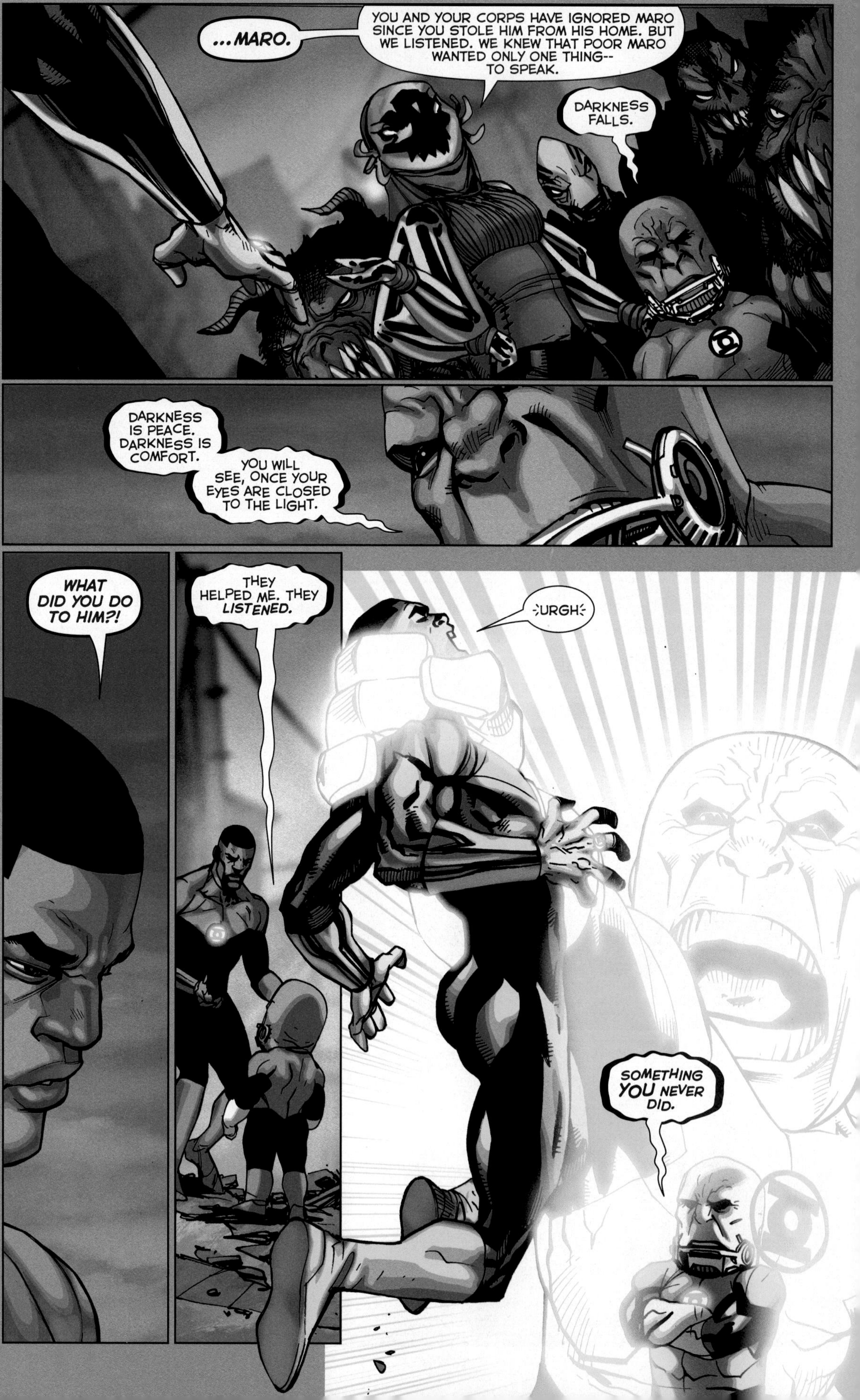
...MARO.
YOU AND YOUR CORPS HAVE IGNORED MARO SINCE YOU STOLE HIM FROM HIS HOME. BUT WE LISTENED. WE KNEW THAT POOR MARO WANTED ONLY ONE THING-- TO SPEAK.
DARKNESS FALLS.
DARKNESS IS PEACE. DARKNESS IS COMFORT.
YOU WILL SEE, ONCE YOUR EYES ARE CLOSED TO THE LIGHT.
WHAT DID YOU DO TO HIM?!
THEY HELPED ME. THEY LISTENED.
URGH
SOMETHING YOU NEVER DID.

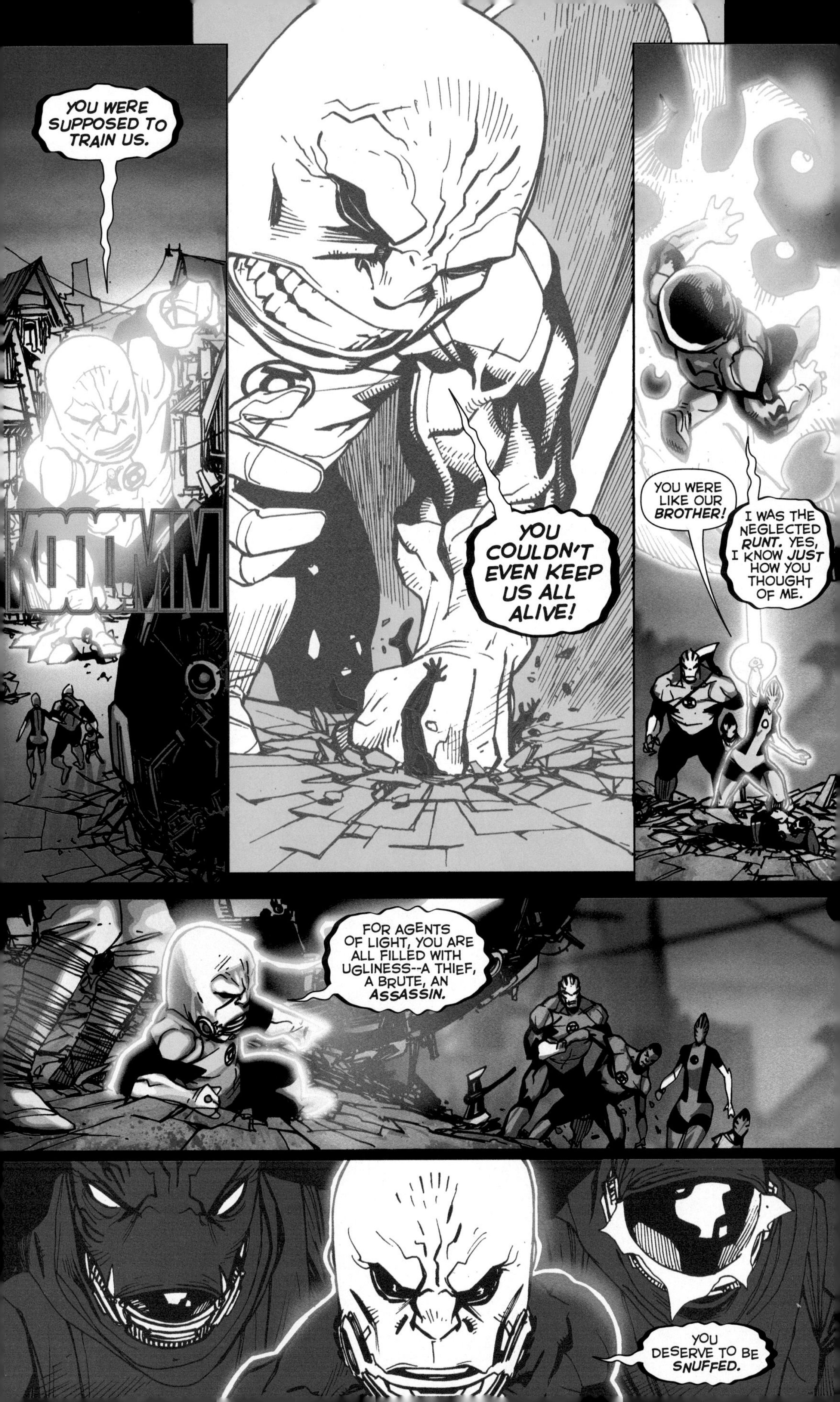
YOU WERE SUPPOSED TO TRAIN US.
KROOMM
YOU COULDN'T EVEN KEEP US ALL ALIVE!
YOU WERE LIKE OUR BROTHER!
I WAS THE NEGLECTED RUNT. YES, I KNOW JUST HOW YOU THOUGHT OF ME.
FOR AGENTS OF LIGHT, YOU ARE ALL FILLED WITH UGLINESS--A THIEF, A BRUTE, AN ASSASSIN.
YOU DESERVE TO BE SNUFFED.

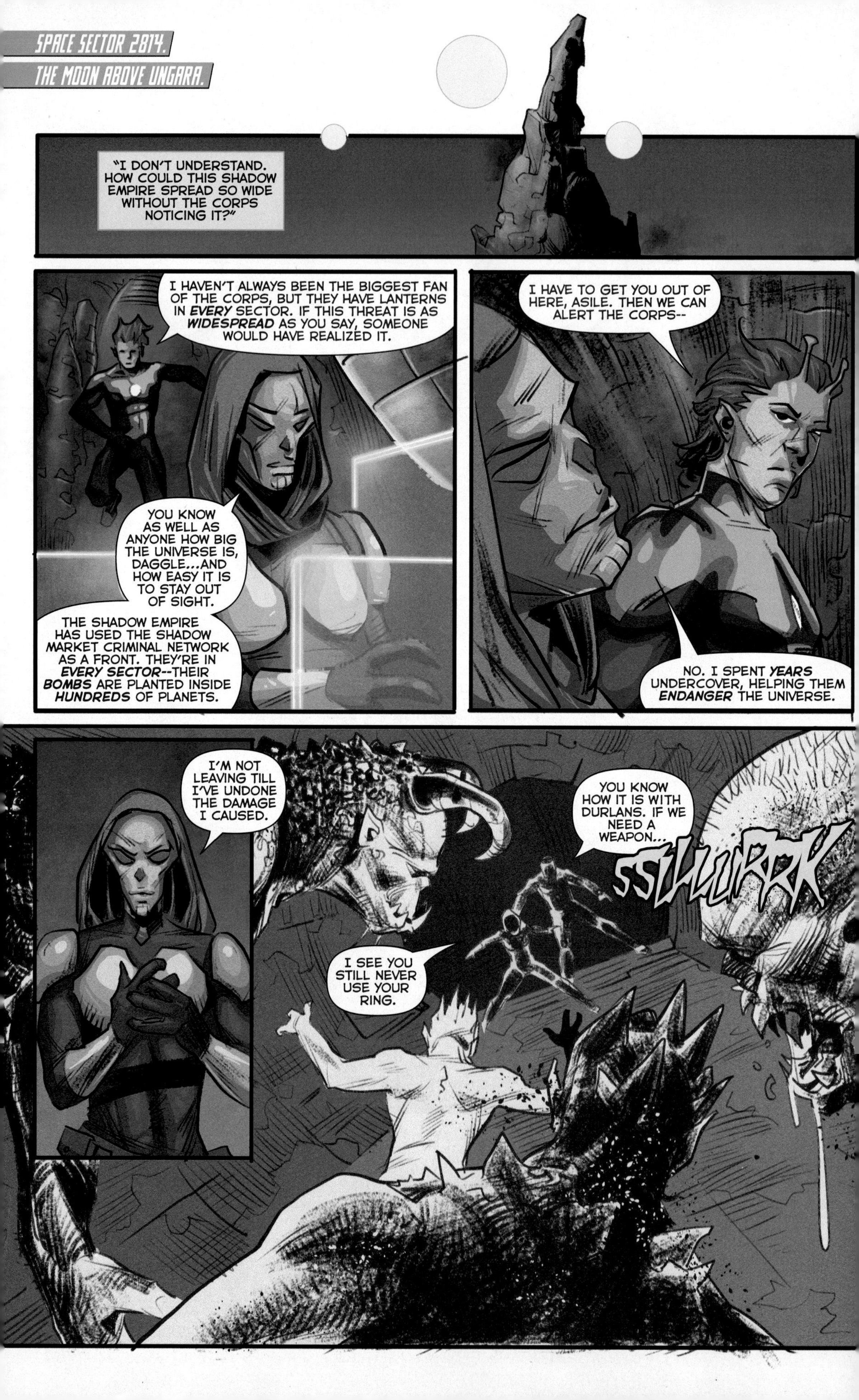
SPACE SECTOR 2814.
THE MOON ABOVE UNGARA.
"I DON'T UNDERSTAND. HOW COULD THIS SHADOW EMPIRE SPREAD SO WIDE WITHOUT THE CORPS NOTICING IT?"
I HAVEN'T ALWAYS BEEN THE BIGGEST FAN OF THE CORPS, BUT THEY HAVE LANTERNS IN EVERY SECTOR. IF THIS THREAT IS AS WIDESPREAD AS YOU SAY, SOMEONE WOULD HAVE REALIZED IT.
YOU KNOW AS WELL AS ANYONE HOW BIG THE UNIVERSE IS, DAGGLE...AND HOW EASY IT IS TO STAY OUT OF SIGHT.
THE SHADOW EMPIRE HAS USED THE SHADOW MARKET CRIMINAL NETWORK AS A FRONT. THEY'RE IN EVERY SECTOR--THEIR BOMBS ARE PLANTED INSIDE HUNDREDS OF PLANETS.
I HAVE TO GET YOU OUT OF HERE, ASILE. THEN WE CAN ALERT THE CORPS--
NO. I SPENT YEARS UNDERCOVER, HELPING THEM ENDANGER THE UNIVERSE.
I'M NOT LEAVING TILL I'VE UNDONE THE DAMAGE I CAUSED.
YOU KNOW HOW IT IS WITH DURLANS. IF WE NEED A WEAPON...
SSLLLURRK
I SEE YOU STILL NEVER USE YOUR RING.

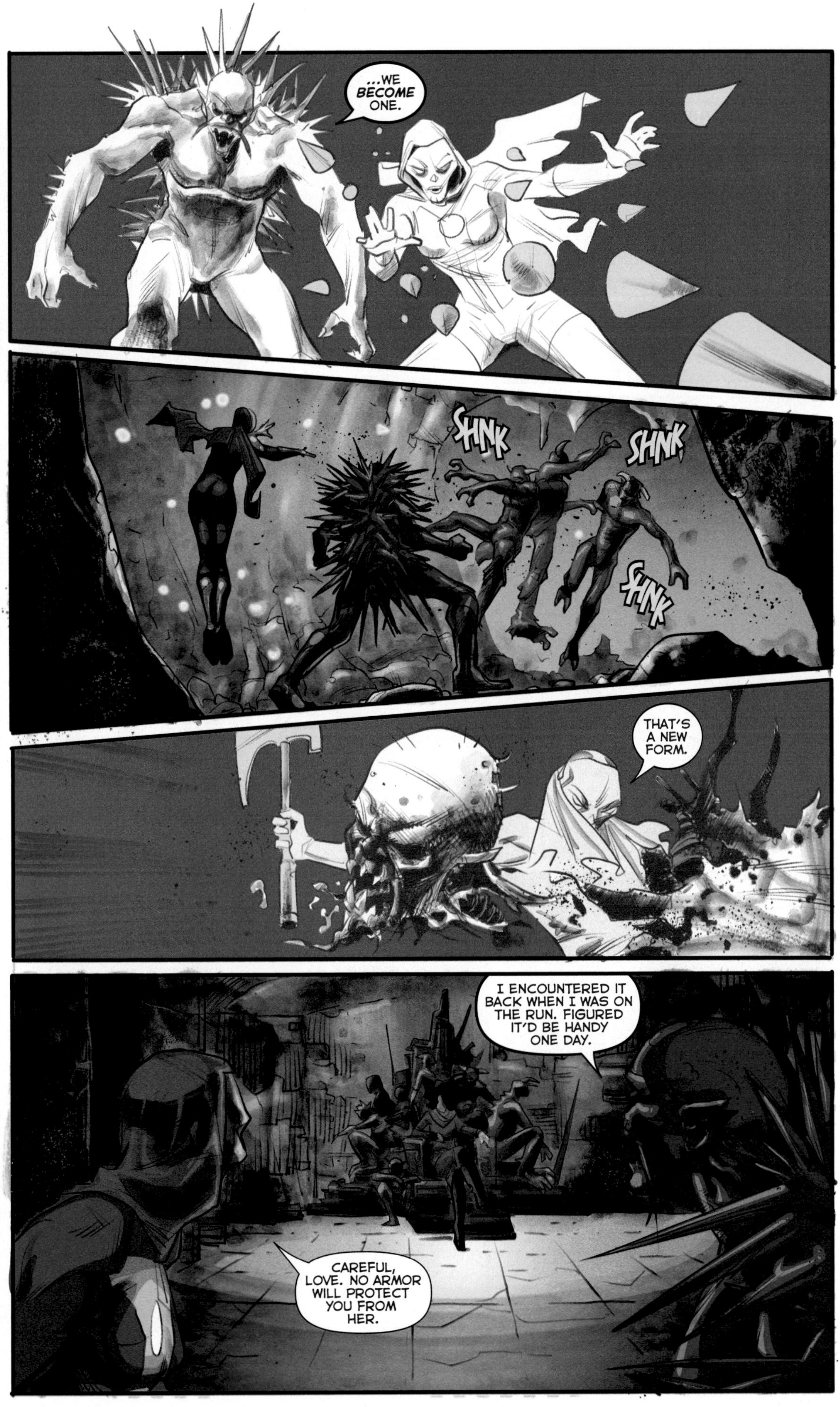
...WE BECOME ONE.
SHNK
SHNK
SHNK
THAT'S A NEW FORM.
I ENCOUNTERED IT BACK WHEN I WAS ON THE RUN. FIGURED IT'D BE HANDY ONE DAY.
CAREFUL, LOVE. NO ARMOR WILL PROTECT YOU FROM HER.

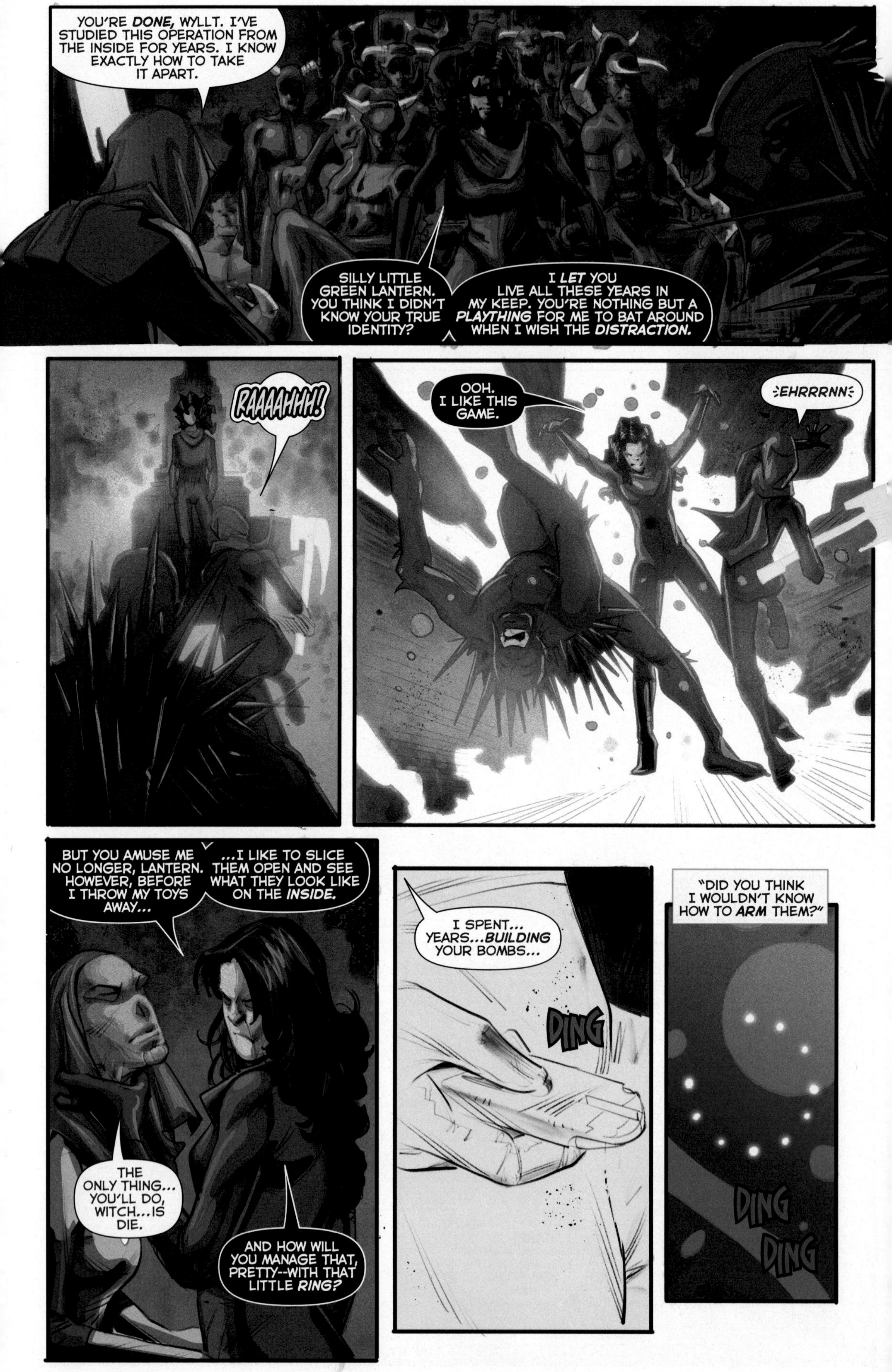
YOU'RE DONE, WYLLT. I'VE STUDIED THIS OPERATION FROM THE INSIDE FOR YEARS. I KNOW EXACTLY HOW TO TAKE IT APART.
SILLY LITTLE GREEN LANTERN. YOU THINK I DIDN'T KNOW YOUR TRUE IDENTITY?
I LET YOU LIVE ALL THESE YEARS IN MY KEEP. YOU'RE NOTHING BUT A PLAYTHING FOR ME TO BAT AROUND WHEN I WISH THE DISTRACTION.
RAAAAHHH!
OOH. I LIKE THIS GAME.
EHRRRNN
BUT YOU AMUSE ME NO LONGER, LANTERN. HOWEVER, BEFORE I THROW MY TOYS AWAY...
...I LIKE TO SLICE THEM OPEN AND SEE WHAT THEY LOOK LIKE ON THE INSIDE.
THE ONLY THING... YOU'LL DO, WITCH...IS DIE.
AND HOW WILL YOU MANAGE THAT, PRETTY--WITH THAT LITTLE RING?
I SPENT... YEARS...BUILDING YOUR BOMBS...
DING
"DID YOU THINK I WOULDN'T KNOW HOW TO ARM THEM?"
DING
DING

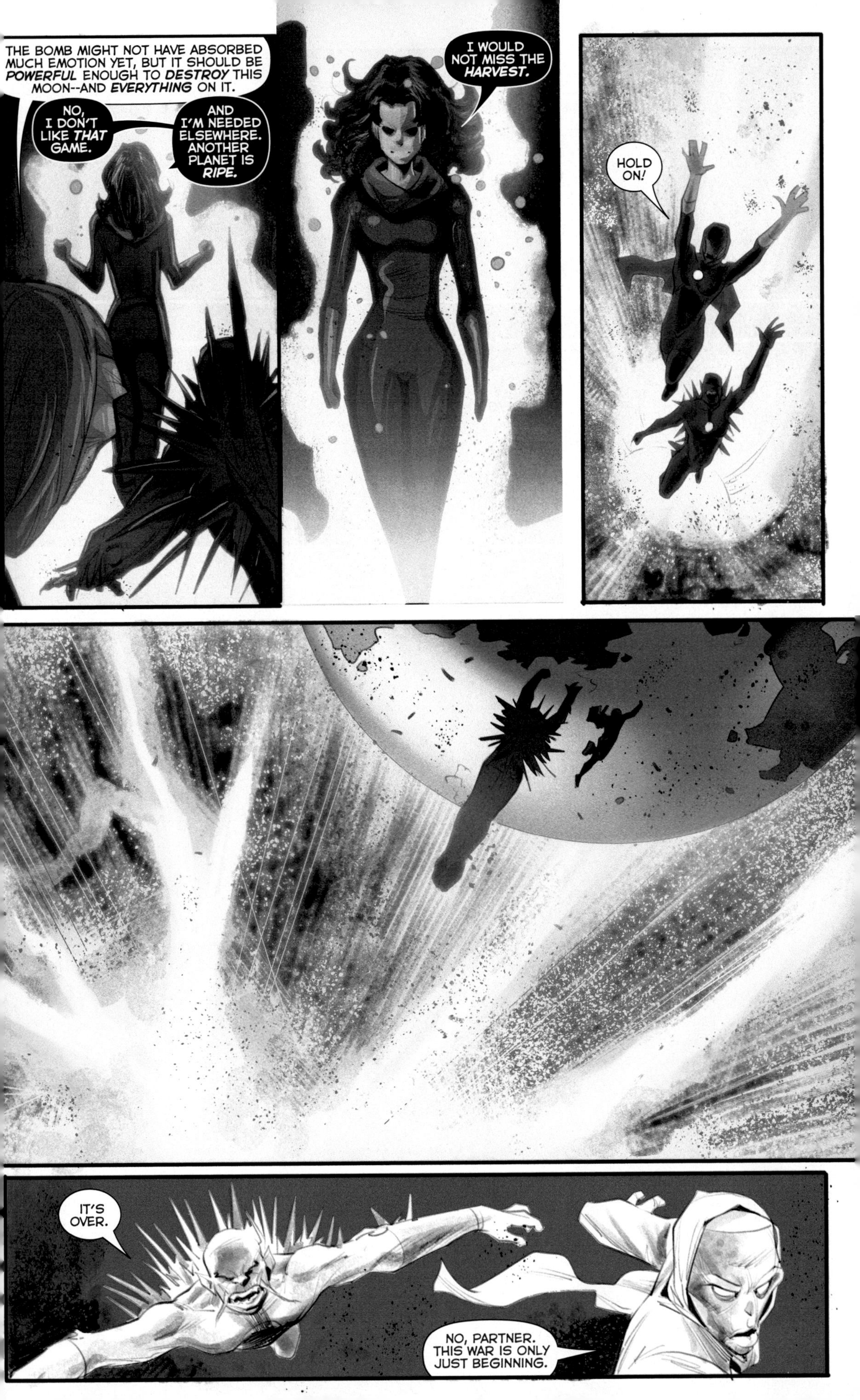
THE BOMB MIGHT NOT HAVE ABSORBED MUCH EMOTION YET, BUT IT SHOULD BE POWERFUL ENOUGH TO DESTROY THIS MOON--AND EVERYTHING ON IT.
NO, I DON'T LIKE THAT GAME.
AND I'M NEEDED ELSEWHERE. ANOTHER PLANET IS RIPE.
I WOULD NOT MISS THE HARVEST.
HOLD ON!
IT'S OVER.
NO, PARTNER. THIS WAR IS ONLY JUST BEGINNING.

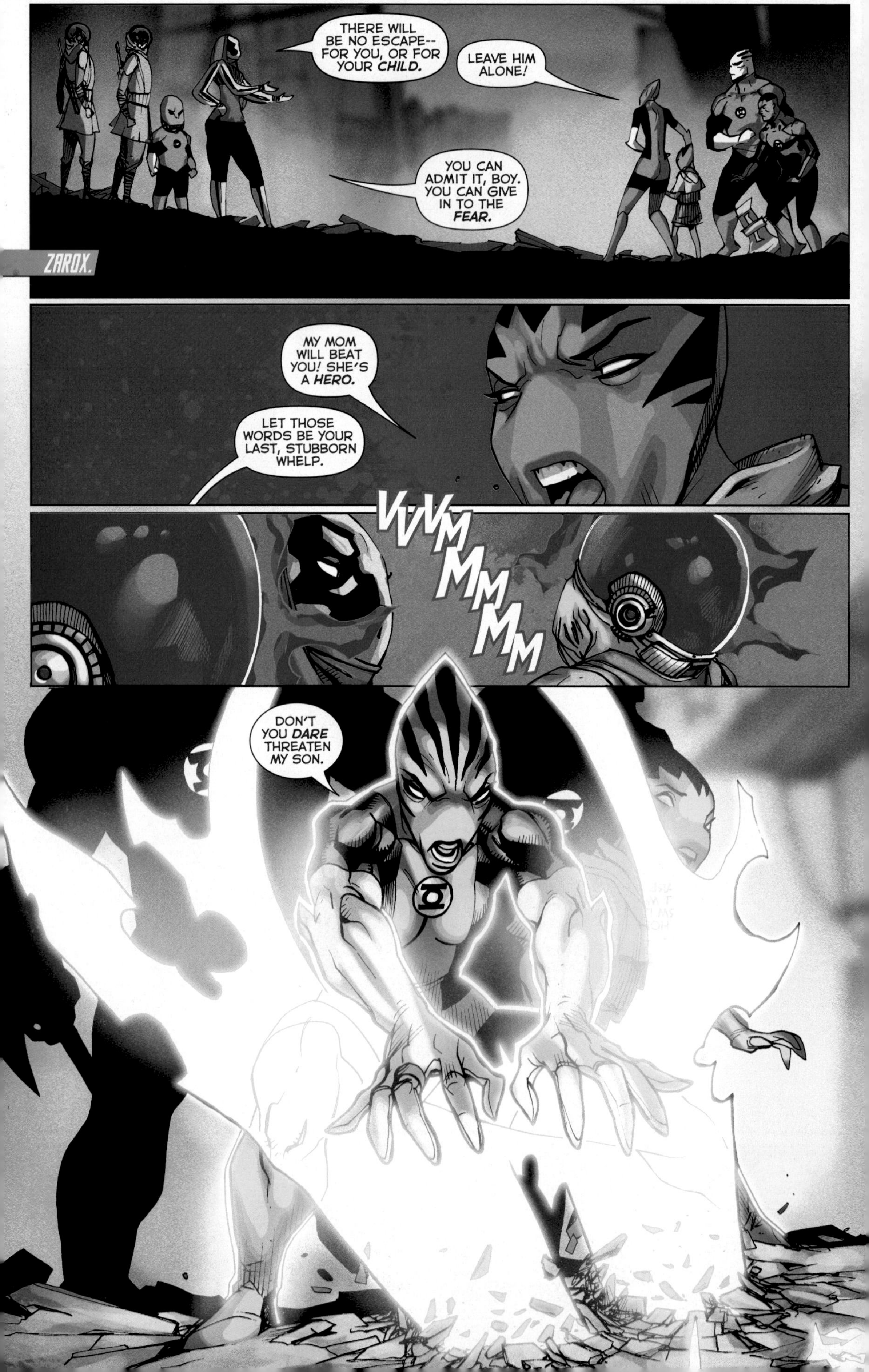
THERE WILL BE NO ESCAPE-- FOR YOU, OR FOR YOUR CHILD.
LEAVE HIM ALONE!
YOU CAN ADMIT IT, BOY. YOU CAN GIVE IN TO THE FEAR.
ZAROX.
MY MOM WILL BEAT YOU! SHE'S A HERO.
LET THOSE WORDS BE YOUR LAST, STUBBORN WHELP.
VVVMMMMMM
DON'T YOU DARE THREATEN MY SON.

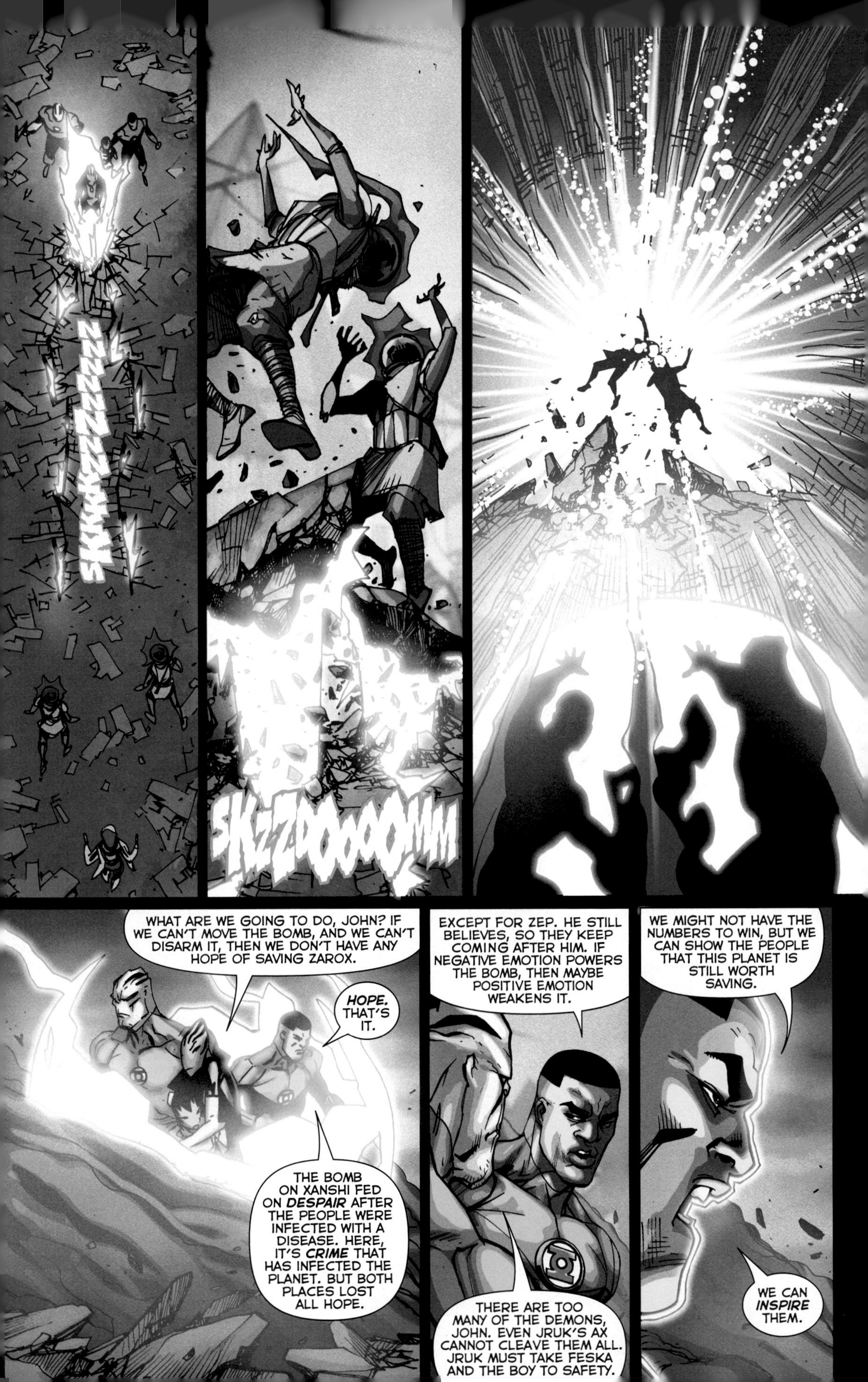
SKKKZZZZZZZZZ
SKZZDOOOOMM
WHAT ARE WE GOING TO DO, JOHN? IF WE CAN'T MOVE THE BOMB, AND WE CAN'T DISARM IT, THEN WE DON'T HAVE ANY HOPE OF SAVING ZAROX.
HOPE. THAT'S IT.
THE BOMB ON XANSHI FED ON DESPAIR AFTER THE PEOPLE WERE INFECTED WITH A DISEASE. HERE, IT'S CRIME THAT HAS INFECTED THE PLANET. BUT BOTH PLACES LOST ALL HOPE.
EXCEPT FOR ZEP. HE STILL BELIEVES, SO THEY KEEP COMING AFTER HIM. IF NEGATIVE EMOTION POWERS THE BOMB, THEN MAYBE POSITIVE EMOTION WEAKENS IT.
THERE ARE TOO MANY OF THE DEMONS, JOHN. EVEN JRUK'S AX CANNOT CLEAVE THEM ALL. JRUK MUST TAKE FESKA AND THE BOY TO SAFETY.
WE MIGHT NOT HAVE THE NUMBERS TO WIN, BUT WE CAN SHOW THE PEOPLE THAT THIS PLANET IS STILL WORTH SAVING.
WE CAN INSPIRE THEM.

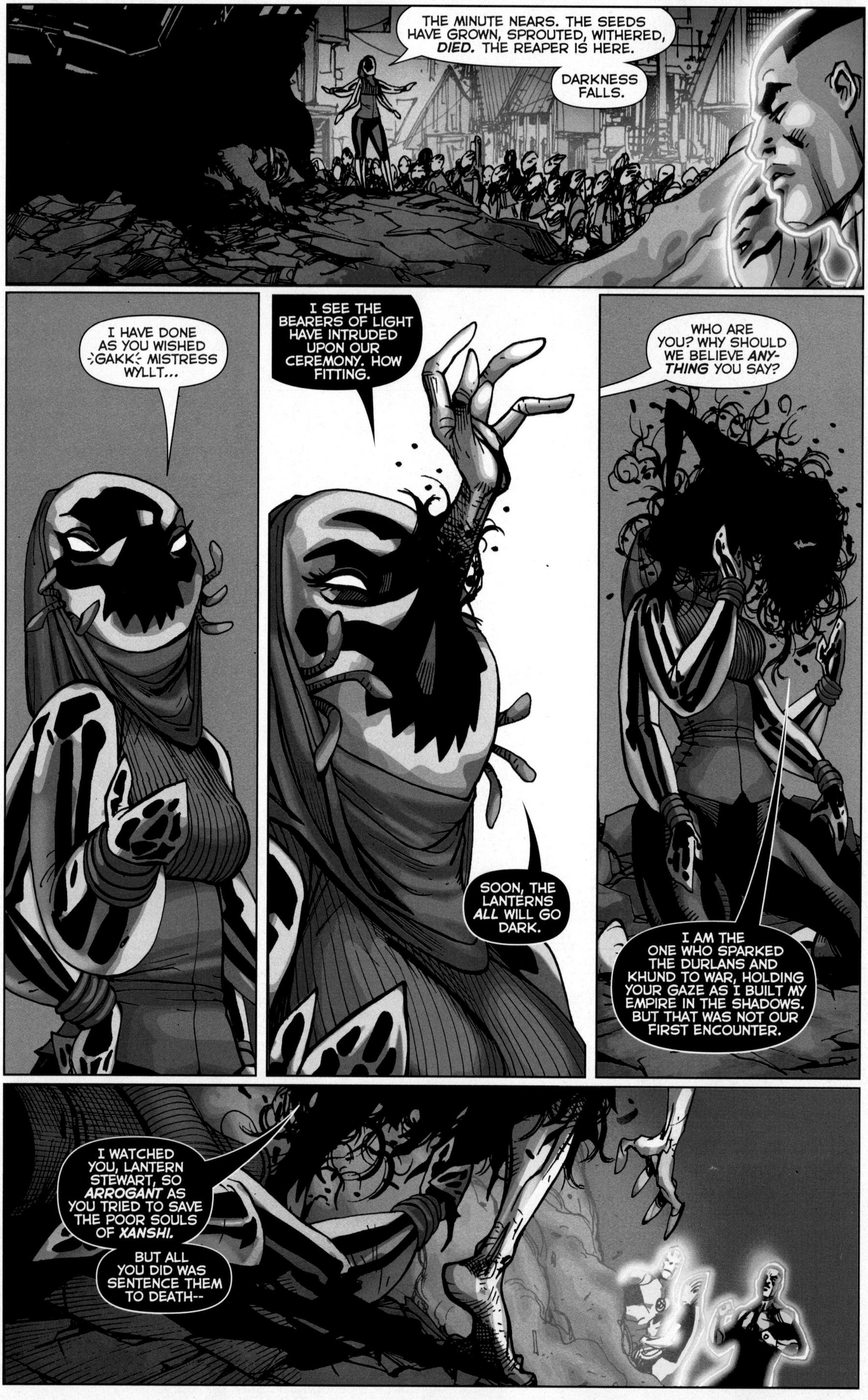
THE MINUTE NEARS. THE SEEDS HAVE GROWN, SPROUTED, WITHERED, *DIED.* THE REAPER IS HERE.
DARKNESS FALLS.
I HAVE DONE AS YOU WISHED -GAKK- MISTRESS WYLLT...
I SEE THE BEARERS OF LIGHT HAVE INTRUDED UPON OUR CEREMONY. HOW FITTING.
SOON, THE LANTERNS *ALL* WILL GO DARK.
WHO ARE YOU? WHY SHOULD WE BELIEVE *ANYTHING* YOU SAY?
I AM THE ONE WHO SPARKED THE DURLANS AND KHUND TO WAR, HOLDING YOUR GAZE AS I BUILT MY EMPIRE IN THE SHADOWS. BUT THAT WAS NOT OUR FIRST ENCOUNTER.
I WATCHED YOU, LANTERN STEWART, SO *ARROGANT* AS YOU TRIED TO SAVE THE POOR SOULS OF *XANSHI.*
BUT ALL YOU DID WAS SENTENCE THEM TO DEATH--

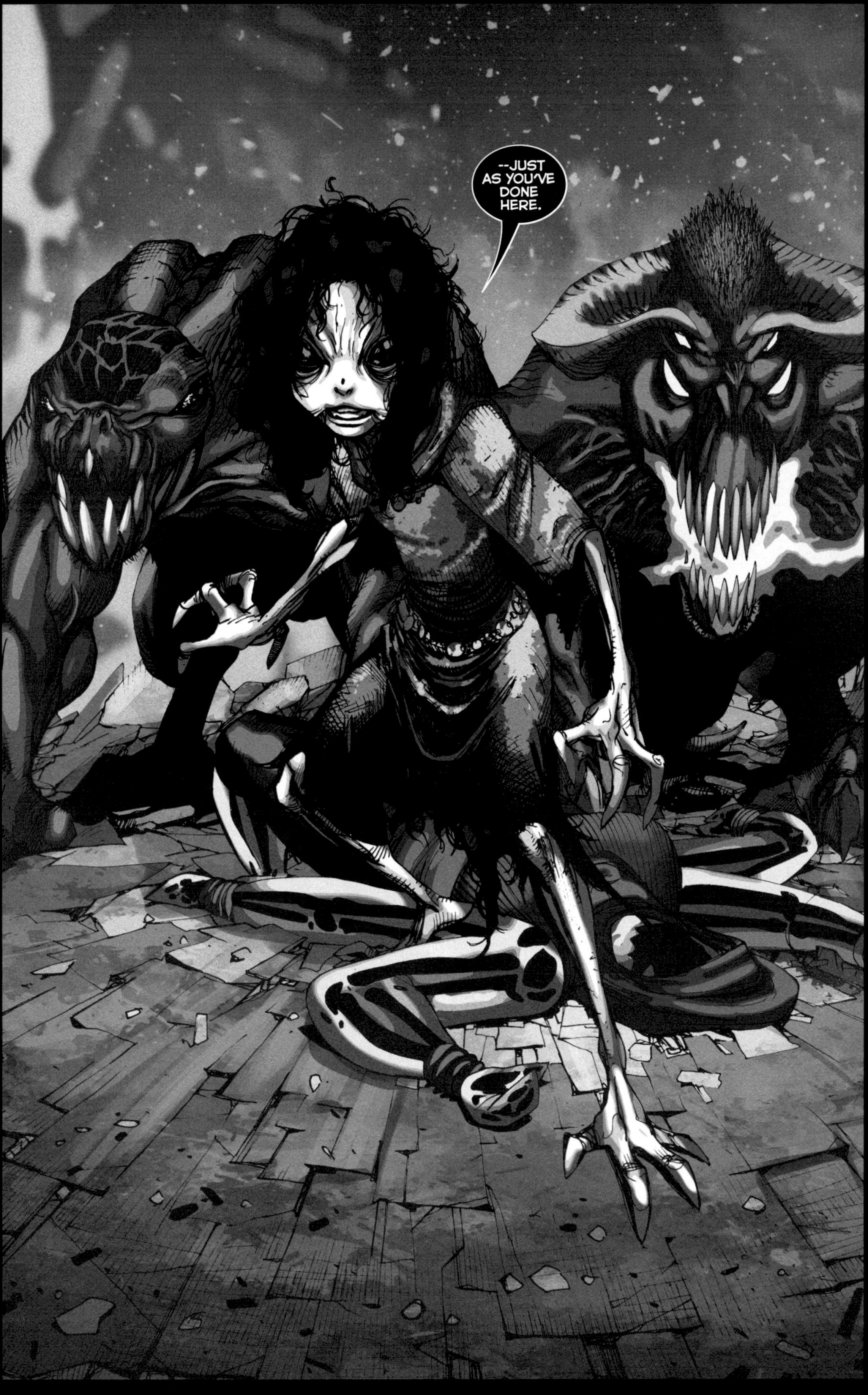
--JUST AS YOU'VE DONE HERE.

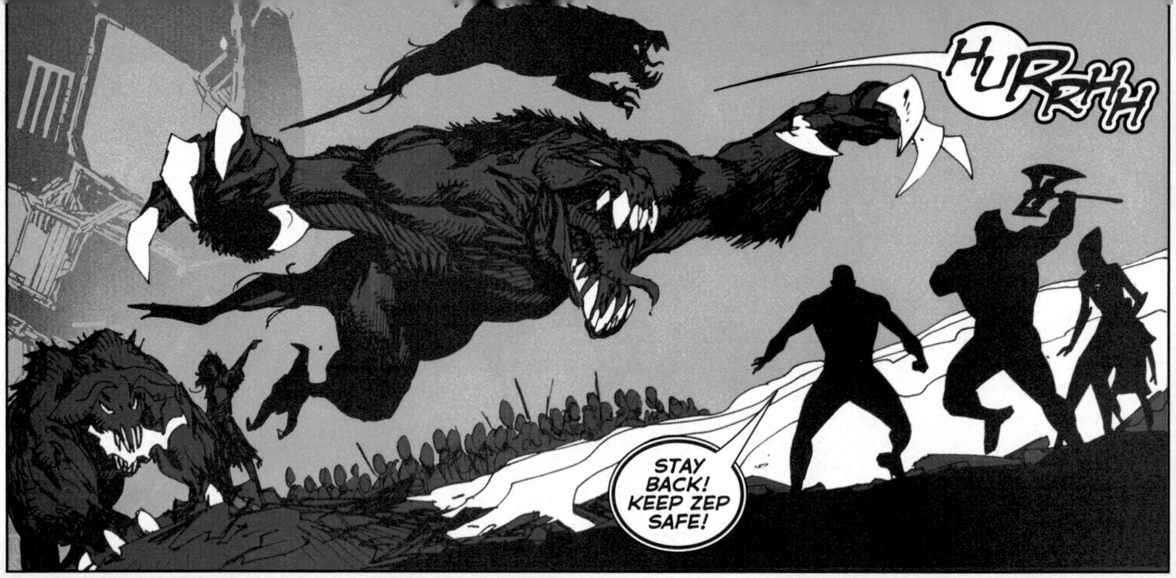
HURRHH
STAY BACK! KEEP ZEP SAFE!

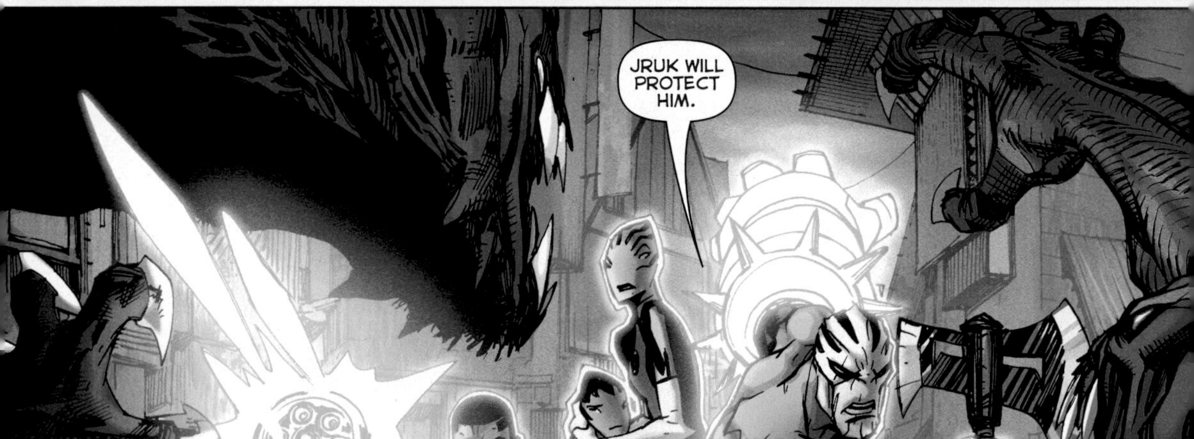
JRUK WILL PROTECT HIM.

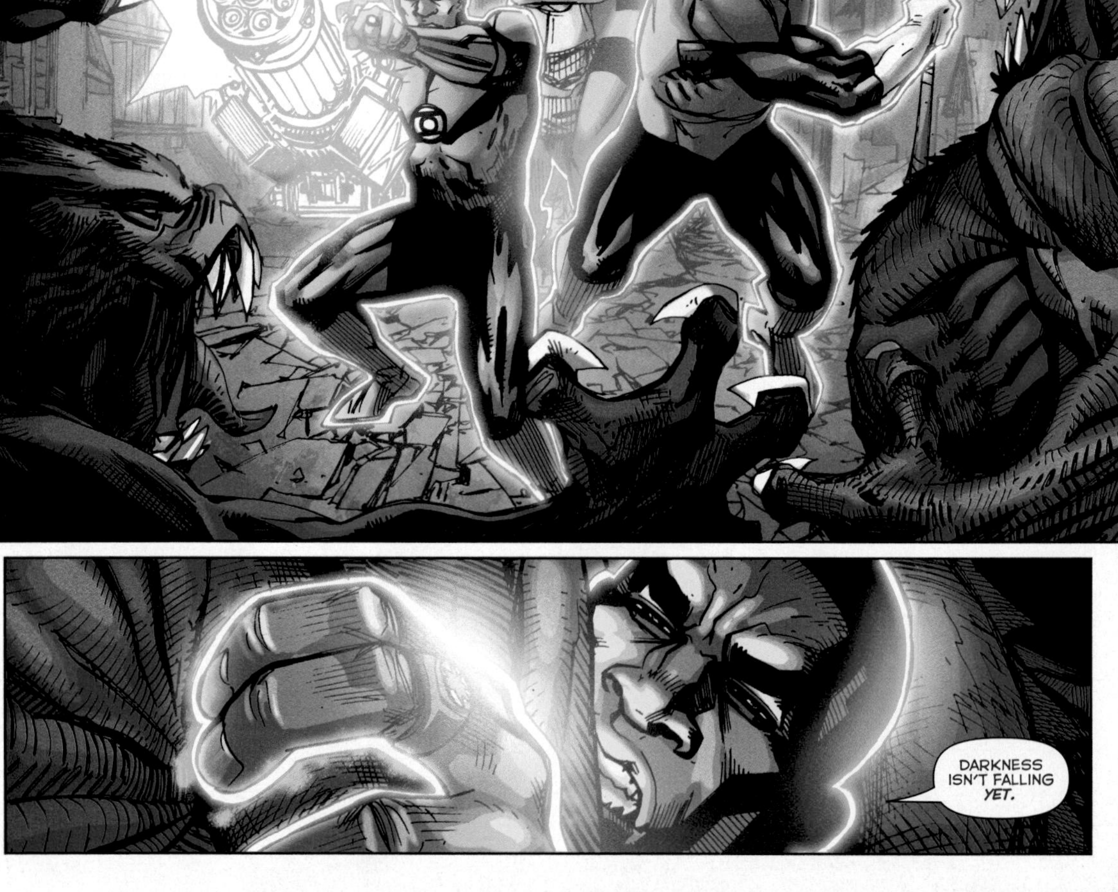
DARKNESS ISN'T FALLING *YET.*

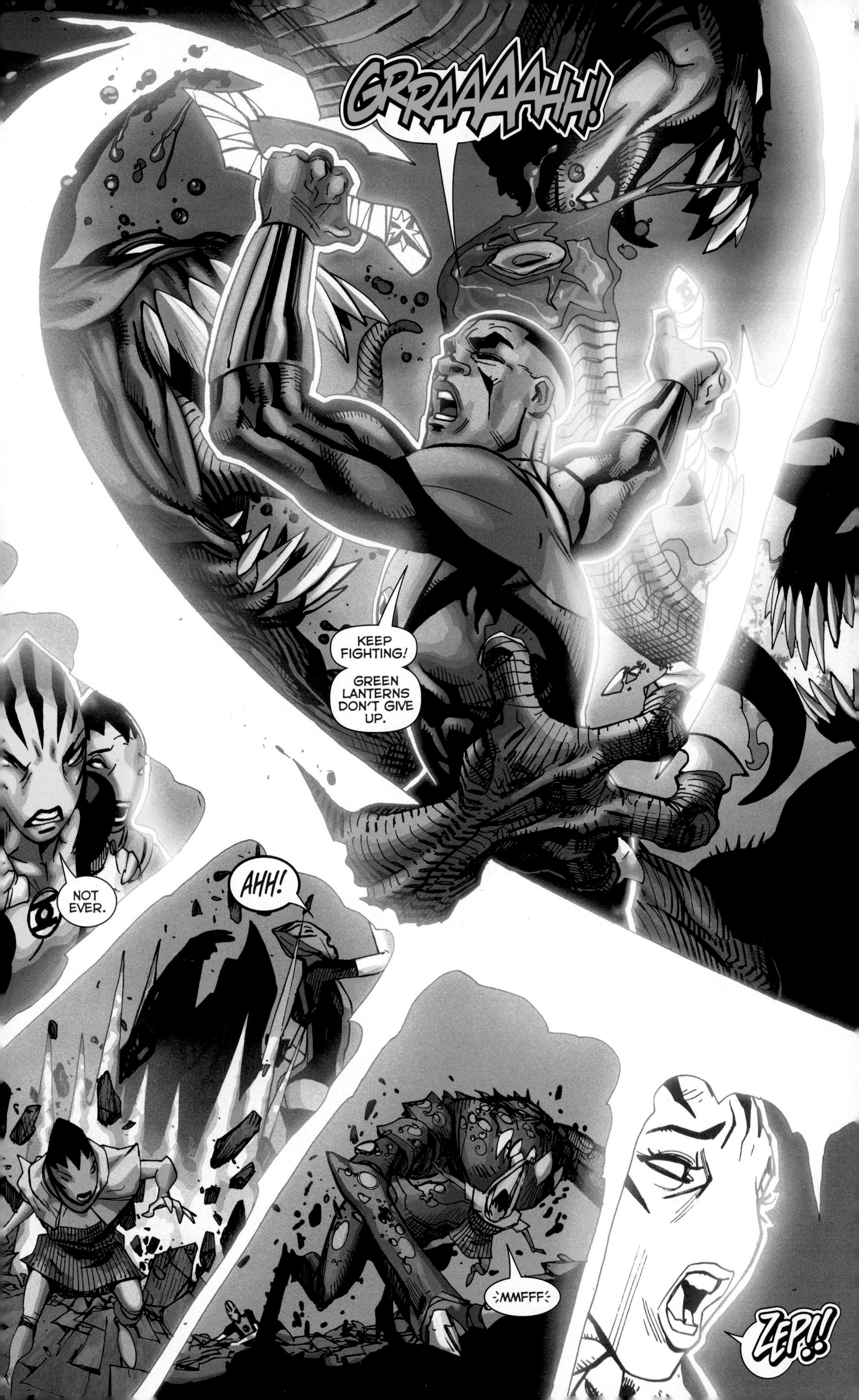
GRRAAAAHH!
KEEP FIGHTING!
GREEN LANTERNS DON'T GIVE UP.
NOT EVER.
AHH!
MMFFF
ZEP!!

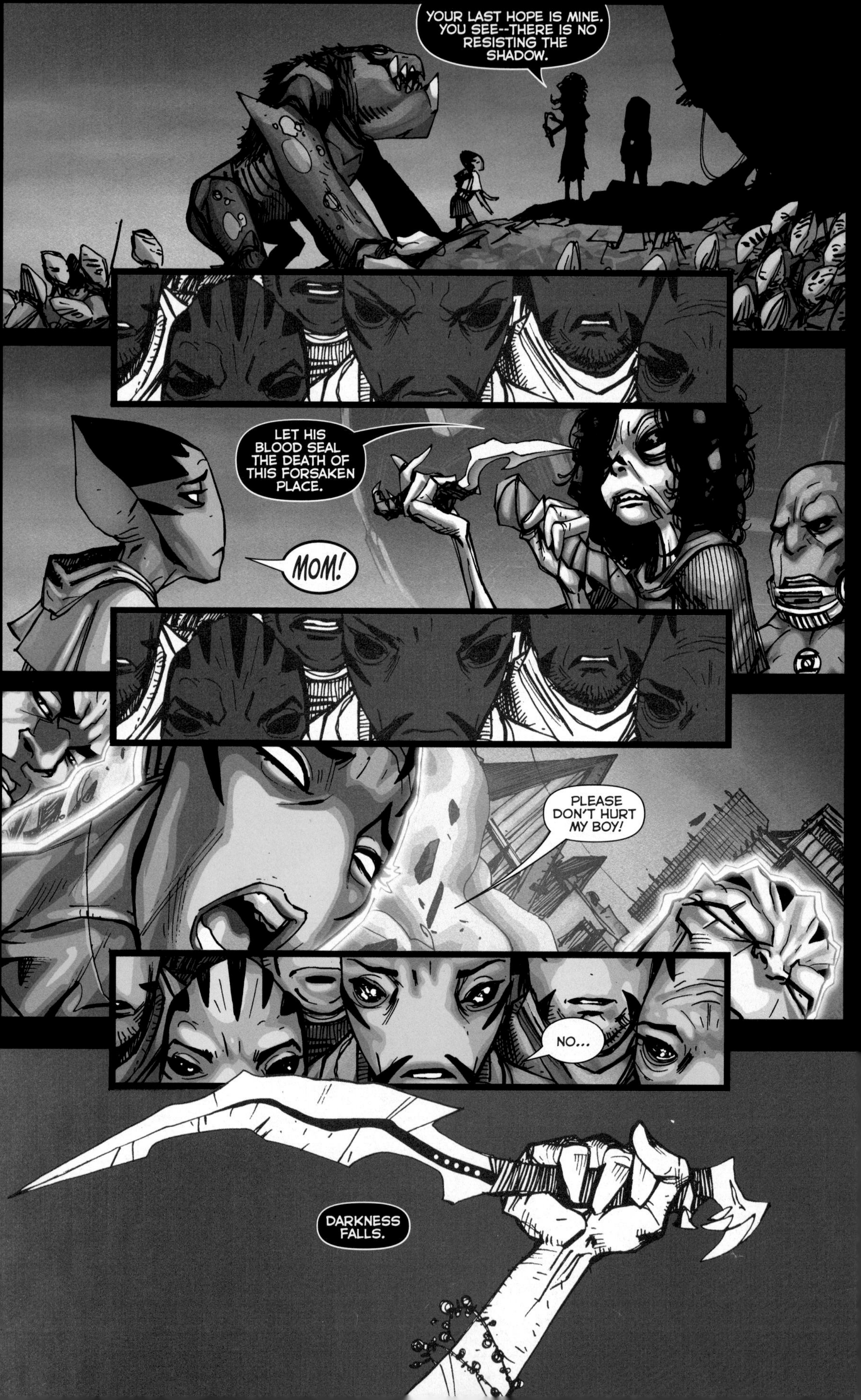
YOUR LAST HOPE IS MINE. YOU SEE--THERE IS NO RESISTING THE SHADOW.
LET HIS BLOOD SEAL THE DEATH OF THIS FORSAKEN PLACE.
MOM!
PLEASE DON'T HURT MY BOY!
NO...
DARKNESS FALLS.

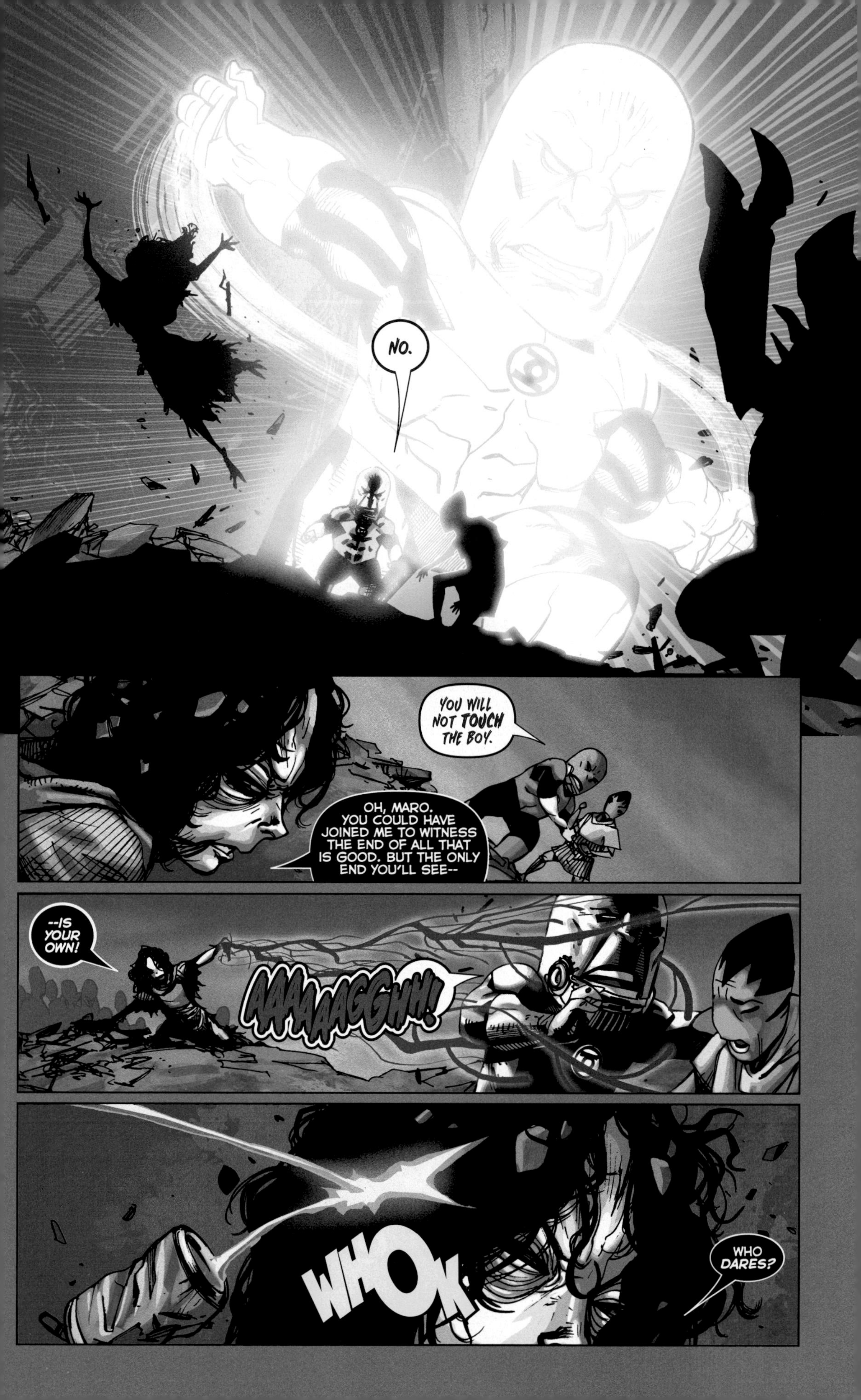
NO.
YOU WILL NOT TOUCH THE BOY.
OH, MARO. YOU COULD HAVE JOINED ME TO WITNESS THE END OF ALL THAT IS GOOD. BUT THE ONLY END YOU'LL SEE--
--IS YOUR OWN!
AAAAAAGGHH!
WHOK
WHO DARES?

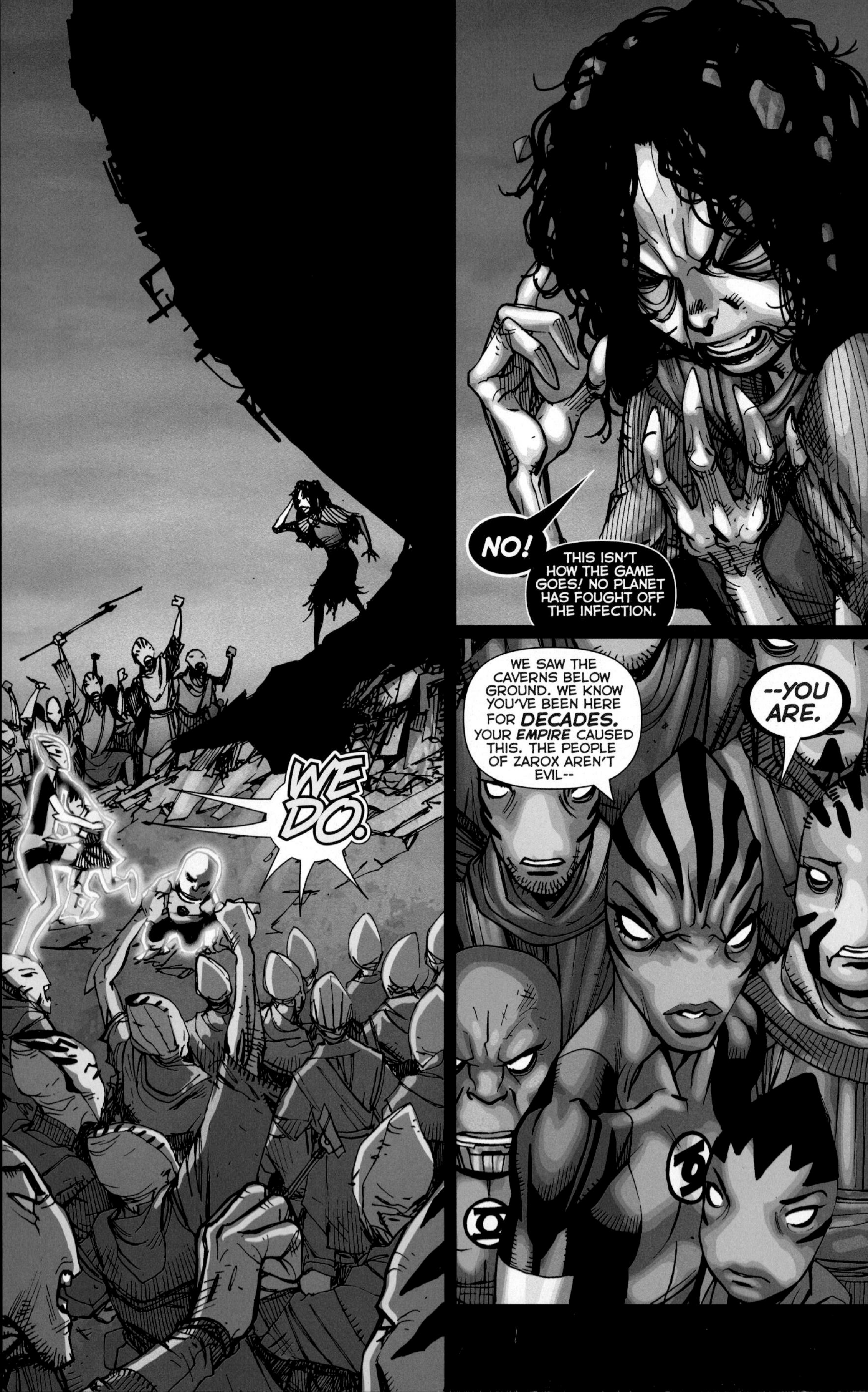
WE DO.
NO!
THIS ISN'T HOW THE GAME GOES! NO PLANET HAS FOUGHT OFF THE INFECTION.
WE SAW THE CAVERNS BELOW GROUND. WE KNOW YOU'VE BEEN HERE FOR DECADES. YOUR EMPIRE CAUSED THIS. THE PEOPLE OF ZAROX AREN'T EVIL--
--YOU ARE.

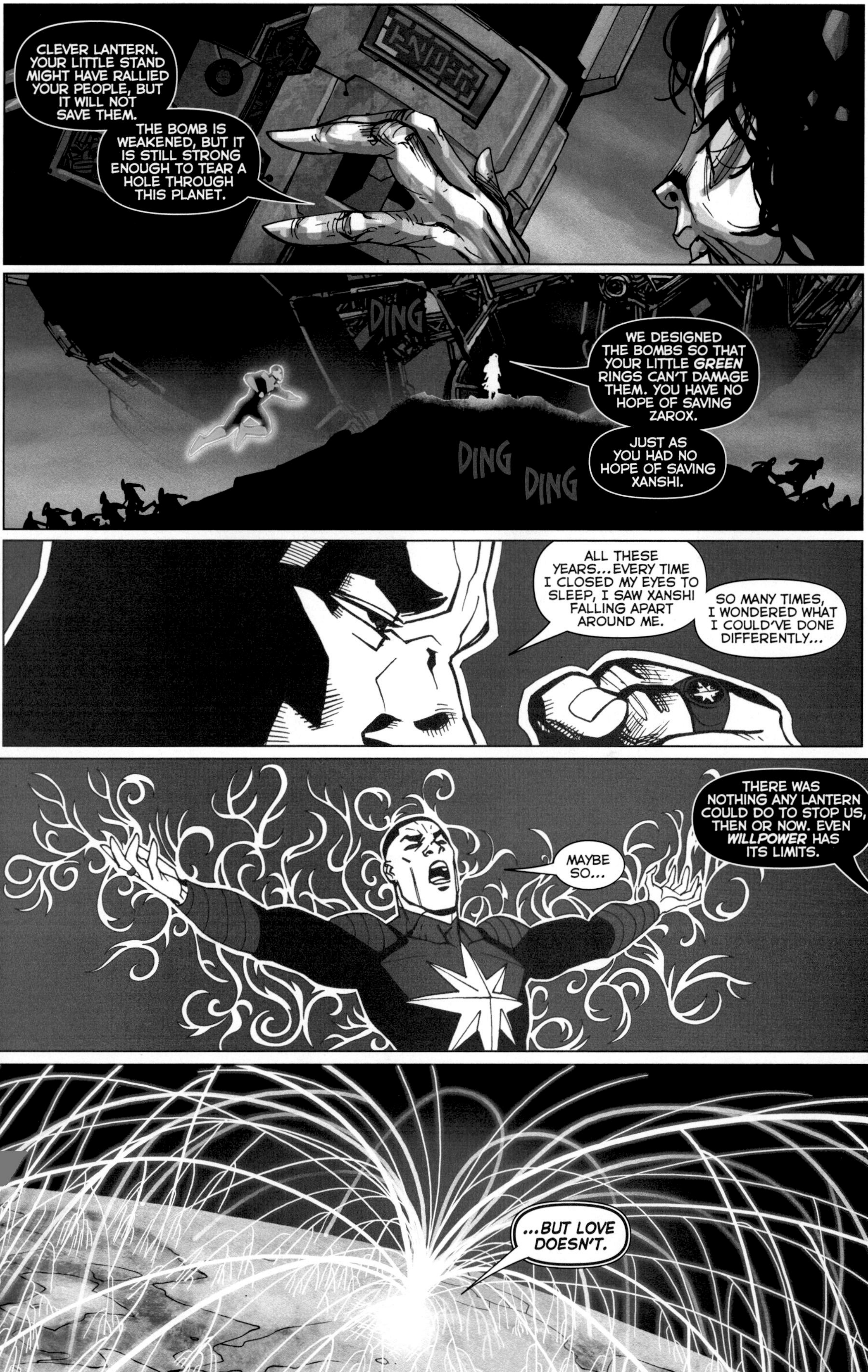
CLEVER LANTERN. YOUR LITTLE STAND MIGHT HAVE RALLIED YOUR PEOPLE, BUT IT WILL NOT SAVE THEM.
THE BOMB IS WEAKENED, BUT IT IS STILL STRONG ENOUGH TO TEAR A HOLE THROUGH THIS PLANET.
DING
WE DESIGNED THE BOMBS SO THAT YOUR LITTLE GREEN RINGS CAN'T DAMAGE THEM. YOU HAVE NO HOPE OF SAVING ZAROX.
JUST AS YOU HAD NO HOPE OF SAVING XANSHI.
DING
DING
ALL THESE YEARS...EVERY TIME I CLOSED MY EYES TO SLEEP, I SAW XANSHI FALLING APART AROUND ME.
SO MANY TIMES, I WONDERED WHAT I COULD'VE DONE DIFFERENTLY...
THERE WAS NOTHING ANY LANTERN COULD DO TO STOP US, THEN OR NOW. EVEN WILLPOWER HAS ITS LIMITS.
MAYBE SO...
...BUT LOVE DOESN'T.

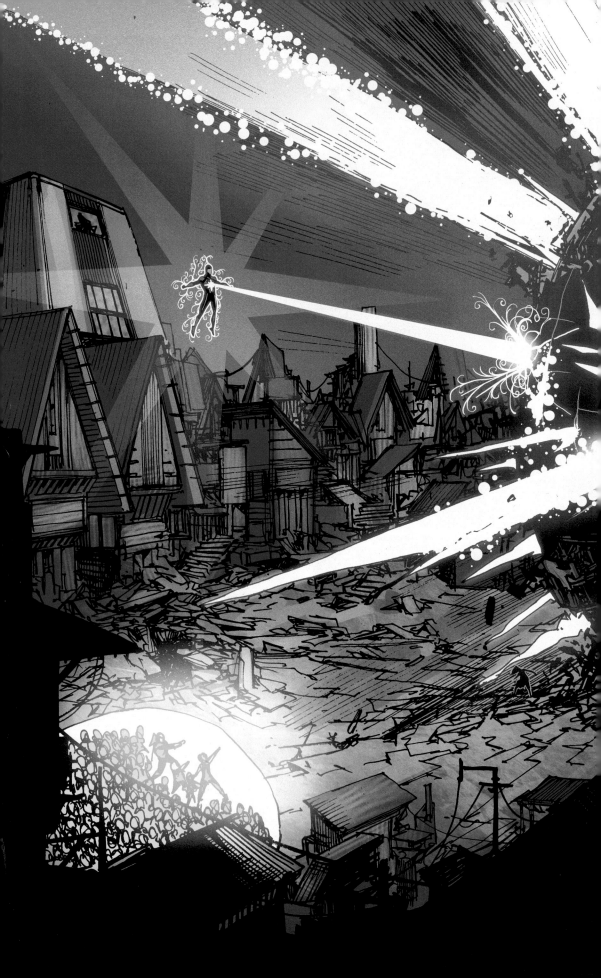

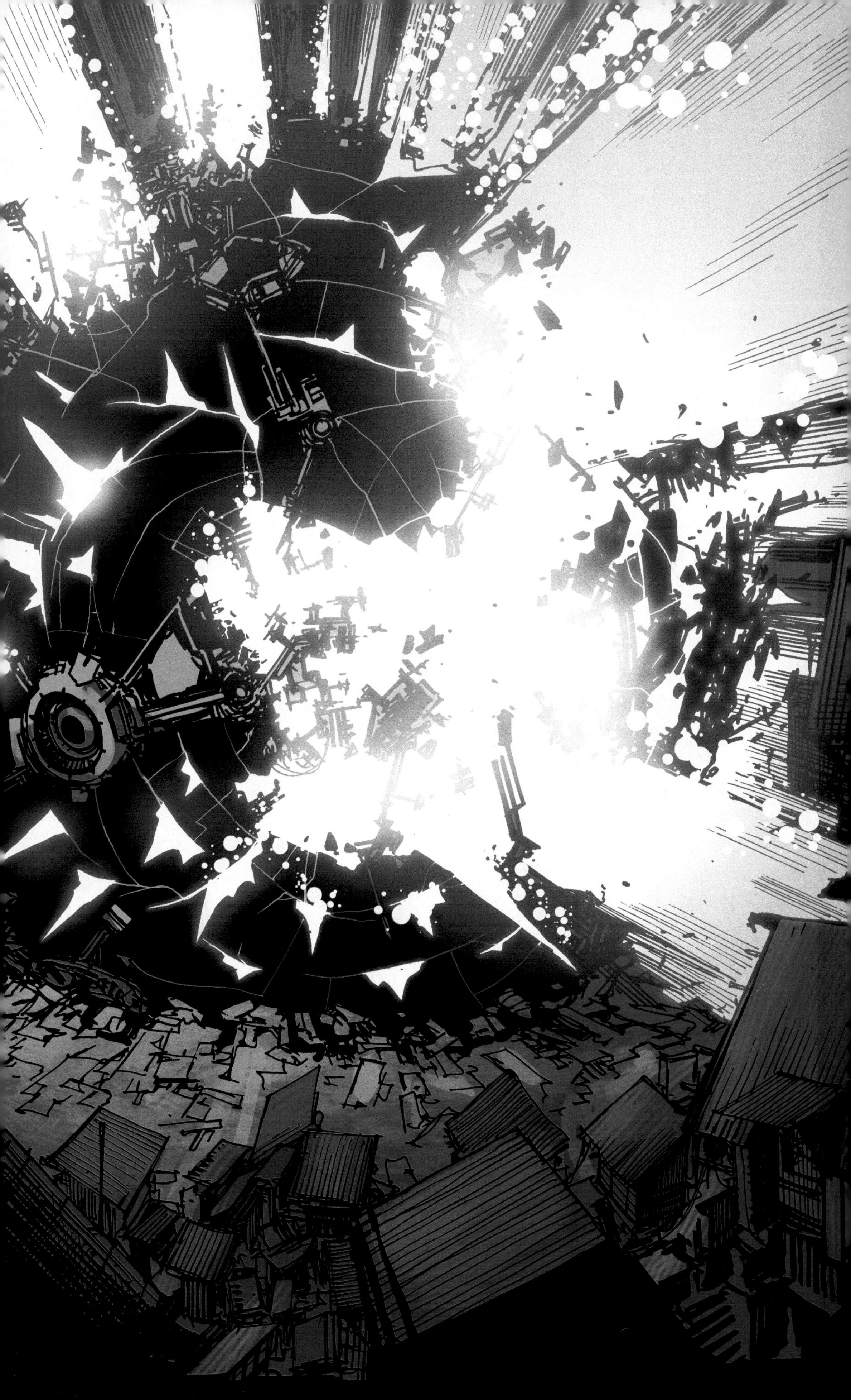

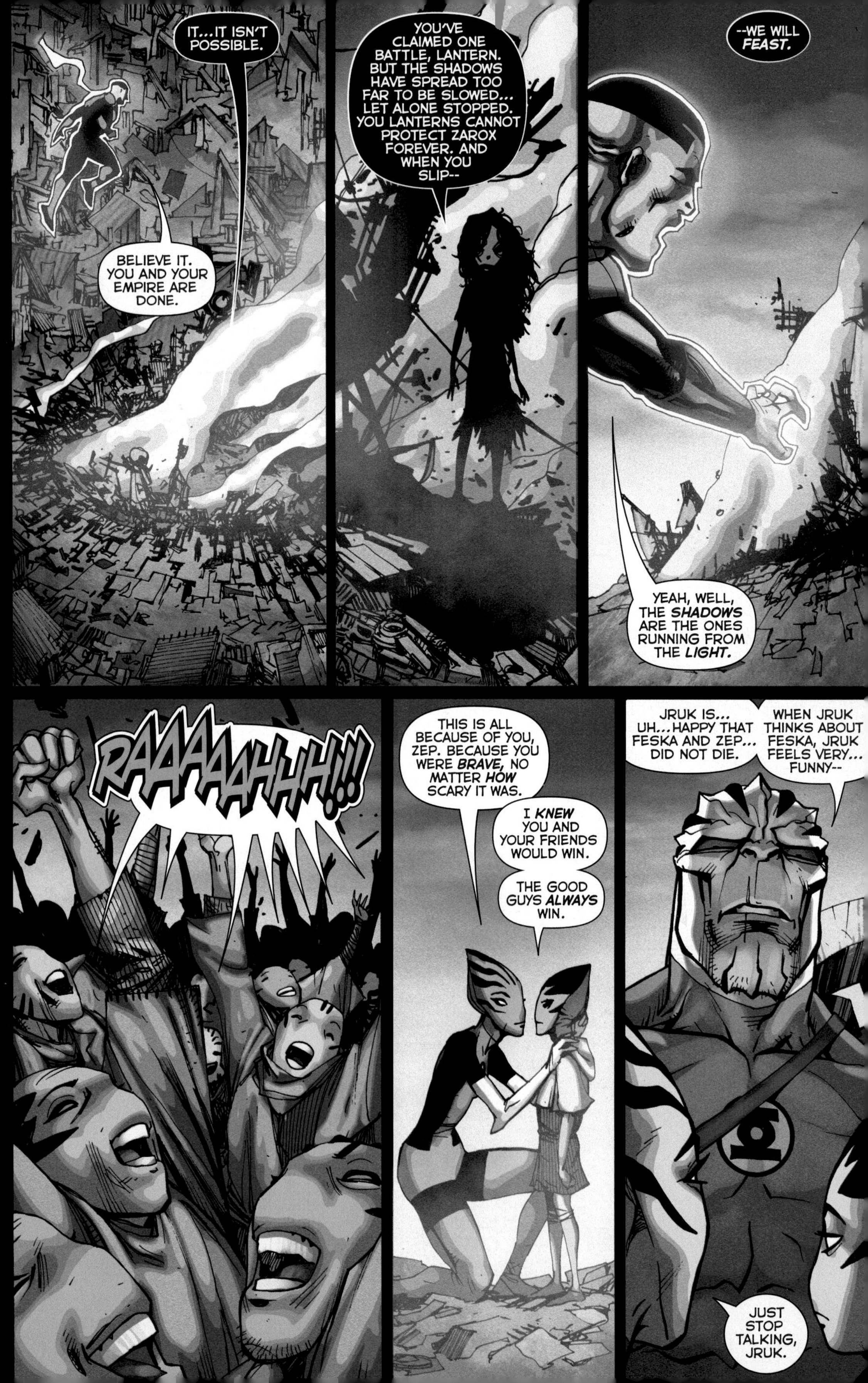
IT...IT ISN'T POSSIBLE.
BELIEVE IT. YOU AND YOUR EMPIRE ARE DONE.
YOU'VE CLAIMED ONE BATTLE, LANTERN. BUT THE SHADOWS HAVE SPREAD TOO FAR TO BE SLOWED... LET ALONE STOPPED. YOU LANTERNS CANNOT PROTECT ZAROX FOREVER. AND WHEN YOU SLIP--
--WE WILL *FEAST.*
YEAH, WELL, THE *SHADOWS* ARE THE ONES RUNNING FROM THE *LIGHT.*
RAAAAAHHH!!!
THIS IS ALL BECAUSE OF YOU, ZEP. BECAUSE YOU WERE *BRAVE,* NO MATTER *HOW* SCARY IT WAS.
I *KNEW* YOU AND YOUR FRIENDS WOULD WIN.
THE GOOD GUYS *ALWAYS* WIN.
JRUK IS... UH...HAPPY THAT FESKA AND ZEP... DID NOT DIE.
WHEN JRUK THINKS ABOUT FESKA, JRUK FEELS VERY... FUNNY--
JUST STOP TALKING, JRUK.

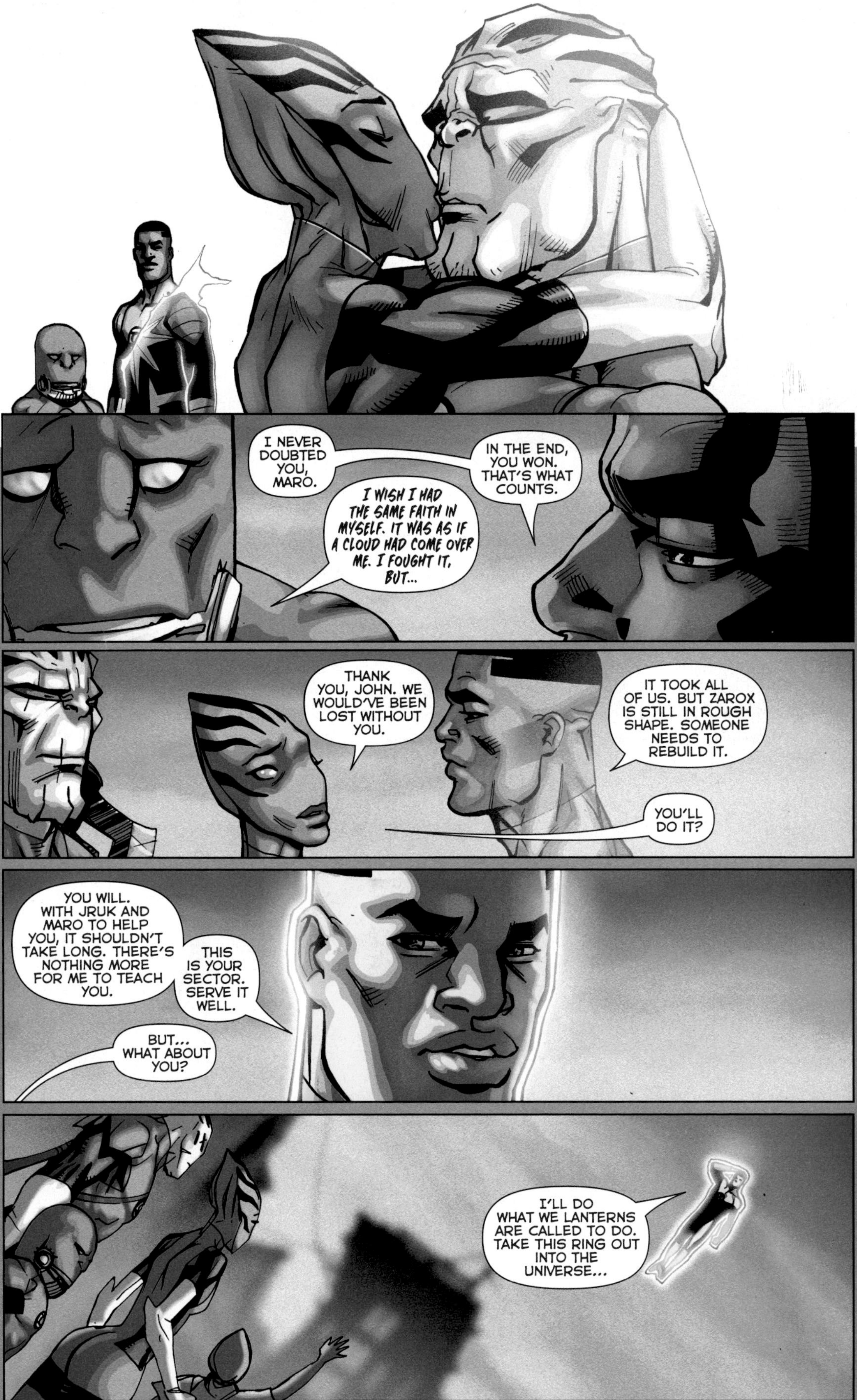
I NEVER DOUBTED YOU, MARO.
I WISH I HAD THE SAME FAITH IN MYSELF. IT WAS AS IF A CLOUD HAD COME OVER ME. I FOUGHT IT, BUT...
IN THE END, YOU WON. THAT'S WHAT COUNTS.
THANK YOU, JOHN. WE WOULD'VE BEEN LOST WITHOUT YOU.
IT TOOK ALL OF US. BUT ZAROX IS STILL IN ROUGH SHAPE. SOMEONE NEEDS TO REBUILD IT.
YOU'LL DO IT?
YOU WILL. WITH JRUK AND MARO TO HELP YOU, IT SHOULDN'T TAKE LONG. THERE'S NOTHING MORE FOR ME TO TEACH YOU.
THIS IS YOUR SECTOR. SERVE IT WELL.
BUT... WHAT ABOUT YOU?
I'LL DO WHAT WE LANTERNS ARE CALLED TO DO. TAKE THIS RING OUT INTO THE UNIVERSE...

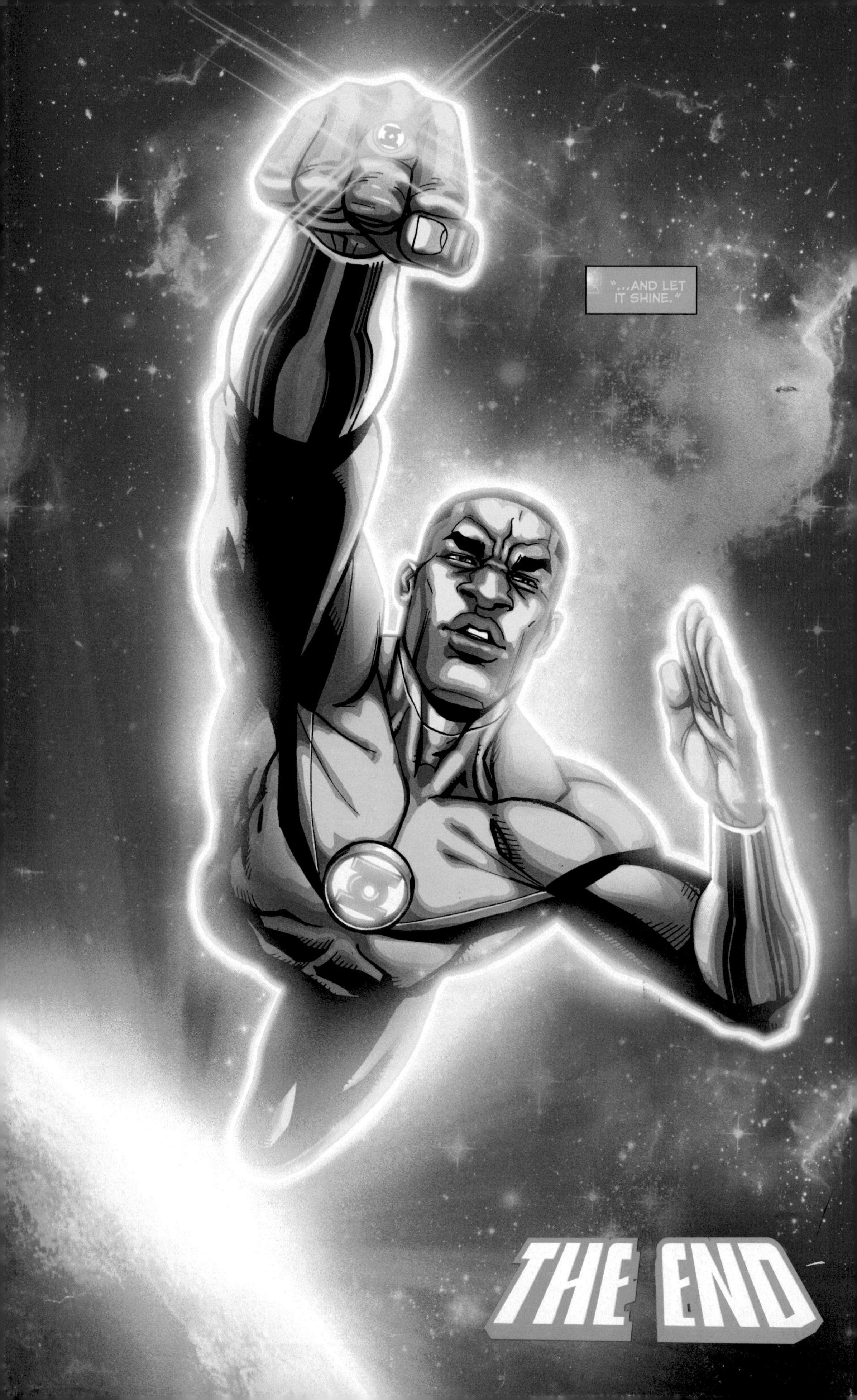
"...AND LET IT SHINE."
THE END